Wiley CIAexcel Exam Review 2018

Wiley CIAexcel Exam Review 2018

Part 1, Internal Audit Basics

S. Rao Vallabhaneni

WILEY

Library of Congress Cataloging-in-Publication Data:

ISBN 978-1-119-48256-7 (Paperback); ISBN 978-1-119-48257-4 (ebk); ISBN 978-1-119-48264-2 (ebk); ISBN 978-1-119-48269-7 (Part 2); ISBN 978-1-119-48285-7 (Part 3)

Printed in the United States of America

10 9 8 7 6 5 4 3 2 1

Contents

Preface

The Certified Internal Auditor (CIA) Examination is a program of The Institute of Internal Auditors (IIA), Inc. The CIA Examination certifies a person as a professional internal auditor and is intended to measure the knowledge, skills, and competency required in the field of internal auditing. The CIA designation is the mark of an expert in internal auditing. The new exam syllabus, effective from the middle of 2013, tests knowledge at two levels of comprehension—proficiency and awareness, as indicated in the IIA's content specifications outlines (www.theiia .org). These levels require allocating more preparation time to proficiency-level topics and less time to awareness-level topics. The scope of the new CIA Exam consists of three parts, which are divided into 14 domains; there are three domains in Part 1, three domains in Part 2, and eight domains in Part 3.

A series of review books has been prepared for the candidate to utilize for all three parts of the new CIA Exam. Each part's review book includes a comprehensive coverage of the subject matter (theory) based on the new exam syllabus followed by some sample practice multiple-choice (M/C) questions with answers and explanations (practice). The sample practice M/C questions included in the review book are taken from Wiley's Web-based online test software to show you the flavor of the questions. Each part's review book contains a glossary section, which is a good source for answering M/C questions on the CIA Exam.

The scope of the Part 1 review book covers internal audit basics. It has three domains: Domain 1 deals with mandatory guidance, including international standards and code of ethics. Domain 2 addresses internal control and risk. Domain 3 covers conducting internal audit engagements with audit tools and techniques. The Part 1 review book contains 81 sample practice M/C questions with answers and explanations and a glossary section.

The objective of this review book is to provide single-source, comprehensive review materials to assist the CIA Exam candidate in successfully preparing for the exam. The major highlights are presented next.

- Easy to navigate, comprehend, learn, and apply the subject matter since it was written from a student's perspective in a textbook style and format.

- The review book contains fully developed theories and concepts with complete thoughts as opposed to mere outlines. The candidate needs to know more than outlines to pass the difficult CIA Exam.

- Each theoretical domain in the review books is shown with a range of percentages to indicate the relative weights given to that domain in the exam. Candidates are expected to plan their study time in proportion to the relative weights suggested (i.e., more time and effort to higher percentages, and vice versa).

- CIA Exam content specifications included at the beginning of the book show the level of difficulty for each topic in the CIA Exam expressed as (A) for Awareness and (P) for Proficiency. Awareness means candidates must exhibit awareness (i.e., knowledge of terminology and fundamentals) in these topic areas. Proficiency means candidates must exhibit proficiency (i.e., thorough understanding and ability to apply concepts) in these topic areas.

- Greater use of comparisons and contrasts of subject matter make the key concepts come alive by providing lasting impressions. These comparisons show interrelationships between key concepts.

- Parts 1 and 2 theory of the review books offer full coverage of all the IIA's new *International Standards*, all of the Practice Advisories, and the Code of Ethics in their entirety, effective from January 2011 (International Professional Practice Framework, IPPF). Note that all the IIA *Standards* included in the review books contain Practice Advisories in the way they were published by the IIA.

Note: Although the IIA's *International Standards* are explicitly covered in the Part 1 exam, a conscious decision was made to include certain IIAs Standards by repeating them in the Part 2 review book to provide a better understanding of the subject matter as it relates to the *Standards*. This helps CIA Exam candidates to read the subject matter and the relevant *Standards* in one convenient place because each part of the exam is tested separately. Note that the IIA *Standards* are implicitly addressed in the Part 2 Exam and that both Part 1 and 2 Exams are highly integrated from a *Standards* viewpoint.

These review books focus on the student—the candidate preparing for the CIA Exam. They provide a positive learning experience for candidates by helping them to remember what they read and recall the subject matter through the use of tree diagrams, line drawings, memory aids (key concepts to remember), tables, charts, and graphic text boxes. In other words, an attempt has been made to bring life to static words through visual aids and compare and contrast approaches (i.e., which is what). The positive learning experience system provided through visual aids and memories will enable candidates to form long-lasting study impressions of the subject matter in their minds. In short, these books are student focused and learning oriented.

The aim of these books is to make learning easier, more convenient, and more enjoyable for our customer, the student. A great deal of planning and thought went into the creation of these books with the single goal of making the student's study program (whether individual or group) more relevant and more meaningful. It is hoped that these books meet or exceed the student's expectations in terms of quality, content coverage, and presentation of the subject matter.

We were excited and challenged while writing these books, and we hope that you too will be excited to study, remember, and achieve lifelong benefit from them. We believe that the knowledge gained from these books will remain with the candidate even after passing the CIA Exam, serving as on-the-job reference material as well as a training source.

Our goal is to be responsive to the CIA Exam candidate's needs and provide customer (student) satisfaction through continuous quality improvement. This goal can be met only through timely feedback from candidates. Please help us to serve you better—your input counts. You can reach us at ciatestbank@wiley.com.

Administrative Matters

We encourage the new, prospective candidate to obtain a copy of the CIA "Information for Candidates" brochure by writing directly to:

> Institute of Internal Auditors
>
> 247 Maitland Avenue
>
> Altamonte Springs, FL 32701-4201 USA
>
> Phone: 407-937-1100, Fax: 407-937-1111
>
> Web site: www.theiia.org

This brochure contains everything the candidate needs to know about the CIA Exam (i.e., application form, fees, dates, and sites).

Acknowledgments

The author is indebted to a number of people and organizations that helped to improve the content and quality of this book: Thanks to the Director of Certification at The Institute of Internal Auditors (IIA), Altamonte Springs, Florida, for providing great assistance during the writing of these books. Special thanks to the IIA for providing previous CIA Exam questions, answers, and explanations, IIA *Standards*, the Code of Ethics, and model exam questions. Many thanks also go to Wiley's editorial content management and marketing teams for their capable assistance in completing the CIA Exam learning system.

CIA Exam January Summary of Standards Changes

The Institute of Internal Auditors (IIA) issued revisions to existing standards eligible for testing on the IIA's Certified Internal Auditor (CIA) exam on and after January 1, 2017. These revisions and changes primarily focus on expanding and clarifying the interpretations of the existing standards.

This document will provide you with a summary of the substantive changes made to those standards that could impact your exam experience.

1. Introduction:

    a. The first purpose of the *Standards* listed was changed from "Delineate basic principles that represent the practice of internal auditing" to "Guide adherence with the mandatory elements of the International Professional Practices Framework" (IPPF).

    b. A paragraph was added that states that the *Standards* and the *Code of Ethics* are considered mandatory elements of the IPPF.

2. 1000—Purpose, Authority, and Responsibility: The IPPF full mandatory guidance includes:

    a. Mission of Internal Audit

    b. Core Principles for the Professional Practice of Internal Auditing

    c. Code of Ethics

    d. *Standards*

    e. Definition of Internal Auditing

3. 1010—Recognizing Mandatory Guidance in the Internal Audit Charter: Clarification of standards to ensure the mandatory guidance listed in standard 1000 is recognized in the internal audit charter.

4. 1110—Organizational Independence: Disclosure requirements of any interference have been added to 1110.A1.

5. 1112—Chief Audit Executive Roles Beyond Internal Auditing: This standard is new. It expresses the need to maintain independence and objectivity of the chief audit executive.

6. 1130—Impairment to Independence or Objectivity: Paragraph 1130.A3 in the interpretations is new. It grants permission to perform assurance services for a former consulting client provided there is no impairment of objectivity.

7. 1210—Proficiency: Interpretation expanded to include "consideration of current activities, trends, and emerging issues."

8. 1300—Quality Assurance and Improvement Program: Interpretation expanded to encourage board oversight of quality assurance and improvement program.

9. 1312—External Assessments: Interpretation expanded to state that the external assessor may comment on operations or strategy and the assessor must comment on the conformance with the Standards and Code of Ethics. The interpretation was also expanded to encourage board oversight of the external assessment.

10. 1320—Reporting on the Quality Assurance and Improvement Program: The Standard was expanded to include four minimum disclosure requirements such as the scope and frequency of assessments, the qualifications and independence of assessors, conclusions of assessors, and corrective action plans.

11. 2000—Managing the Internal Audit Activity: The interpretation has narrowed the term *individuals* to *individual members*. The interpretation was also expanded to include the consideration of impactful trends and emerging issues as a fourth interpretation of an effectively managed internal audit activity. The final paragraph of the interpretation was expanded to include the consideration of "strategies, objectives, and risks" in a value-adding internal audit activity.

12. 2050—Coordination and Reliance: "and Reliance" was added to the standard title. An interpretation was added to help better understand the standard.

13. 2060—Reporting to Senior Management and the Board: The Standard was expanded to include a statement on the conformance with the Standards and the Code of Ethics in the report to senior management and the board. The interpretation was expanded to include required report information.

14. 2100—Nature of Work: The interpretation was expanded to include a statement that the credibility and value of the work is enhanced when the internal auditor is proactive and considers future impact in their evaluations.

15. 2110—Governance: The standard was expanded to include two additional governance tasks: the process for making strategic and operational decisions as well as the process for risk management and control oversight.

16. 2200—Engagement Planning: The standard was expanded to explicitly state that the engagement plan must include the organization's strategies, objectives, and risks.

17. 2210—Engagement Objectives: The interpretation of this standard was expanded to include three types of evaluation criteria such as internal, external, and leading practices.

18. 2230—Engagement Resource Allocation: An interpretation was added to this standard.

19. 2330—Documenting Information: The standard was expanded to include "sufficient, reliable, and useful" in the description of "relevant information."

20. 2410—Criteria for Communicating: Additions were made to 2410.A1 to be more specific and make mandatory the inclusion of any applicable conclusions, recommendations, and/or action plans in the final engagement communication.

21. 2450—Overall Opinions: The standard was expanded to include "strategies, objectives, and risks" in the overall opinion. The interpretation was expanded to require that a summary of the information that supports the opinion be included.

22. Glossary Changes: The following glossary terms have been clarified or added:

    a. Board

    b. Chief Audit Executive

    c. Core Principles for the Professional Practice of Internal Auditing (new)

    d. International Professional Practices Framework

Two new terms, *Mission* and *Core Principles*, are added to the new IPPF of 2017, as follows:

The *Mission of Internal Audit* articulates what internal audit aspires to accomplish within an organization. Its place in the new IPPF of 2017 is deliberate, demonstrating how practitioners should leverage the entire framework to facilitate their ability to achieve the Mission.

> The mission of internal audit is to enhance and protect organizational value by providing risk-based and objective assurance, advice, and insight.

A set of ten *Core Principles* (CPs) comprise the fundamentals essential to the effective practice of internal auditing. They are the foundational underpinnings of the Code of Ethics and the Standards, reflecting the primary requirements for the professional practice of internal auditing now and in the future. The Core Principles can be used as a benchmark against which to gauge the effectiveness of an internal audit activity. Thus, the Core Principles should be well expressed throughout the Code of Ethics and the Standards.

> CP1: Demonstrates integrity
>
> CP2: Demonstrates competence and due professional care
>
> CP3: Is objective and free from undue influence (independent)
>
> CP4: Aligns with the strategies, objectives, and risks of the organization
>
> CP5: Is appropriately positioned and adequately resourced
>
> CP6: Demonstrates quality and continuous improvement
>
> CP7: Communicates effectively
>
> CP8: Provides risk-based assurance
>
> CP9: Is insightful, proactive, and future-focused
>
> CP10: Promotes organizational improvement

CIA Exam Study Preparation Resources

To succeed in the exam, we recommend the following study plan and three review products for each part of the CIA Exam:

- Read each part's review book (theory).
- Practice the Web-based online test bank software (practice).
- Reinforce the theoretical concepts by studying the Focus Notes (theory).

A series of **review books** has been prepared for the candidate to utilize for all three parts of the new CIA Exam. Each part's review book includes a comprehensive coverage of the subject matter (theory) followed by some sample practice multiple-choice (M/C) questions with answers and explanations (practice). The sample practice M/C questions included in the review book are taken from Wiley's Web-based online test software to show you the flavor of questions. Each part's review book contains a glossary section, which is a good source for answering M/C questions on the CIA Exam.

The **Web-based online test bank software** is a robust review product that simulates the format of the actual CIA Exam in terms of look and feel, thus providing intense practice and greater confidence to the CIA Exam candidates. The thousands of sample practice questions (5,275 plus) included in the online test bank can assure CIA Exam candidates that they are preparing well for all the required subject matter topics in the exam. All practice questions include explanations for the correct answer and are organized by domain topics within each part. See www.wileycia.com.

A part summary showing the number of sample practice questions included in the online test bank and the number of questions tested in the actual CIA Exam is presented next.

Part Summary	Wiley Sample Practice Questions	CIA Exam Actual Test Questions
Part 1	750+	125
Part 2	725+	100
Part 3	3,800+	100
Total Questions in Three Parts	**5,275+**	**325**

Focus Notes provide a quick review and reinforcement of the important theoretical concepts. They are presented in a summary manner taken from the details of the review books. The Focus Notes can be studied just before the exam, during travel time, or any other time.

When combined, these three review products provide a great value to CIA Exam students.

We suggest a sequential study approach in four steps for each part of the exam, as follows:

Step 1. Read the glossary section at the end of each part's review book for a better understanding of key technical terms.

Step 2. Study the theory from the each part's review book.

Step 3. Practice the multiple-choice questions from the online test bank for each part.

Step 4. Read the Focus Notes for each part for a quick review and reinforcement of the important theoretical concepts.

In addition, CIA Exam candidates should read **Practice Guides** from the IIA because these guides provide detailed guidance for conducting internal audit activities. They include detailed processes and procedures, such as tools and techniques, audit work programs, and step-by-step audit approaches, as well as examples of audit deliverables. These Practice Guides are not included in the Wiley Review Books due to their size and the fact that they are available from www.theiia.org.

CIA Exam-Taking Tips and Techniques

The types of questions a candidate can expect to see in the CIA Exam are objective and scenario-based multiple-choice (M/C) questions. Answering the M/C questions requires a good amount of practice and effort.

The following tips and techniques will be helpful in answering the CIA Exam questions.

- Stay with your first impression of the correct choice.

- Know the subject area or topic. Don't read too much into the question.

- Remember that questions are independent of specific country, products, practices, vendors, hardware, software, or industry.

- Read the last sentence of the question first followed by all choices and then the body (stem) of the question.

- Read the question twice or read the underlined or circled keywords twice, and watch for tip-off words, such as **not, except, all, every, always, never, least, or most,** which denote absolute conditions.

- Do not project the question into your organizational environment, practices, policies, procedures, standards, and guidelines. The examination is focusing on the IIA's professional *Standards* and publications and on the CIA's exam syllabus (i.e., content specifications).

- Try to eliminate wrong choices as quickly as possible. When you get down to two semifinal choices, take a big-picture approach. For example, if choices A and D are the semifinalists, and choice D could be a part of choice A, then select choice A; or if choice D could be a more complete answer, then select choice D.

- Don't spend too much time on one question. If you are not sure of an answer, move on, and go back to it if time permits. The last resort is to guess the answer. There is no penalty for guessing the wrong answer.

Remember that success in any professional examination depends on several factors required of any student, such as time management skills, preparation time and effort levels, education and experience levels, memory recall of the subject matter, state of the mind before or during the exam, and decision-making skills.

CIA Exam Content Specifications

Part 1 of the CIA Exam is called **internal audit basics.** The exam duration is 2.5 hours (150 minutes) with 125 multiple-choice questions. A breakdown of topics in the Part 1 follows.

Domain I: Mandatory Guidance (35–45%)*

A. Definition of Internal Auditing (P)†

B. Code of Ethics (P)

C. International Standards (P)

Domain II: Internal Control and Risk (25–35%)

A. Types of Controls (e.g., preventive, detective, input, and output) (P)

B. Management Control Techniques (A)

C. Internal Control Framework Characteristics and Use (e.g., COSO and Cadbury) (A)

D. Alternative Control Frameworks (A)

E. Risk Vocabulary And Concepts (A)

F. Fraud Risk Awareness (A)

- ☐ Types of fraud (A)

- ☐ Fraud red flags (A)

Domain III: Conducting Internal Audit Engagements—Audit Tools and Techniques (28–38%)

A. Data Gathering

- ☐ Review prior audit reports and other relevant documentation as part of a preliminary survey of the engagement area (P)

- ☐ Develop checklists/internal control questionnaires as part of a preliminary survey of the engagement area (P)

  - • Conduct interviews as part of a preliminary survey of the engagement area (P)

- Use observation to gather data (P)

- Conduct engagement to assure identification of key risks and controls (P)

- Use nonstatistical (judgmental) sampling method (P)

B. Data Analysis and Interpretation

☐ Use computerized audit tools and techniques (e.g., data mining and extraction, and continuous monitoring) (P)

☐ Conduct spreadsheet analysis (P)

☐ Use analytical review techniques (e.g., ratio estimation, variance analysis, budget versus actual, trend analysis, and other reasonableness tests) (P)

☐ Draw conclusions (P)

C. Data Reporting

☐ Report test results to auditors in charge (P)

D. Documentation and Work Papers

☐ Develop work papers (P)

E. Process Mapping (P)

F. Evaluate Relevance, Sufficiency, and Competence of Evidence (P)

☐ Identify potential sources of evidence (P)

*Indicates the relative range of weights assigned to this topic area for both theory and practice sections in the CIA Exam.

†Indicates the level of difficulty for each topic in the CIA Exam expressed as (A) for Awareness and (P) for Proficiency. (A) = Candidates must exhibit awareness (i.e., knowledge of terminology and fundamentals) in these topic areas. (P) = Candidates must exhibit proficiency (i.e., thorough understanding and ability to apply concepts) in these topic areas.

The Institute of Internal Auditors (IIA) issued revisions to existing standards eligible for testing on the IIA Certified Internal Auditor (CIA) exam on and after January 1, 2017. The changes primarily focus on expanding the interpretations of these standards. To see a summary of the changes to the standards as well as a copy of the new standards, visit https://www.efficientlearning.com/updates.

These revisions do not yet appear in this text. Where you see this icon, please refer to the website above to review relevant revisions.

Mandatory Guidance (35–45%)

1.1 Definition of Internal Auditing

The globally accepted definition of internal auditing states the fundamental purpose, nature, and scope of internal auditing:

> Internal auditing is an independent, objective assurance and consulting activity designed to add value and improve an organization's operations. It helps an organization accomplish its objectives by bringing a systematic, disciplined approach to evaluate and improve the effectiveness of risk management, control, and governance processes.

1.2 International Standards

Internal auditing is conducted in diverse legal and cultural environments; within organizations that vary in purpose, size, complexity, and structure; and by persons within or outside the organization. While differences may affect the practice of internal auditing in each environment, conformance with The Institute of Internal Auditors' *International Standards for the Professional Practice of Internal Auditing* (*Standards*) is essential in meeting the responsibilities of internal auditors and the internal audit activity.

If internal auditors or the internal audit activity is prohibited by law or regulation from conformance with certain parts of the *Standards*, conformance with all other parts of the *Standards* and appropriate disclosures are needed.

If the *Standards* are used in conjunction with standards issued by other authoritative bodies, internal audit communications may also cite the use of other standards, as appropriate. In such a case, if inconsistencies exist between the *Standards* and other standards, internal auditors and the internal audit activity must conform with the *Standards* and may conform with the other standards if they are more restrictive.

The purpose of the *Standards* is to:

- Delineate basic principles that represent the practice of internal auditing.
- Provide a framework for performing and promoting a broad range of value-added internal auditing.
- Establish the basis for the evaluation of internal audit performance.
- Foster improved organizational processes and operations.

The *Standards* are principles-focused, mandatory requirements consisting of:

- Statements of basic requirements for the professional practice of internal auditing and for evaluating the effectiveness of performance that are internationally applicable at organizational and individual levels.
- Interpretations that clarify terms or concepts within the Statements.

The *Standards* employ terms that have been given specific meanings that are included in the Glossary. Specifically, the *Standards* use the word "must" to specify an unconditional requirement and the word "should" where conformance is expected unless, when applying professional judgment, circumstances justify deviation.

It is necessary to consider the Statements and their Interpretations as well as the specific meanings from the Glossary to understand and apply the *Standards* correctly.

The structure of the *Standards* is divided between Attribute and Performance *Standards*. **Attribute *Standards*** address the attributes of organizations and individuals performing internal auditing (numbered from 1000 to 1322). **Performance *Standards*** describe the nature of internal auditing and provide quality criteria against which the performance of these services can be measured (numbered from 2000 to 2600). The Attribute and Performance *Standards* are also provided to apply to all internal audit services.

Implementation *Standards* are also provided to expand on the Attribute and Performance *Standards*, by providing the requirements applicable to assurance (A) or consulting (C) activities.

Assurance services involve the internal auditor's objective assessment of evidence to provide an independent opinion or conclusions regarding an entity, operation, function, process, system, or other subject matter. The nature and scope of the assurance engagement are determined by the internal auditor. Generally there are three parties involved in assurance services: (1) the person or group directly involved with the entity, operation, function, process, system, or other subject matter—the process owner; (2) the person or group making the assessment—the internal auditor; and (3) the person or group using the assessment—the user.

Consulting services are advisory in nature and generally are performed at the specific request of an engagement client. The nature and scope of the consulting engagement are subject to agreement with the engagement client. Consulting services generally involve two parties: (1) the person or group offering the advice—the internal auditor; and (2) the person or group seeking and receiving the advice—the engagement client. When performing consulting services, the internal auditor should maintain objectivity and not assume management responsibility.

(a) Attribute Standards (1000 to 1322)

1000—Purpose, Authority, and Responsibility

The purpose, authority, and responsibility of the internal audit activity must be formally defined in an internal audit charter, consistent with the definition of Internal auditing, the Code of Ethics, and the *Standards*. The chief audit executive (CAE) must periodically review the internal audit charter and present it to senior management and the board for approval.

Interpretation: *The internal audit charter is a formal document that defines the internal audit activity's purpose, authority, and responsibility. The internal audit charter establishes the internal audit activity's position within the organization, including the nature of the CAE's functional reporting relationship with the board; authorizes access to records, personnel, and physical properties relevant to the performance of engagements; and defines the scope of internal audit activities. Final approval of the internal audit charter resides with the board.*

> **1000.A1**—The nature of assurance services provided to the organization must be defined in the internal audit charter. If assurances are to be provided to parties outside the organization, the nature of these assurances must also be defined in the internal audit charter.

> **1000.C1**—The nature of consulting services must be defined in the internal audit charter.

Practice Advisory 1000-1: Internal Audit Charter

1. Providing a formal, written internal audit charter is critical in managing the internal audit activity. The internal audit charter provides a recognized statement for review and acceptance by management and for approval, as documented in the minutes, by the board. It also facilitates a periodic assessment of the adequacy of the internal audit activity's purpose, authority, and responsibility, which establishes the role of the internal audit activity. If a question should arise, the internal audit charter provides a formal, written agreement with management and the board about the organization's internal audit activity.

2. The CAE is responsible for periodically assessing whether the internal audit activity's purpose, authority, and responsibility, as defined in the internal audit charter, continue to be adequate to enable the activity to accomplish its objectives. The CAE is also responsible for communicating the result of this assessment to senior management and the board.

1010–Recognition of the Definition of Internal Auditing, the Code of Ethics, and the *Standards* in the Internal Audit Charter

The mandatory nature of the Definition of Internal Auditing, the Code of Ethics, and the *Standards* must be recognized in the internal audit charter. The CAE should discuss the definition of internal auditing, the Code of Ethics, and the *Standards* with senior management and the board.

No Practice Advisory for Standard 1010

1100–Independence and Objectivity

The internal audit activity must be independent, and internal auditors must be objective in performing their work.

Interpretation: *Independence is the freedom from conditions that threaten the ability of the internal audit activity to carry out internal audit responsibilities in an unbiased manner. To achieve the* *degree of independence necessary to effectively carry out the responsibilities of the internal audit activity, the CAE has direct and unrestricted access to senior management and the board. This can be achieved through a dual-reporting relationship. Threats to independence must be managed at the individual auditor, engagement, functional, and organizational levels.*

Objectivity is an unbiased mental attitude that allows internal auditors to perform engagements in such a manner that they believe in their work product and that no quality compromises are made. Objectivity requires that internal auditors do not subordinate their judgment on audit matters to others. Threats to objectivity must be managed at the individual auditor, engagement, functional, and organizational levels.

No Practice Advisory for Standard 1100

1110–Organizational Independence

The CAE must report to a level within the organization that allows the internal audit activity to fulfill its responsibilities. The CAE must confirm to the board, at least annually, the organizational independence of the internal audit activity.

Interpretation: *Organizational independence is effectively achieved when the CAE reports functionally to the board. Examples of functional reporting to the board involve the board:*

- *Approving the internal audit charter.*
- *Approving the risk based internal audit plan.*
- *Receiving communications from the CAE on the internal audit activity's performance relative to its plan and other matters.*
- *Approving decisions regarding the appointment and removal of the CAE.*
- *Making appropriate inquiries of management and the CAE to determine whether there are inappropriate scope or resource limitations.*

    1110.A1–The internal audit activity must be free from interference in determining the scope of internal auditing, performing work, and communicating results.

Practice Advisory 1110-1: Organizational Independence

1. Support from senior management and the board assists the internal audit activity in gaining the cooperation of engagement clients and performing their work free from interference.

2. The CAE, reporting functionally to the board and administratively to the organization's chief executive officer (CEO), facilitates organizational independence. At a minimum, the CAE needs to report to an individual in the organization with sufficient authority to promote independence and to ensure broad audit coverage, adequate consideration of engagement communications, and appropriate action on engagement recommendations.

3. Functional reporting to the board typically involves the board:

- ☐ Approving the internal audit activity's overall charter.
- ☐ Approving the internal audit risk assessment and related audit plan.
- ☐ Receiving communications from the CAE on the results of the internal audit activities or other matters that the CAE determines are necessary, including private meetings with the CAE without management present, as well as annual confirmation of the internal audit activity's organizational independence.

- ❑ Approving all decisions regarding the performance evaluation, appointment, or removal of the CAE.

- ❑ Approving the annual compensation and salary adjustment of the CAE.

- ❑ Making appropriate inquiries of management and the CAE to determine whether there is audit scope or budgetary limitations that impede the ability of the internal audit activity to execute its responsibilities.

4. Administrative reporting is the reporting relationship within the organization's management structure that facilitates the day-to-day operations of the internal audit activity. Administrative reporting typically includes:

- ❑ Budgeting and management accounting.

- ❑ Human resource administration, including personnel evaluations and compensation.

- ❑ Internal communications and information flows.

- ❑ Administration of the internal audit activity's policies and procedures.

1111–Direct Interaction with the Board

The CAE must communicate and interact directly with the board.

Practice Advisory 1111-1: Board Interaction

1. Direct communication occurs when the CAE regularly attends and participates in board meetings that relate to the board's oversight responsibilities for auditing, financial reporting, organizational governance, and control. The CAE's attendance and participation at these meetings provide an opportunity to be apprised of strategic business and operational developments and to raise high-level risk, systems, procedures, or control issues at an early stage. Meeting attendance also provides an opportunity to exchange information concerning the internal audit activity's plans and activities and to keep each other informed on any other matters of mutual interest.

2. Such communication and interaction also occurs when the CAE meets privately with the board, at least annually.

1120–Individual Objectivity

Internal auditors must have an impartial, unbiased attitude and avoid any conflict of interest.

Interpretation: *"Conflict of interest" is a situation in which an internal auditor who is in a position of trust has a competing professional or personal interest. Such competing interests can make it difficult to fulfill his or her duties impartially. A conflict of interest exists even if no unethical or improper act results. A conflict of interest can create an appearance of impropriety that can undermine confidence in the internal auditor, the internal audit activity, and the profession. A conflict of interest could impair an individual's ability to perform his or her duties and responsibilities objectively.*

Practice Advisory 1120-1: Individual Objectivity

1. "Individual objectivity" means the internal auditors perform engagements in such a manner that they have an honest belief in their work product and that no significant quality compromises are made. Internal auditors are not to be placed in situations that could impair their ability to make objective professional judgments.

2. Individual objectivity involves the CAE organizing staff assignments that prevent potential and actual conflict of interest and bias, periodically obtaining information from the internal audit staff concerning potential conflict of interest and bias, and, when practicable, rotating internal audit staff assignments periodically.

3. Review of internal audit work results before the related engagement communications are released assists in providing reasonable assurance that the work was performed objectively.

4. The internal auditor's objectivity is not adversely affected when the auditor recommends standards of control for systems or reviews procedures before they are implemented. The auditor's objectivity is considered to be impaired if the auditor designs, installs, drafts procedures for, or operates such systems.

5. The occasional performance of non-audit work by the internal auditor, with full disclosure in the reporting process, would not necessarily impair objectivity. However, it would require careful consideration by management and the internal auditor to avoid adversely affecting the internal auditor's objectivity.

1130–Impairment to Independence or Objectivity

If independence or objectivity is impaired in fact or appearance, the details of the impairment must be disclosed to appropriate parties. The nature of the disclosure will depend on the impairment.

Interpretation: *"Impairment to organizational independence and individual objectivity" may include, but is not limited to, personal conflict of interest, scope limitations, restrictions on access to records, personnel, and properties, and resource limitations, such as funding.*

The determination of appropriate parties to which the details of an impairment to independence or objectivity must be disclosed is dependent on the expectations of the internal audit activity's and the CAE's responsibilities to senior management and the board as described in the internal audit charter, as well as the nature of the impairment.

1130.A1. Internal auditors must refrain from assessing specific operations for which they were previously responsible. Objectivity is presumed to be impaired if an internal auditor provides assurance services for an activity for which he or she had responsibility within the previous year.

1130.A2–Assurance engagements for functions over which the CAE has responsibility must be overseen by a party outside the internal audit activity.

1130.C1–Internal auditors may provide consulting services relating to operations for which they had previous responsibilities.

1130.C2–If internal auditors have potential impairments to independence or objectivity relating to proposed consulting services, disclosure must be made to the engagement client prior to accepting the engagement.

Practice Advisory 1130-1: Impairment to Independence or Objectivity

1. Internal auditors are to report to the CAE any situations in which an actual or potential impairment to independence or objectivity may reasonably be inferred or if they have questions about whether a situation constitutes an impairment to objectivity or independence. If the CAE determines that impairment exists or may be inferred, he or she needs to reassign the auditor(s).

2. A scope limitation is a restriction placed on the internal audit activity that precludes the activity from accomplishing its objectives and plans. Among other things, a scope limitation may restrict the:

- ☐ Scope defined in the internal audit charter.
- ☐ Internal audit activity's access to records, personnel, and physical properties relevant to the performance of engagements.
- ☐ Approved engagement work schedule.

☐ Performance of necessary engagement procedures.

☐ Approved staffing plan and financial budget.

3. A scope limitation, along with its potential effect, needs to be communicated, preferably in writing, to the board. The CAE needs to consider whether it is appropriate to inform the board regarding scope limitations that were previously communicated to and accepted by the board. This may be necessary particularly when there have been organization, board, senior management, or other changes.

4. Internal auditors are not to accept fees, gifts, or entertainment from an employee, client, customer, supplier, or business associate that may create the appearance that the auditors' objectivity has been impaired. The appearance that objectivity has been impaired may apply to current and future engagements conducted by the auditors. The status of engagements is not to be considered as justification for receiving fees, gifts, or entertainment. The receipt of promotional items (such as pens, calendars, or samples) that are available to employees and the general public and have minimal value do not hinder internal auditors' professional judgments. Internal auditors are to report immediately to their supervisors the offer of all material fees or gifts.

Practice Advisory 1130.A1-1: Assessing Operations for Which Internal Auditors Were Previously Responsible

1. Persons transferred to, or temporarily engaged by, the internal audit activity should not be assigned to audit those activities they previously performed or for which they had management responsibility until at least one year has elapsed. Such assignments are presumed to impair objectivity, and additional consideration should be exercised when supervising the engagement work and communicating engagement results.

Practice Advisory 1130.A2-1: Internal Audit's Responsibility for Other (Non-Audit) Functions

1. Internal auditors are not to accept responsibility for non-audit functions or duties that are subject to periodic internal audit assessments. If they have this responsibility, then they are not functioning as internal auditors.

2. When the internal audit activity, CAE, or individual internal auditor is responsible for, or management is considering assigning, an operational responsibility that the internal audit activity might audit, the internal auditor's independence and objectivity may be impaired. At a minimum, the CAE needs to consider the next factors in assessing the impact on independence and objectivity:

☐ Requirements of the Code of Ethics and the *Standards*.

☐ Expectations of stakeholders, who may include the shareholders, board of directors, management, legislative bodies, public entities, regulatory bodies, and public interest groups.

☐ Allowances and/or restrictions contained in the internal audit charter.

☐ Disclosures required by the *Standards*.

☐ Audit coverage of the activities or responsibilities undertaken by the internal auditor.

☐ Significance of the operational function to the organization (in terms of revenue, expenses, reputation, and influence).

☐ Length or duration of the assignment and scope of responsibility.

☐ Adequacy of separation of duties.

☐ Whether there is any history or other evidence that the internal auditor's objectivity may be at risk.

3. If the internal audit charter contains specific restrictions or limiting language regarding the assignment of non-audit functions to the internal auditor, then disclosure and discussion

with management of such restrictions is necessary. If management insists on such an assignment, then disclosure and discussion of this matter with the board is necessary. If the internal audit charter is silent on this matter, the guidance noted in the points listed below are to be considered. All the points noted below are subordinate to the language of the internal audit charter.

4. When the internal audit activity accepts operational responsibilities and that operation is part of the internal audit plan, the CAE needs to:

- Minimize the impairment to objectivity by using a contracted, third-party entity or external auditors to complete audits of those areas reporting to the CAE.

- Confirm that individuals with operational responsibility for those areas reporting to the CAE do not participate in internal audits of the operation.

- Ensure that internal auditors conducting the assurance engagement of those areas reporting to the CAE are supervised by, and report the results of the assessment, to senior management and the board.

- Disclose the operational responsibilities of the internal auditor for the function, the significance of the operation to the organization (in terms of revenue, expenses, or other pertinent information), and the relationship of those who audited the function.

5. The auditor's operational responsibilities need to be disclosed in the related audit report of those areas reporting to the CAE and in the internal auditor's standard communication to the board. Results of the internal audit may also be discussed with management and/or other appropriate stakeholders. Impairment disclosure does not negate the requirement that assurance engagements for functions over which the CAE has responsibility need to be overseen by a party outside the internal audit activity.

1200–Proficiency and Due Professional Care

Engagements must be performed with proficiency and due professional care.

Practice Advisory 1200-1: Proficiency and Due Professional Care

1. Proficiency and due professional care are the responsibility of the CAE and each internal auditor. As such, the CAE ensures that persons assigned to each engagement collectively possess the necessary knowledge, skills, and other competencies to conduct the engagement appropriately.

2. Due professional care includes conforming with the Code of Ethics and, as appropriate, the organization's code of conduct as well as the codes of conduct for other professional designations the internal auditors may hold. The Code of Ethics extends beyond the definition of internal auditing to include two essential components:

- Principles that are relevant to the profession and practice of internal auditing: integrity, objectivity, confidentiality, and competency.

- Rules of conduct that describe behavioral norms expected of internal auditors. These rules are an aid to interpreting the principles into practical applications and are intended to guide the ethical conduct of internal auditors.

1210–Proficiency

Internal auditors must possess the knowledge, skills, and other competencies needed to perform their individual responsibilities. The internal audit activity collectively must possess or obtain the knowledge, skills, and other competencies needed to perform its responsibilities.

Interpretation: *"Knowledge, skills, and other competencies" is a collective term that refers to the professional proficiency required of internal auditors to effectively carry out their professional responsibilities. Internal auditors are encouraged to demonstrate their proficiency by obtaining appropriate professional certifications and qualifications, such as the Certified Internal Auditor (CIA) designation and other designations offered by The Institute of Internal Auditors (the IIA) and other appropriate professional organizations.*

1210.A1–The CAE must obtain competent advice and assistance if the internal auditors lack the knowledge, skills, or other competencies needed to perform all or part of the engagement.

1210.A2–Internal auditors must have sufficient knowledge to evaluate the risk of fraud and the manner in which it is managed by the organization but are not expected to have the expertise of a person whose primary responsibility is detecting and investigating fraud.

1210.A3–Internal auditors must have sufficient knowledge of key information technology (IT) risks and controls and available technology-based audit techniques to perform their assigned work. However, not all internal auditors are expected to have the expertise of an internal auditor whose primary responsibility is IT auditing.

1210.C1–The CAE must decline the consulting engagement or obtain competent advice and assistance if the internal auditors lack the knowledge, skills, or other competencies needed to perform all or part of the engagement.

Practice Advisory 1210-1: Proficiency

1. The knowledge, skills, and other competencies referred to in the standard include:

- □ Proficiency in applying internal audit standards, procedures, and techniques in performing engagements. "Proficiency" means the ability to apply knowledge to situations likely to be encountered and to deal with them appropriately without extensive recourse to technical research and assistance.

- □ Proficiency in accounting principles and techniques if internal auditors work extensively with financial records and reports.

- □ Knowledge to identify the indicators of fraud.

- □ Knowledge of key IT risks and controls and available technology-based audit techniques.

- □ An understanding of management principles to recognize and evaluate the materiality and significance of deviations from good business practices. "An understanding" means the ability to apply broad knowledge to situations likely to be encountered, to recognize significant deviations, and to be able to carry out the research necessary to arrive at reasonable solutions.

- □ An appreciation of the fundamentals of business subjects such as accounting, economics, commercial law, taxation, finance, quantitative methods, IT, risk management, and fraud. "An appreciation" means the ability to recognize the existence of problems or potential problems and to identify the additional research to be undertaken or the assistance to be obtained.

- □ Skills in dealing with people, understanding human relations, and maintaining satisfactory relationships with engagement clients.

- □ Skills in oral and written communications to clearly and effectively convey such matters as engagement objectives, evaluations, conclusions, and recommendations.

2. Suitable criteria of education and experience for filling internal audit positions is established by the CAE, who gives due consideration to the scope of work and level of responsibility and obtains reasonable assurance as to each prospective auditor's qualifications and proficiency.

3. The internal audit activity needs to collectively possess the knowledge, skills, and other competencies essential to the practice of the profession within the organization. Performing an annual analysis of an internal audit activity's knowledge, skills, and other competencies helps identify areas of opportunity that can be addressed by continuing professional development, recruiting, or co-sourcing.

4. Continuing professional development is essential to help ensure internal audit staff remains proficient.

5. The CAE may obtain assistance from experts outside the internal audit activity to support or complement areas where the internal audit activity is not sufficiently proficient.

Practice Advisory 1210.A1-1: Obtaining External Service Providers to Support or Complement the Internal Audit Activity

1. Each member of the internal audit activity need not be qualified in all disciplines. The internal audit activity may use external service providers or internal resources that are qualified in disciplines such as accounting, auditing, economics, finance, statistics, IT, engineering, taxation, law, environmental affairs, and other areas as needed to meet the internal audit activity's responsibilities.

2. An external service provider is a person or firm, independent of the organization, who has special knowledge, skill, and experience in a particular discipline. External service providers include actuaries, accountants, appraisers, culture or language experts, environmental specialists, fraud investigators, lawyers, engineers, geologists, security specialists, statisticians, IT specialists, the organization's external auditors, and other audit organizations. An external service provider may be engaged by the board, senior management, or the CAE.

3. External service providers may be used by the internal audit activity in connection with, among other things:

- Achievement of the objectives in the engagement work schedule.

- Audit activities where a specialized skill and knowledge are needed, such as IT, statistics, taxes, or language translations.

- Valuations of assets, such as land and buildings, works of art, precious gems, investments, and complex financial instruments.

- Determination of quantities or physical condition of certain assets, such as mineral and petroleum reserves.

- Measuring the work completed and to be completed on contracts in progress.

- Fraud and security investigations.

- Determination of amounts by using specialized methods, such as actuarial determinations of employee benefit obligations.

- Interpretation of legal, technical, and regulatory requirements.

- Evaluation of the internal audit activity's quality assurance and improvement program in conformance with the *Standards*.

- Mergers and acquisitions.

- Consulting on risk management and other matters.

4. When the CAE intends to use and rely on the work of an external service provider, the CAE needs to consider the competence, independence, and objectivity of the external service provider as it relates to the particular assignment to be performed. The assessment of competency, independence, and objectivity is also needed when the external service provider is selected by senior management or the board, and the CAE intends to use and rely on the external service provider's work. When the selection is made by others and the CAE's assessment indicates that he or she should not use and rely on the work of the external service provider, communication of such results is needed to senior management or the board, as appropriate.

5. The CAE determines that the external service provider possesses the necessary knowledge, skills, and other competencies to perform the engagement by considering:

- Professional certification, license, or other recognition of the external service provider's competence in the relevant discipline.

- Membership of the external service provider in an appropriate professional organization and adherence to that organization's code of ethics.

- The reputation of the external service provider. This may include contacting others familiar with the external service provider's work.

- The external service provider's experience in the type of work being considered.

- The extent of education and training received by the external service provider in disciplines that pertain to the particular engagement.

- The external service provider's knowledge and experience in the industry in which the organization operates.

6. The CAE needs to assess the relationship of the external service provider to the organization and to the internal audit activity to ensure that independence and objectivity are maintained throughout the engagement. In performing the assessment, the CAE verifies that there are no financial, organizational, or personal relationships that will prevent the external service provider from rendering impartial and unbiased judgments and opinions when performing or reporting on the engagement.

7. The CAE assesses the independence and objectivity of the external service provider by considering:

- The financial interest the external service provider may have in the organization.

- The personal or professional affiliation the external service provider may have to the board, senior management, or others within the organization.

- The relationship the external service provider may have had with the organization or the activities being reviewed.

- The extent of other ongoing services the external service provider may be performing for the organization.

- Compensation or other incentives that the external service provider may have.

8. If the external service provider is also the organization's external auditor and the nature of the engagement is extended audit services, the CAE needs to ascertain that work performed does not impair the external auditor's independence. "Extended audit services" refer to those services beyond the requirements of audit standards generally accepted by external auditors. If the organization's external auditors act or appear to act as members of senior management, management, or as employees of the organization, then their independence is impaired. Additionally, external auditors may provide the organization with other services, such as tax and

consulting. Independence needs to be assessed in relation to the full range of services provided to the organization.

9. To ascertain that the scope of work is adequate for the purposes of the internal audit activity, the CAE obtains sufficient information regarding the scope of the external service provider's work. It may be prudent to document these and other matters in an engagement letter or contract. To accomplish this, the CAE reviews the next items with the external service provider:

- Objectives and scope of work including deliverables and time frames.
- Specific matters expected to be covered in the engagement communications.
- Access to relevant records, personnel, and physical properties.
- Information regarding assumptions and procedures to be employed.
- Ownership and custody of engagement working papers, if applicable.
- Confidentiality and restrictions on information obtained during the engagement.
- Where applicable, conformance with the *Standards* and the internal audit activity's standards for working practices.

10. In reviewing the work of an external service provider, the CAE evaluates the adequacy of work performed, which includes sufficiency of information obtained to afford a reasonable basis for the conclusions reached and the resolution of exceptions or other unusual matters.

11. When the CAE issues engagement communications and an external service provider was used, the CAE may, as appropriate, refer to such services provided. The external service provider needs to be informed, and, if appropriate, concurrence should be obtained before making such reference in engagement communications.

1220–Due Professional Care

Internal auditors must apply the care and skill expected of a reasonably prudent and competent internal auditor. Due professional care does not imply infallibility.

Practice Advisory 1220-1: Due Professional Care

1. Due professional care calls for the application of the care and skill expected of a reasonably prudent and competent internal auditor in the same or similar circumstances. Due professional care is therefore appropriate to the complexities of the engagement being performed. Exercising due professional care involves internal auditors being alert to the possibility of fraud, intentional wrongdoing, errors and omissions, inefficiency, waste, ineffectiveness, and conflicts of interest as well as being alert to those conditions and activities where irregularities are most likely to occur. This also involves internal auditors identifying inadequate controls and recommending improvements to promote conformance with acceptable procedures and practices.

2. Due professional care implies reasonable care and competence, not infallibility or extraordinary performance. As such, due professional care requires the internal auditor to conduct examinations and verifications to a reasonable extent. Accordingly, internal auditors cannot give absolute assurance that noncompliance or irregularities do not exist. Nevertheless, the possibility of material irregularities or noncompliance needs to be considered whenever an internal auditor undertakes an internal audit assignment.

1220.A1–Internal auditors must exercise due professional care by considering the:

- Extent of work needed to achieve the engagement's objectives.
- Relative complexity, materiality, or significance of matters to which assurance procedures are applied.

□ Adequacy and effectiveness of governance, risk management, and control processes.

□ Probability of significant errors, fraud, or noncompliance.

□ Cost of assurance in relation to potential benefits.

1220.A2–In exercising due professional care, internal auditors must consider the use of technology-based audit and other data analysis techniques.

1220.A3–Internal auditors must be alert to the significant risks that might affect objectives, operations, or resources. However, assurance procedures alone, even when performed with due professional care, do not guarantee that all significant risks will be identified.

1220.C1–Internal auditors must exercise due professional care during a consulting engagement by considering the:

□ Needs and expectations of clients, including the nature, timing, and communication of engagement results.

□ Relative complexity and extent of work needed to achieve the engagement's objectives.

□ Cost of the consulting engagement in relation to potential benefits.

1230–Continuing Professional Development

Internal auditors must enhance their knowledge, skills, and other competencies through continuing professional development.

Practice Advisory 1230-1: Continuing Professional Development

1. Internal auditors are responsible for continuing their education to enhance and maintain their proficiency. Internal auditors need to stay informed about improvements and current developments in internal audit standards, procedures, and techniques, including the IIA's *International Professional Practices Framework* guidance. Continuing professional education (CPE) may be obtained through membership, participation, and volunteering in professional organizations, such as the IIA; attendance at conferences, seminars, and in-house training programs; completion of college and self-study courses; and involvement in research projects.

2. Internal auditors are encouraged to demonstrate their proficiency by obtaining appropriate professional certification, such as the Certified Internal Auditor (CIA) designation, other designations offered by the IIA, and additional designations related to internal auditing.

3. Internal auditors are encouraged to pursue CPE (related to their organization's activities and industry) to maintain their proficiency with regard to the governance, risk, and control processes of their unique organization.

4. Internal auditors who perform specialized audit and consulting work—such as IT, tax, actuarial, or systems design—may undertake specialized CPE to allow them to perform their internal audit work with proficiency.

5. Internal auditors with professional certifications are responsible for obtaining sufficient CPE to satisfy requirements related to the professional certification held.

6. Internal auditors not currently holding appropriate certifications are encouraged to pursue an educational program and/or individual study to obtain professional certification.

1300–Quality Assurance and Improvement Program

The CAE must develop and maintain a quality assurance and improvement program (QAIP) that covers all aspects of the internal audit activity.

Interpretation: *A QAIP is designed to enable an evaluation of the internal audit activity's conformance with the definition of internal auditing and the* Standards *and an evaluation of whether internal auditors apply the Code of Ethics. The program also assesses the efficiency and effectiveness of the internal audit activity and identifies opportunities for improvement.*

Practice Advisory 1300-1: Quality Assurance and Improvement Program

1. The CAE is responsible for establishing an internal audit activity whose scope of work includes the activities in the *Standards* and in the definition of internal auditing. To ensure that this occurs, Standard 1300 requires that the CAE develop and maintain a QAIP.

2. The CAE is accountable for implementing processes designed to provide reasonable assurance to the various stakeholders that the internal audit activity:

- Performs in accordance with the internal audit charter, which is consistent with the definition of internal auditing, the Code of Ethics, and the *Standards*.
- Operates in an effective and efficient manner.
- Is perceived by those stakeholders as adding value and improving the organization's operations.

These processes include appropriate supervision, periodic internal assessments and ongoing monitoring of quality assurance, and periodic external assessments.

3. The QAIP needs to be sufficiently comprehensive to encompass all aspects of operation and management of an internal audit activity, as found in the definition of internal auditing, the Code of Ethics, the *Standards*, and best practices of the profession. The QAIP process is performed by or under direct supervision of the CAE. Except in small internal audit activities, the CAE would usually delegate most QAIP responsibilities to subordinates. In large or complex environments (e.g., numerous business units and/or locations), the CAE establishes a formal QAIP function—headed by an internal audit executive—independent of the audit and consulting segments of the internal audit activity. This executive (and limited staff) administers and monitors the activities needed for a successful QAIP.

1310–Requirements of the Quality Assurance and Improvement Program

The quality assurance and improvement program must include both internal and external assessments.

Practice Advisory 1310-1: Requirements of the Quality Assurance and Improvement Program

1. A QAIP is an ongoing and periodic assessment of the entire spectrum of audit and consulting work performed by the internal audit activity. These ongoing and periodic assessments are composed of rigorous, comprehensive processes; continuous supervision and testing of internal audit and consulting work; and periodic validations of conformance with the definition of internal auditing, the Code of Ethics, and the *Standards*. This also includes ongoing measurements and analyses of performance metrics (e.g., internal audit plan accomplishment, cycle time, recommendations accepted, and customer satisfaction). If the assessments' results indicate areas for improvement by the internal audit activity, the CAE will implement the improvements through the QAIP.

2. Assessments evaluate and conclude on the quality of the internal audit activity and lead to recommendations for appropriate improvements. QAIPs include an evaluation of:

- Conformance with the definition of internal auditing, the Code of Ethics, and the *Standards*, including timely corrective actions to remedy any significant instances of nonconformance.

□ Adequacy of the internal audit activity's charter, goals, objectives, policies, and procedures.

□ Contribution to the organization's governance, risk management, and control processes.

□ Compliance with applicable laws, regulations, and government or industry standards.

□ Effectiveness of continuous improvement activities and adoption of best practices.

□ The extent to which the internal audit activity adds value and improves the organization's operations.

3. The QAIP efforts also include follow-up on recommendations involving appropriate and timely modification of resources, technology, processes, and procedures.

4. To provide accountability and transparency, the CAE communicates the results of external and, as appropriate, internal quality program assessments to the various stakeholders of the activity (such as senior management, the board, and external auditors). At least annually, the CAE reports to senior management and the board on the quality program efforts and results.

1311–Internal Assessments

Internal assessments must include:

□ Ongoing monitoring of the performance of the internal audit activity.

□ Periodic reviews performed through self-assessment or by other persons within the organization with sufficient knowledge of internal audit practices.

Interpretation: *Ongoing monitoring is an integral part of the day-to-day supervision, review, and measurement of the internal audit activity. Ongoing monitoring is incorporated into the routine policies and practices used to manage the internal audit activity and uses processes, tools, and information considered necessary to evaluate conformance with the definition of internal auditing, the Code of Ethics, and the* Standards.

Periodic reviews are assessments conducted to evaluate conformance with the definition of internal auditing, the Code of Ethics, and the Standards.

Sufficient knowledge of internal audit practices requires at least an understanding of all elements of the International Professional Practices Framework.

Practice Advisory 1311-1: Internal Assessments

1. The processes and tools used in ongoing internal assessments include:

□ Engagement supervision;

□ Checklists and procedures (e.g., in an audit and procedures manual) are being followed;

□ Feedback from audit customers and other stakeholders;

□ Selective peer reviews of working papers by staff not involved in the respective audits;

□ Project budgets, timekeeping systems, audit plan completion, and cost recoveries; and/or

□ Analyses of other performance metrics (such as cycle time and recommendations accepted).

2. Conclusions are developed as to the quality of ongoing performance, and follow-up action is taken to ensure that appropriate improvements are implemented.

3. The IIA's *Quality Assessment Manual*, or a comparable set of guidance and tools, should serve as the basis for periodic internal assessments.

4. Periodic internal assessments may:

☐ Include more in-depth interviews and surveys of stakeholder groups.

☐ Be performed by members of the internal audit activity (self-assessment).

☐ Be performed by CIAs or other competent audit professionals currently assigned elsewhere in the organization.

☐ Encompass a combination of self-assessment and preparation of materials subsequently reviewed by CIAs or other competent audit professionals.

☐ Include benchmarking of the internal audit activity's practices and performance metrics against relevant best practices of the internal audit profession.

5. A periodic internal assessment performed within a short time before an external assessment can serve to facilitate and reduce the cost of the external assessment. If the periodic internal assessment is performed by a qualified, independent external reviewer or review team, the assessment results should not communicate any assurances on the outcome of the subsequent external quality assessment. The report may offer suggestions and recommendations to enhance the internal audit activities' practices. If the external assessment takes the form of a self-assessment with independent validation, the periodic internal assessment can serve as the self-assessment portion of this process.

6. Conclusions are developed as to quality of performance, and appropriate action are initiated to achieve improvements and conformity to the *Standards*, as necessary.

7. The CAE establishes a structure for reporting results of internal assessments that maintains appropriate credibility and objectivity. Generally, those assigned responsibility for conducting ongoing and periodic reviews report to the CAE while performing the reviews and communicate results directly to the CAE.

8. At least annually, the CAE reports the results of internal assessments, necessary action plans, and their successful implementation to senior management and the board.

1312–External Assessments

External assessments must be conducted at least once every five years by a qualified, independent reviewer or review team from outside the organization. The CAE must discuss with the board:

■ The need for more frequent external assessments.

■ The qualifications and independence of the external reviewer or review team, including any potential conflict of interest.

Interpretation: *A qualified reviewer or review team demonstrates competence in two areas: the professional practice of internal auditing and the external assessment process. Competence can be demonstrated through a mixture of experience and theoretical learning. Experience gained in organizations of similar size, complexity, sector or industry, and technical issues is more valuable than less relevant experience. In the case of a review team, not all members of the team need to have all the competencies; it is the team as a whole that is qualified. The CAE uses professional judgment when assessing whether a reviewer or review team demonstrates sufficient competence to be qualified.*

An "independent reviewer or review team" means not having either a real or an apparent conflict of interest and not being a part of, or under the control of, the organization to which the internal audit activity belongs.

Practice Advisory 1312-1: External Assessments

1. External assessments cover the entire spectrum of audit and consulting work performed by the internal audit activity and should not be limited to assessing its quality assurance and improvement program. To achieve optimum benefits from an external assessment, the scope of work should include benchmarking, identification, and reporting of leading practices that could assist the internal audit activity in becoming more efficient and/or effective. This can be accomplished in two ways: through (a) a full external assessment by a qualified, independent external reviewer or review team or (b) a comprehensive internal self-assessment with independent validation by a qualified, independent external reviewer or review team. Nonetheless, the CAE is to ensure that the scope clearly states the expected deliverables of the external assessment in each case.

2. External assessments of an internal audit activity contain an expressed opinion as to the entire spectrum of assurance and consulting work performed (or that should have been performed based on the internal audit charter) by the internal audit activity, including its conformance with the definition of internal auditing, the Code of Ethics, and the *Standards* and, as appropriate, includes recommendations for improvement. Apart from conformance with the definition of internal auditing, the Code of Ethics, and the *Standards*, the scope of the assessment is adjusted at the discretion of the CAE, senior management, or the board. These assessments can have considerable value to the CAE and other members of the internal audit activity, especially when benchmarking and best practices are shared.

3. On completion of the review, a formal communication is to be given to senior management and the board.

4. There are two approaches to external assessments. The first approach is a full external assessment conducted by a qualified, independent external reviewer or review team. This approach involves an outside team of competent professionals under the leadership of an experienced and professional project manager. The second approach involves the use of a qualified, independent external reviewer or review team to conduct an independent validation of the internal self-assessment and a report completed by the internal audit activity. Independent external reviewers should be well versed in leading internal audit practices.

5. Individuals who perform the external assessment are free from any obligation to, or interest in, the organization whose internal audit activity is the subject of the external assessment or the personnel of such organization. Particular matters relating to independence, which are to be considered by the CAE in consultation with the board, in selecting a qualified, independent external reviewer or review team, include:

- ☐ Any real or apparent conflict of interest of firms that provide:

  - The external audit of financial statements.

  - Significant consulting services in the areas of governance, risk management, financial reporting, internal control, and other related areas.

  - Assistance to the internal audit activity. The significance and amount of work performed by the professional service provider is to be considered in the deliberation.

- ☐ Any real or apparent conflict of interest of former employees of the organization who would perform the assessment. Consideration should be given to the length of time the individual has been independent of the organization.

- ☐ Individuals who perform the assessment are independent of the organization whose internal audit activity is the subject of the assessment and do not have any real or apparent conflict of interest. "Independent of the organization" means not a part of, or under the control of, the organization to which the internal audit activity belongs. In the selection of a qualified, independent external reviewer or review team, consideration is to be given to any real or apparent conflict of interest the reviewer may have due to present or past relationships with the organization or its internal audit activity, including the reviewer's participation in internal quality assessments.

□ Individuals in another department of the subject organization or in a related organization, although organizationally separate from the internal audit activity, are not considered independent for purposes of conducting an external assessment. A related organization may be a parent organization; an affiliate in the same group of entities; or an entity with regular oversight, supervision, or quality assurance responsibilities with respect to the subject organization.

□ Real or apparent conflict involving peer review arrangements. Peer review arrangements among three or more organizations (e.g., within an industry or other affinity group, regional association, or other group of organizations—except as precluded by the "related organization" definition in the previous point) may be structured in a manner that alleviates independence concerns, but care must be taken to ensure that the issue of independence does not arise. Peer reviews between two organizations would not pass the independence test.

□ To overcome concerns regarding the appearance or reality of impairment of independence in instances such as those discussed in this section, one or more independent individuals could be part of the external assessment team to independently validate the work of that external assessment team.

6. Integrity requires the reviewer to be honest and candid within the constraints of confidentiality. Service and the public trust should not be subordinated to personal gain and advantage. Objectivity is a state of mind and a quality that lends value to a reviewer's services. The principle of objectivity imposes the obligation to be impartial, intellectually honest, and free of conflict of interest.

7. Performing and communicating the results of an external assessment require the exercise of professional judgment. Accordingly, an individual serving as an external reviewer should:

□ Be a competent, CIA professional who possesses current, in-depth knowledge of the *Standards*.

□ Be well versed in the best practices of the profession.

□ Have at least three years of recent experience in the practice of internal auditing or related consulting at a management level.

Leaders of independent review teams and external reviewers who independently validate the results of the self-assessment should have an additional level of competence and experience gained from working previously as team members on an external quality assessment, successful completion of the IIA's quality assessment training course or similar training, and CAE or comparable senior internal audit management experience.

8. The reviewer should possess relevant technical expertise and industry experience. Individuals with expertise in other specialized areas may assist the team. For example, specialists in enterprise risk management, IT auditing, statistical sampling, operations monitoring systems, or control self-assessment may participate in certain segments of the assessment.

9. The CAE involves senior management and the board in determining the approach and selection of an external quality assessment provider.

10. The external assessment consists of a broad scope of coverage that includes the following elements of the internal audit activity:

☐ Conformance with the definition of internal auditing; the Code of Ethics; and the *Standards*; and the internal audit activity's charter, plans, policies, procedures, practices, and applicable legislative and regulatory requirements.

☐ Expectations of the internal audit activity expressed by the board, senior management, and operational managers.

☐ Integration of the internal audit activity into the organization's governance process, including the relationships between and among the key groups involved in the process.

☐ Tools and techniques employed by the internal audit activity.

☐ Mix of knowledge, experience, and disciplines within the staff, including staff focus on process improvement.

☐ Determination as to whether the internal audit activity adds value and improves the organization's operations.

11. The preliminary results of the review are discussed with the CAE during and at the conclusion of the assessment process. Final results are communicated to the CAE or other official who authorized the review for the organization, preferably with copies sent directly to appropriate members of senior management and the board.

12. The communication includes:

☐ An opinion on the internal audit activity's conformance with the definition of internal auditing, the Code of Ethics, and the *Standards* based on a structured rating process. The term "conformance" means the practices of the internal audit activity, taken as a whole, satisfy the requirements of the definition of internal auditing, the Code of Ethics, and the *Standards*. Similarly, "nonconformance" means the impact and severity of the deficiencies in the practices of the internal audit activity are so significant they impair the internal audit activity's ability to discharge its responsibilities. The degree of "partial conformance" with the definition of internal auditing, the Code of Ethics, and/or individual *Standards*, if relevant to the overall opinion, should also be expressed in the report on the independent assessment. The expression of an opinion on the results of the external assessment requires the application of sound business judgment, integrity, and due professional care.

☐ An assessment and evaluation of the use of best practices, both those observed during the assessment and others potentially applicable to the activity.

☐ Recommendations for improvement, where appropriate.

☐ Responses from the CAE that include an action plan and implementation dates.

13. To provide accountability and transparency, the CAE communicates the results of external quality assessments, including specifics of planned remedial actions for significant issues and subsequent information as to accomplishment of those planned actions, to the various stakeholders of the activity, such as senior management, the board, and external auditors.

Practice Advisory 1312-2: External Assessments: Self-Assessment with Independent Validation

1. An external assessment by a qualified, independent reviewer or review team may be troublesome for smaller internal audit activities, or there may be circumstances in other organizations where a full external assessment by an independent team is not deemed appropriate or necessary. For example, the internal audit activity may (a) be in an industry subject to extensive regulation and/or supervision, (b) be otherwise subject to extensive external oversight and direction relating

to governance and internal controls, (c) have been recently subjected to external review(s) and/or consulting services in which there was extensive benchmarking with best practices, or (d) in the judgment of the CAE, the benefits of self-assessment for staff development and the strength of the internal quality assurance and improvement program currently outweigh the benefits of a quality assessment by an external team.

2. A self-assessment with independent (external) validation includes:

☐ A comprehensive and fully documented self-assessment process, which emulates the external assessment process, at least with respect to evaluation of conformance with the definition of internal auditing, the Code of Ethics, and the *Standards*.

☐ An independent, on-site validation by a qualified, independent reviewer.

☐ Economical time and resource requirements—for example, the primary focus would be on conformance with the *Standards*.

☐ Limited attention to other areas—such as benchmarking, review and consultation as to employment of leading practices, and interviews with senior and operating management—may be reduced. However, the information produced by these parts of the assessment is one of the benefits of an external assessment.

3. The same guidance and criteria as set forth in Practice Advisory 1312-1 would apply for a self-assessment with independent validation.

4. A team under the direction of the CAE performs and fully documents the self-assessment process. A draft report, similar to that for an external assessment, is prepared including the CAE's judgment on conformance with the *Standards*.

5. A qualified, independent reviewer or review team performs sufficient tests of the self-assessment so as to validate the results and express the indicated level of the activity's conformance with the definition of internal auditing, the Code of Ethics, and the *Standards*. The independent validation follows the process outlined in the IIA's *Quality Assessment Manual* or a similar comprehensive process.

6. As part of the independent validation, the independent external reviewer—upon completion of a rigorous review of the self-assessment team's evaluation of conformance with the definition of internal auditing, the Code of Ethics, and the *Standards*:

☐ Reviews the draft report and attempts to reconcile unresolved issues (if any).

☐ If in agreement with the opinion of conformance with the definition of internal auditing, the Code of Ethics, and the *Standards*, adds wording (as needed) to the report, concurring with the self-assessment process and opinion and—to the extent deemed appropriate—with the report's findings, conclusions, and recommendations.

☐ If not in agreement with the evaluation, adds dissenting wording to the report, specifying the points of disagreement with it and—to the extent deemed appropriate—with the significant findings, conclusions, recommendations, and opinions in the report.

☐ Alternatively, may prepare a separate independent validation report—concurring or expressing disagreement as outlined above—to accompany the report of the self-assessment.

7. The final report(s) of the self-assessment with independent validation is signed by the self-assessment team and the qualified, independent external reviewer(s) and issued by the CAE to senior management and the board.

8. To provide accountability and transparency, the CAE communicates the results of external quality assessments—including specifics of planned remedial actions for significant issues and subsequent information as to accomplishment of those planned actions—with the various stakeholders of the activity, such as senior management, the board, and external auditors.

1320–Reporting on the Quality Assurance and Improvement Program

The CAE must communicate the results of the QAIP to senior management and the board.

Interpretation: *The form, content, and frequency of communicating the results of the QAIP is established through discussions with senior management and the board and considers the responsibilities of the internal audit activity and CAE as contained in the internal audit charter. To demonstrate conformance with the definition of internal auditing, the Code of Ethics, and the* Standards, *the results of external and periodic internal assessments are communicated upon completion of such assessments and the results of ongoing monitoring are communicated at least annually. The results include the reviewer's or review team's assessment with respect to the degree of conformance.*

> No Practice Advisory for Standard 1320

1321–Use of "Conforms with the *International Standards for the Professional Practice of Internal Auditing*"

The CAE may state that the internal audit activity conforms with the *International Standards for the Professional Practice of Internal Auditing* only if the results of the QAIP support this statement.

Interpretation: *The internal audit activity conforms with the* Standards *when it achieves the outcomes described in the definition of internal auditing, Code of Ethics, and* Standards.

The results of the QAIP include the results of both internal and external assessments. All internal audit activities will have the results of internal assessments. Internal audit activities in existence for at least five years will also have the results of external assessments.

Practice Advisory 1321-1: Use of "Conforms with the *International Standards for the Professional Practice of Internal Auditing*"

1. Ongoing monitoring and external and internal assessments of an internal audit activity are performed to evaluate and express an opinion as to the internal audit activity's conformance with the definition of internal auditing, the Code of Ethics, and the *Standards* and, as appropriate, should include recommendations for improvement.

2. The phrase to be used may be "in conformance with the *Standards*" or "in conformity to the *Standards.*" To use one of these phrases, an external assessment is required at least once during each five-year period, along with ongoing monitoring and periodic internal assessments, and these activities need to have concluded that the internal audit activity is in conformance with the definition of internal auditing, the Code of Ethics, and the *Standards*. Initial use of the conformance phrase is not appropriate until an external review has demonstrated that the internal audit activity is in conformance with the definition of internal auditing, the Code of Ethics, and the *Standards*.

3. The CAE is responsible for disclosing instances of nonconformance that impact the overall scope or operation of the internal audit activity, including failure to obtain an external assessment within a five-year period, to senior management and the board.

4. Before the internal audit activity's use of the conformance phrase, any instances of nonconformance that have been disclosed by a quality assessment (internal or external) which impair the internal audit activity's ability to discharge its responsibilities needs to be adequately remedied. In addition, the following are needed:

□ Remedial actions need to be documented and reported to the relevant assessor(s) to obtain concurrence that the nonconformance has been adequately remedied.

□ Remedial actions and agreement of the relevant assessor(s) therewith need to be reported to senior management and the board.

1322–Disclosure of Nonconformance

When nonconformance with the definition of internal auditing, the Code of Ethics, or the *Standards* impacts the overall scope or operation of the internal audit activity, the CAE must disclose the nonconformance and the impact to senior management and the board.

No Practice Advisory for Standard 1322

(b) Performance Standards (2000 to 2600)

2000–Managing the Internal Audit Activity

The CAE must effectively manage the internal audit activity to ensure it adds value to the organization.

Interpretation: *The internal audit activity is effectively managed when:*

■ *The results of the internal audit activity's work achieve the purpose and responsibility included in the internal audit charter.*

■ *The internal audit activity conforms with the definition of internal auditing and the* Standards.

■ *The individuals who are part of the internal audit activity demonstrate conformance with the Code of Ethics and the* Standards.

The internal audit activity adds value to the organization (and its stakeholders) when it provides objective and relevant assurance, and contributes to the effectiveness and efficiency of governance, risk management, and control processes.

No Practice Advisory for Standard 2000

2010–Planning

The CAE must establish risk-based plans to determine the priorities of the internal audit activity, consistent with the organization's goals.

Interpretation: *The CAE is responsible for developing a risk-based plan. The CAE takes into account the organization's risk management framework, including using **risk appetite** levels set by management for the different activities or parts of the organization. If a framework does not exist, the CAE uses his or her own judgment of risks after consultation with senior management and the board.*

> 2010.A1–The internal audit activity's plan of engagements must be based on a documented risk assessment, undertaken at least annually. The input of senior management and the board must be considered in this process.

2010.A2–The CAE must identify and consider the expectations of senior management, the board, and other stakeholders for internal audit opinions and other conclusions.

2010.C1–The CAE should consider accepting proposed consulting engagements based on the engagement's potential to improve management of risks, add value, and improve the organization's operations. Accepted engagements must be included in the plan.

Practice Advisory 2010-1: Linking the Audit Plan to Risk and Exposures

1. In developing the internal audit activity's audit plan, many CAEs find it useful to first develop or update the audit universe. The audit universe is a list of all the possible audits that could be performed. The CAE may obtain input on the audit universe from senior management and the board.

2. The audit universe can include components from the organization's strategic plan. By incorporating components of the organization's strategic plan, the audit universe will consider and reflect the business's overall objectives. Strategic plans also likely reflect the organization's attitude toward risk and the degree of difficulty to achieving planned objectives. The audit universe will normally be influenced by the results of the risk management process. The organization's strategic plan considers the environment in which the organization operates. These same environmental factors would likely impact the audit universe and assessment of relative risk.

3. The CAE prepares the internal audit activity's audit plan based on the audit universe, input from senior management and the board, and an assessment of risk and exposures affecting the organization. Key audit objectives are usually to provide senior management and the board with assurance and information to help them accomplish the organization's objectives, including an assessment of the effectiveness of management's risk management activities.

4. The audit universe and related audit plan are updated to reflect changes in management direction, objectives, emphasis, and focus. It is advisable to assess the audit universe on at least an annual basis to ensure that it reflects the most current strategies and direction of the organization. In some situations, audit plans may need to be updated more frequently (e.g., quarterly) in response to changes in the organization's business, operations, programs, systems, and controls.

5. Audit work schedules are based on, among other factors, an assessment of risk and exposures. Prioritizing is needed to make decisions for applying resources. A variety of risk models exist to assist the CAE. Most risk models use risk factors such as impact, likelihood, materiality, asset liquidity, management competence, quality of and adherence to internal controls, degree of change or stability, timing and results of last audit engagement, complexity, and employee and government relations.

Practice Advisory 2010-2: Using the Risk Management Process in Internal Audit Planning

1. Risk management is a critical part of providing sound governance that touches all the organization's activities. Many organizations are moving to adopt consistent and holistic risk management approaches that should, ideally, be fully integrated into the management of the organization. Risk management applies at all levels—enterprise, function, and business unit—of the organization. Management typically uses a risk management framework to conduct the assessment and document the assessment results.

2. An effective risk management process can assist in identifying key controls related to significant inherent risks. Enterprise risk management (ERM) is a term in common use. The Committee of Sponsoring Organizations (COSO) of the Treadway Commission defines "ERM" as "a process, effected by an entity's board of directors, management, and other personnel, applied in strategy setting and across the enterprise, designed to identify potential events that may affect the entity, and manage risk to be within its risk appetite, to provide reasonable assurance regarding the achievement of entity objectives." Implementation of controls is one common method

management can use to manage risk within its risk appetite. Internal auditors audit the key controls and provide assurance on the management of significant risks.

3. The IIA *Standards* defines "control" as "any action taken by management, the board, and other parties to manage risk and increase the likelihood that established objectives and goals will be achieved. Management plans, organizes, and directs the performance of sufficient actions to provide reasonable assurance that objectives and goals will be achieved."

4. Two fundamental risk concepts are inherent risk and residual risk (also known as current risk). Financial/external auditors have long had a concept of inherent risk that can be summarized as the susceptibility of information or data to a material misstatement, assuming that there are no related mitigating controls. The *Standards* define "residual risk" as "the risk remaining after management takes action to reduce the impact and likelihood of an adverse event, including control activities in responding to a risk." "Current risk" is often defined as the risk managed within existing controls or control systems.

5. "Key controls" can be defined as controls or groups of controls that help to reduce an otherwise unacceptable risk to a tolerable level. Controls can be most readily conceived as organizational processes that exist to address risks. In an effective risk management process (with adequate documentation), the key controls can be readily identified from the difference between inherent and residual risk across all affected systems that are relied on to reduce the rating of significant risks. If a rating has not been given to inherent risk, the internal auditor estimates the inherent risk rating. When identifying key controls (and assuming the internal auditor has concluded that the risk management process is mature and reliable), the internal auditor would look for:

- ☐ Individual risk factors where there is a significant reduction from inherent to residual risk (particularly if the inherent risk was very high). This highlights controls that are important to the organization.

- ☐ Controls that serve to mitigate a large number of risks.

6. Internal audit planning needs to make use of the organizational risk management process, where one has been developed. In planning an engagement, the internal auditor considers the significant risks of the activity and the means by which management mitigates the risk to an acceptable level. The internal auditor uses risk assessment techniques in developing the internal audit activity's plan and in determining priorities for allocating internal audit resources. Risk assessment is used to examine auditable units and select areas for review to include in the internal audit activity's plan that have the greatest risk exposure.

7. Internal auditors may not be qualified to review every risk category and the ERM process in the organization (e.g., internal audits of workplace health and safety, environmental auditing, or complex financial instruments). The CAE ensures that internal auditors with specialized expertise or external service providers are used appropriately.

8. Risk management processes and systems are set up differently throughout the world. The maturity level of the organization related to risk management varies among organizations. Where organizations have a centralized risk management activity, the role of this activity includes coordinating with management regarding its continuous review of the internal control structure and updating the structure according to evolving risk appetites. The risk management processes in use in different parts of the world might have different logic, structures, and terminology. Internal auditors therefore make an assessment of the organization's risk management process and determine what parts can be used in developing the internal audit activity's plan and what parts can be used for planning individual internal audit assignments.

9. Factors the internal auditor considers when developing the internal audit plan include:

- ☐ Inherent risks. Are they identified and assessed?

- ☐ Residual risks. Are they identified and assessed?

- ☐ Mitigating controls, contingency plans, and monitoring activities. Are they linked to the individual events and/or risks?

- ☐ Risk registers. Are they systematic, completed, and accurate?

- ☐ Documentation. Are the risks and activities documented?

In addition, the internal auditor coordinates with other assurance providers and considers planned reliance on their work. Refer to the IIA's *Practice Advisory 2050-2: Assurance Maps*.

10. The internal audit charter normally requires the internal audit activity to focus on areas of high risk, including both inherent and residual risk. The internal audit activity needs to identify areas of high inherent risk, high residual risks, and the key control systems on which the organization is most reliant. If the internal audit activity identifies areas of unacceptable residual risk, management needs to be notified so that the risk can be addressed. The internal auditor will, as a result of conducting a strategic audit planning process, be able to identify different kinds of activities to include in the internal audit activity's plan, including:

- ☐ Control reviews/assurance activities, where the internal auditor reviews the adequacy and efficiency of the control systems and provides assurance that the controls are working and the risks are effectively managed.

- ☐ Inquiry activities, where organizational management has an unacceptable level of uncertainty about the controls related to a business activity or identified risk area and the internal auditor performs procedures to gain a better understanding of the residual risk.

- ☐ Consulting activities, where the internal auditor advises organizational management in the development of the control systems to mitigate unacceptable current risks.

Internal auditors also try to identify unnecessary, redundant, excessive, or complex controls that inefficiently reduce risk. In these cases, the cost of the control may be greater than the benefit realized, and therefore there is an opportunity for efficiency gains in the design of the control.

11. To ensure that relevant risks are identified, the approach to risk identification is systematic and clearly documented. Documentation can range from the use of a spreadsheet in small organizations to vendor-supplied software in more sophisticated organizations. The crucial element is that the risk management framework is documented in its entirety.

12. The documentation of risk management in an organization can be at various levels below the strategic level of the risk management process. Many organizations have developed **risk registers** that document risks below the strategic level, providing documentation of significant risks in an area and related inherent and residual risk ratings, key controls, and mitigating factors. An alignment exercise can then be undertaken to identify more direct links between risk "categories" and "aspects" described in the risk registers and, where applicable, the items already included in the audit universe documented by the internal audit activity.

13. Some organizations may identify several high (or higher) inherent risk areas. While these risks may warrant the internal audit activity's attention, it is not always possible to review all of them. Where the risk register shows a high, or above, ranking for inherent risk in a particular area, and the residual risk remains largely unchanged and no action by management or the internal audit activity is planned, the CAE reports those areas separately to the board with details of the risk analysis and reasons for the lack of, or ineffectiveness of, internal controls.

14. A selection of audits of lower-risk-level business units or branches need to periodically be included in the internal audit activity's plan to give them coverage and confirm that their risks have not changed. Also, the internal audit activity establishes a method for prioritizing outstanding risks not yet subject to an internal audit.

15. An internal audit activity's plan will normally focus on:

□ Unacceptable current risks where management action is required. These would be areas with minimal key controls or mitigating factors that senior management wants audited immediately.

□ Control systems on which the organization is most reliant.

□ Areas where the differential is great between inherent risk and residual risk.

□ Areas where the inherent risk is very high.

16. When planning individual internal audits, the internal auditor identifies and assesses risks relevant to the area under review.

2020–Communication and Approval

The CAE must communicate the internal audit activity's plans and resource requirements, including significant interim changes, to senior management and the board for review and approval. The CAE must also communicate the impact of resource limitations.

Practice Advisory 2020-1: Communication and Approval

1. The CAE will submit annually to senior management and the board for review and approval a summary of the internal audit plan, work schedule, staffing plan, and financial budget. This summary will inform senior management and the board of the scope of internal audit work and of any limitations placed on that scope. The CAE will also submit all significant interim changes for approval and information.

2. The approved engagement work schedule, staffing plan, and financial budget, along with all significant interim changes, are to contain sufficient information to enable senior management and the board to ascertain whether the internal audit activity's objectives and plans support those of the organization and the board and are consistent with the internal audit charter.

2030–Resource Management

The CAE must ensure that internal audit resources are appropriate, sufficient, and effectively deployed to achieve the approved plan.

Interpretation: *"Appropriate" refers to the mix of knowledge, skills, and other competencies needed to perform the plan. "Sufficient" refers to the quantity of resources needed to accomplish the plan. Resources are effectively deployed when they are used in a way that optimizes the achievement of the approved plan.*

Practice Advisory 2030-1: Resource Management

1. The CAE is primarily responsible for the sufficiency and management of internal audit resources in a manner that ensures the fulfillment of internal audit's responsibilities, as detailed in the internal audit charter. This includes effective communication of resource needs and reporting of status to senior management and the board. Internal audit resources may include employees, external service providers, financial support, and technology-based audit techniques. Ensuring the adequacy of internal audit resources is ultimately a responsibility of the organization's senior management and board; the CAE should assist them in discharging this responsibility.

2. The skills, capabilities, and technical knowledge of the internal audit staff are to be appropriate for the planned activities. The CAE will conduct a periodic skills assessment or inventory to determine the specific skills required to perform the internal audit activities. The skills assessment

is based on and considers the various needs identified in the risk assessment and audit plan. This includes assessments of technical knowledge, language skills, business acumen, fraud detection and prevention competency, and accounting and audit expertise.

3. Internal audit resources need to be sufficient to execute the audit activities in the breadth, depth, and timeliness expected by senior management and the board, as stated in the internal audit charter. Resource planning considerations include the audit universe, relevant risk levels, the internal audit plan, coverage expectations, and an estimate of unanticipated activities.

4. The CAE also ensures that resources are deployed effectively. This includes assigning auditors who are competent and qualified for specific assignments. It also includes developing a resourcing approach and organizational structure appropriate for the business structure, risk profile, and geographical dispersion of the organization.

5. From an overall resource management standpoint, the CAE considers succession planning, staff evaluation and development programs, and other human resource disciplines. The CAE also addresses the resourcing needs of the internal audit activity, whether those skills are present within the internal audit activity itself or not. Other approaches to addressing resource needs include external service providers, employees from other departments within the organization, or specialized consultants.

6. Because of the critical nature of resources, the CAE maintains ongoing communications and dialog with senior management and the board on the adequacy of resources for the internal audit activity. The CAE periodically presents a summary of status and adequacy of resources to senior management and the board. To that end, the CAE develops appropriate metrics, goals, and objectives to monitor the overall adequacy of resources. This can include comparisons of resources to the internal audit plan, the impact of temporary shortages or vacancies, educational and training activities, and changes to specific skill needs based on changes in the organization's business, operations, programs, systems, and controls.

2040–Policies and Procedures

The CAE must establish policies and procedures to guide the internal audit activity.

Interpretation: *The form and content of policies and procedures are dependent on the size and structure of the internal audit activity and the complexity of its work.*

Practice Advisory 2040-1: Policies and Procedures

1. The CAE develops policies and procedures. Formal administrative and technical audit manuals may not be needed by all internal audit activities. A small internal audit activity may be managed informally. Its audit staff may be directed and controlled through daily, close supervision and memoranda that state policies and procedures to be followed. In a large internal audit activity, more formal and comprehensive policies and procedures are essential to guide the internal audit staff in the execution of the internal audit plan.

2050–Coordination

The CAE should share information and coordinate activities with other internal and external providers of assurance and consulting services to ensure proper coverage and minimize duplication of efforts.

Practice Advisory 2050-1: Coordination

1. Oversight of the work of external auditors, including coordination with the internal audit activity, is the responsibility of the board. Coordination of internal and external audit work is the responsibility of the CAE. The CAE obtains the support of the board to coordinate audit work effectively.

2. Organizations may use the work of external auditors to provide assurance related to activities within the scope of internal auditing. In these cases, the CAE takes the steps necessary to understand the work performed by the external auditors, including:

☐ The nature, extent, and timing of work planned by external auditors, to be satisfied that the external auditors' planned work, in conjunction with the internal auditors' planned work, satisfies the requirements of Standard 2100.

☐ The external auditor's assessment of risk and materiality.

☐ The external auditors' techniques, methods, and terminology to enable the CAE to (a) coordinate internal and external auditing work; (b) evaluate, for purposes of reliance, the external auditors' work; and (c) communicate effectively with external auditors.

☐ Access to the external auditors' programs and working papers, to be satisfied that the external auditors' work can be relied upon for internal audit purposes. Internal auditors are responsible for respecting the confidentiality of those programs and working papers.

3. External auditors may rely on the work of the internal audit activity in performing their work. In this case, the CAE needs to provide sufficient information to enable external auditors to understand the internal auditors' techniques, methods, and terminology to facilitate reliance by external auditors on work performed. Access to the internal auditors' programs and working papers is provided to external auditors in order for external auditors to be satisfied as to the acceptability for external audit purposes of relying on the internal auditors' work.

4. It may be efficient for internal and external auditors to use similar techniques, methods, and terminology to coordinate their work effectively and to rely on the work of one another.

5. Planned audit activities of internal and external auditors need to be discussed to ensure that audit coverage is coordinated and duplicate efforts are minimized where possible. Sufficient meetings are to be scheduled during the audit process to ensure coordination of audit work and efficient and timely completion of audit activities and to determine whether observations and recommendations from work performed to date require that the scope of planned work be adjusted.

6. The internal audit activity's final communications, management's responses to those communications, and subsequent follow-up reviews are to be made available to external auditors. These communications assist external auditors in determining and adjusting the scope and timing of their work. In addition, internal auditors need access to the external auditors' presentation materials and management letters. Matters discussed in presentation materials and included in management letters need to be understood by the CAE and used as input to internal auditors in planning the areas to emphasize in future internal audit work. After review of management letters and initiation of any needed corrective action by appropriate members of senior management and the board, the CAE ensures that appropriate follow-up and corrective actions have been taken.

7. The CAE is responsible for regular evaluations of the coordination between internal and external auditors. Such evaluations may also include assessments of the overall efficiency and effectiveness of internal and external audit activities, including aggregate audit cost. The CAE communicates the results of these evaluations to senior management and the board, including relevant comments about the performance of external auditors.

Practice Advisory 2050-2: Assurance Maps

1. One of the key responsibilities of the board is to gain assurance that processes are operating within the parameters it has established to achieve the defined objectives. It is necessary to determine whether risk management processes are working effectively and whether key or business-critical risks are being managed to an acceptable level.

2. Increased focus on the roles and responsibilities of senior management and boards has prompted many organizations to place a greater emphasis on assurance activities. The *Standards* Glossary defines "assurance" as "an objective examination of evidence for the purpose of providing an independent assessment on governance, risk management, and control processes for the organization." The board will use multiple sources to gain reliable assurance. Assurance from management is fundamental and should be complemented by the provision of objective assurance from internal audit and other third parties. Risk managers, internal auditors, and compliance practitioners are asking: "Who does what and why?" Boards in particular are beginning to question who is providing assurance, where the delineation between the functions is, and if there are any overlaps.

3. There are fundamentally three classes of assurance providers, differentiated by the stakeholders they serve, their level of independence from the activities over which they provide assurance, and the robustness of that assurance.

    a. Those who report to management and/or are part of management (management assurance), including individuals who perform control self-assessments, quality auditors, environmental auditors, and other management- designated assurance personnel.

    b. Those who report to the board, including internal audit.

    c. Those who report to external stakeholders (external audit assurance), which is a role traditionally fulfilled by the independent/statutory auditor.

The level of assurance desired, and who should provide that assurance, will vary depending on the risk.

    4. There are many assurance providers for an organization. These include

      ☐ Line management and employees. (Management provides assurance as a first line of defense over the risks and controls for which they are responsible.)

      ☐ Senior management.

      ☐ Internal and external auditors.

      ☐ Compliance.

      ☐ Quality assurance.

      ☐ Risk management.

      ☐ Environmental auditors.

      ☐ Workplace health and safety auditors.

      ☐ Government performance auditors.

      ☐ Financial reporting review teams.

      ☐ Subcommittees of the board (e.g., audit, actuarial, credit, governance).

      ☐ External assurance providers, including surveys, specialist reviews (health and safety), etc.

5. The internal audit activity will normally provide assurance over the entire organization, including risk management processes (both their design and operating effectiveness), management of those risks classified as "key" (including the effectiveness of the controls and other responses to them), and verification of the reliability and appropriateness of the risk assessment and reporting of the risk and control status.

6. With responsibility for assurance activities traditionally being shared among management, internal audit, risk management, and compliance, it is important that assurance activities are

coordinated to ensure that resources are used in the most efficient and effective way. Many organizations operate with traditional (and separate) internal audit, risk, and compliance activities. It is common for organizations to have a number of separate groups performing different risk management, compliance, and assurance functions independently of one another. Without effective coordination and reporting, work can be duplicated or key risks may be missed or misjudged.

7. While many organizations monitor the activities of internal audit, risk, and compliance, not all view all their activities in a holistic way. An assurance mapping exercise involves mapping assurance coverage against the key risks in an organization. This process allows an organization to identify and address any gaps in the risk management process and gives stakeholders comfort that risks are being managed and reported on and that regulatory and legal obligations are being met. Organizations will benefit from a streamlined approach, which ensures the information is available to management about the risks they face and how the risks are being addressed. The mapping is done across the organization to understand where the overall risk and assurance roles and accountabilities reside. The aim is to ensure that there is a comprehensive risk and assurance process with no duplicated effort or potential gaps.

8. Often an organization will have defined the significant risk categories that make up its risk management framework. In such cases, the **assurance map** would be based on the structure of this framework. For example, an assurance map could have these columns:

- ☐ Significant risk category
- ☐ Management role responsible for the risk (risk owner)
- ☐ Inherent risk rating
- ☐ Residual risk rating
- ☐ External audit coverage
- ☐ Internal audit coverage
- ☐ Other assurance provider coverage

In this example, the CAE would populate the internal audit coverage column with recent coverage. Often each significant risk has a risk owner or a person responsible for coordinating assurance activities for that risk; that person would populate the other assurance provider coverage column. Each significant unit within an organization could have its own assurance map. Alternatively, the internal audit activity may play a coordinating role in developing and completing the organization's assurance map.

9. Once the assurance map for the organization has been completed, significant risks with inadequate assurance coverage, or areas of duplicated assurance coverage, can be identified. Senior management and the board need to consider changes in assurance coverage for these risks. The internal audit activity needs to consider areas of inadequate coverage when developing the internal audit plan.

10. It is the responsibility of the CAE to understand the independent assurance requirements of the board and the organization and to clarify the role the internal audit activity fills and the level of assurance it provides. The board needs to be confident that the overall assurance process is adequate and sufficiently robust to validate that the risks of the organization are being managed and reported on effectively.

11. The board needs to receive information about assurance activities, both implemented and planned, in regard to each category of risk. The internal audit activity and other assurance providers offer the board the appropriate level of assurance for the nature and levels of risk that exist in the organization under the respective categories.

12. In organizations requiring an overall opinion from the CAE, the CAE needs to understand the nature, scope, and extent of the integrated assurance map to consider the work of other assurance providers (and rely on it as appropriate) before presenting an overall opinion on the organization's governance, risk management, and control processes. The IIA's Practice Guide titled *Formulating and Expressing Internal Audit Opinions* provides additional guidance.

13. In instances where the organization does not expect an overall opinion, the CAE can act as the coordinator of assurance providers to ensure that there are either no gaps in assurance or the gaps are known and accepted. The CAE reports on any lack of input/involvement/ oversight/assurance over other assurance providers. If the CAE believes that the assurance coverage is inadequate or ineffective, senior management and the board need to be advised accordingly.

14. The CAE is directed by Standard 2050 to coordinate activities with other assurance providers; the use of an assurance map will help achieve this. Assurance maps offer an effective way of communicating this coordination.

Practice Advisory 2050-3: Relying on the Work of Other Assurance Providers

1. The internal auditor may rely on or use the work of other internal or external assurance providers in providing governance, risk management, and control assurance to the board. Internal assurance providers could include company functions such as compliance, information security, quality, and labor health and safety as well as management monitoring activities. External assurance providers could include external auditors, joint venture partners, specialist reviews, or third-party audit firms, including those providing reports in accordance with *International Standard on Assurance Engagements 3402: Assurance Reports on Controls at a Service Organization*.

2. The decision to rely on the work of other assurance providers can be made for a variety of reasons, including to address areas that fall outside of the competence of the internal audit activity, to gain knowledge transfer from other assurance providers, or to efficiently enhance coverage of risk beyond the internal audit plan.

3. An internal audit charter and/or engagement letter should specify that the internal audit activity have access to the work of other internal and external assurance providers.

4. Where the internal auditor is hiring the assurance provider, the auditor should document engagement expectations in a contract or agreement. Minimum expectations should be provided for the nature and ownership of deliverables, methods/techniques, the nature of procedures and data/information to be used, progress reports/supervision to ensure the work is adequate, and reporting requirements.

5. If management within the organization provides the contracting of, and direction to, a third-party assurance provider, the internal auditor should be satisfied that the instruction is appropriate, understood, and executed.

6. The internal auditor should consider the independence and objectivity of the other assurance providers when considering whether to rely on or use their work. If an assurance provider is hired by and/or is under the direction of management instead of internal auditing, the impact of this arrangement on the assurance provider's independence and objectivity should be evaluated.

7. The internal auditor should assess the competencies and qualifications of the provider performing the assurance work. Examples of competency include verifying that the assurer holds appropriate professional experience and qualifications, has a current registration with the relevant professional body or institute, and has a reputation for competency and integrity in the sector.

8. The internal auditor should consider the other assurance provider's elements of practice to have reasonable assurance the findings are based on sufficient, reliable, relevant, and useful information, as required by *Standard 2310: Identifying Information*. Standard 2310 must be met by the CAE regardless of the degree to which the work of other assurance providers is used.

9. The internal auditor should ensure that the work of the other assurance provider is appropriately planned, supervised, documented, and reviewed. The auditor should consider whether the

audit evidence is appropriate and sufficient to determine the extent of use and reliance on the work of the other assurance providers. Based on an assessment of the work of the other assurance provider, additional work or test procedures may be needed to gain appropriate and sufficient audit evidence. The internal auditor should be satisfied, based on knowledge of the business, environment, techniques, and information used by the assurance provider, that the findings appear to be reasonable.

10. The level of reliance that can be placed on another assurance provider will be impacted by the factors mentioned earlier: independence, objectivity, competencies, elements of practice, adequacy of execution of audit work, and sufficiency of audit evidence to support the given level of assurance. As the risk or significance of the activity reviewed by the other assurance provider increases, the internal auditor should gather more information on these factors and may need to obtain additional audit evidence to supplement the work done by the other assurance provider. To increase the level of reliance on the results, the internal audit activity may retest results of the other assurance provider.

11. The internal auditor should incorporate the assurance provider's results into the overall report of assurance that the internal auditor reports to the board or other key stakeholders. Significant issues raised by the other assurance provider can be incorporated in detail or summarized in internal audit reports. The internal auditor should include reference to other assurance providers where reports rely on such information.

12. Follow-up is a process by which internal auditors evaluate the adequacy, effectiveness, and timeliness of actions taken by management on reported observations and recommendations, including those made by other assurance providers. In reviewing actions taken to address recommendations made by other assurance providers, the internal auditor should determine whether management has implemented the recommendations or assumed the risk of not implementing them.

13. Significant findings from other assurance providers should be considered in the assurance and communications internal auditing is providing the organization. In addition, results of work performed by others may impact the internal audit risk assessment as to whether the findings impact the evaluation of risk and the level of audit work necessary in response to that risk.

14. In evaluating the effectiveness of, and contributing to the improvement of, risk management processes (*Standard 2120: Risk Management*), the internal audit activity may review the processes of these internal assurance providers, including company functions such as compliance, information security, quality, and labor health and safety as well as management monitoring activities. There should be coverage of risk areas by internal auditing, but when another assurance function exists, the internal audit activity may review the performance of that process rather than duplicate the detailed specific work of that other function.

15. Assessment from the other assurance provider on significant risks should be reported to relevant areas of the organization to be included in considerations regarding the organization's risk management framework and assurance map. See *Practice Advisory 2050-2: Assurance Maps*.

2060–Reporting to Senior Management and the Board

The CAE must report periodically to senior management and the board on the internal audit activity's purpose, authority, responsibility, and performance relative to its plan. Reporting must also include significant risk exposures and control issues, including fraud risks, governance issues, and other matters needed or requested by senior management and the board.

Interpretation: *The frequency and content of reporting are determined in discussion with senior management and the board and depend on the importance of the information to be communicated and the urgency of the related actions to be taken by senior management or the board.*

Practice Advisory 2060-1: Reporting to Senior Management and the Board

1. The purpose of reporting is to provide assurance to senior management and the board regarding governance processes (Standard 2110), risk management (Standard 2120), and control

(Standard 2130). Standard 1111 states: "The CAE must communicate and interact directly with the board."

2. The CAE should agree with the board about the frequency and nature of reporting on the internal audit activity's charter (e.g., purpose, authority, and responsibility) and performance. Performance reporting should be relative to the most recently approved plan to inform senior management and the board of significant deviations from the approved audit plan, staffing plans, and financial budgets; reasons for the deviations; and action needed or taken. Standard 1320 states: "The chief audit executive must communicate the results of the quality assurance and improvement program to senior management and the board."

3. Significant risk exposures and control issues are those conditions that, according to the CAE's judgment, could adversely affect the organization and its ability to achieve its strategic, financial reporting, operational, and compliance objectives. Significant issues may carry unacceptable exposure to internal and external risks, including conditions related to control weaknesses, fraud, irregularities, illegal acts, errors, inefficiency, waste, ineffectiveness, conflicts of interest, and financial viability.

4. Senior management and the board make decisions on the appropriate action to be taken regarding significant issues. They may decide to assume the risk of not correcting the reported condition because of cost or other considerations. Senior management should inform the board of decisions about all significant issues raised by internal auditing.

5. When the CAE believes that senior management has accepted a level of risk that the organization considers unacceptable, the CAE must discuss the matter with senior management as stated in Standard 2600. The CAE should understand management's basis for the decision, identify the cause of any disagreement, and determine whether management has the authority to accept the risk. Disagreements may relate to risk likelihood and potential exposure, understanding of risk appetite, cost, and level of control. Preferably, the CAE should resolve the disagreement with senior management.

6. If the CAE and senior management cannot reach an agreement, Standard 2600 directs the CAE to inform the board. If possible, the CAE and management should make a joint presentation about the conflicting positions. For financial reporting matters, CAEs should consider discussing these issues with the external auditors in a timely manner.

2070–External Service Provider and Organizational Responsibility for Internal Auditing

When an external service provider serves as the internal audit activity, the provider must make the organization aware that the organization has the responsibility for maintaining an effective internal audit activity.

Interpretation: *This responsibility is demonstrated through the QAIP, which assesses conformance with the definition of internal auditing, the Code of Ethics, and the* Standards.

> No Practice Advisory for Standard 2070

2100–Nature of Work

The internal audit activity must evaluate and contribute to the improvement of governance, risk management, and control processes using a systematic and disciplined approach.

> No Practice Advisory for Standard 2100

2110–Governance

The internal audit activity must assess and make appropriate recommendations for improving the governance process in its accomplishment of the following objectives:

☐ Promoting appropriate ethics and values within the organization.

☐ Ensuring effective organizational performance management and accountability.

☐ Communicating risk and control information to appropriate areas of the organization.

☐ Coordinating the activities of and communicating information among the board, external and internal auditors, and management.

2110.A1–The internal audit activity must evaluate the design, implementation, and effectiveness of the organization's ethics-related objectives, programs, and activities.

2110.A2–The internal audit activity must assess whether the IT governance of the organization supports the organization's strategies and objectives.

Practice Advisory 2110-1: Governance: Definition

1. The role of internal auditing as noted in the definition of internal auditing includes the responsibility to evaluate and improve governance processes as part of the assurance function.

2. The term "governance" has a range of definitions, depending on a variety of environmental, structural, and cultural circumstances as well as legal frameworks. The *Standards* define "governance" as "the combination of processes and structures implemented by the board to inform, direct, manage, and monitor the activities of the organization toward the achievement of its objectives." The CAE may use a different definition for audit purposes when the organization has adopted a different governance framework or model.

3. Globally, there are a variety of governance models that have been published by other organizations and legal and regulatory bodies. For example, the Organisation for Economic Co-operation and Development defines "governance" as "a set of relationships between a company's management, its board, its shareholders, and other stakeholders. Corporate governance provides the structure through which the objectives of the company are set and the means of attaining those objectives and monitoring performance are determined." The Australian Securities Exchange Corporate Governance Council defines "governance" as "the system by which companies are directed and managed. It influences how the objectives of the company are set and achieved, how risk is monitored and assessed, and how performance is optimized." In most instances, there is an indication that governance is a process or system and is not static. What distinguishes the approach in the *Standards* is the specific emphasis on the board and its governance activities.

4. The frameworks and requirements for governance vary according to organization type and regulatory jurisdictions. Examples include publicly traded companies, not-for-profit organizations, associations, government or quasi-government entities, academic institutions, private companies, commissions, and stock exchanges.

5. How an organization designs and practices the principles of effective governance also vary depending on the size, complexity, and life cycle maturity of the organization, its stakeholder structure, legal and cultural requirements, and so on.

6. As a consequence of the variation in the design and structure of governance, the CAE should work with the board and the executive management team, as appropriate, to determine how governance should be defined for audit purposes.

7. Internal auditing is integral to the organization's governance framework. The unique position of internal auditors within the organization enables them to observe and formally assess the governance structure, its design, and its operational effectiveness while remaining independent.

8. The relationship among governance, risk management, and internal control should be considered. This item is addressed in Practice Advisory 2110-2. Practice Advisory 2110-3 discusses assessing governance.

Practice Advisory 2110-2: Governance: Relationship with Risk and Control

1. The *Standards* define "governance" as "the combination of processes and structures implemented by the board to inform, direct, manage, and monitor the activities of the organization toward the achievement of its objectives."

2. Governance does not exist as a set of distinct and separate processes and structures. Rather, there are relationships among governance, risk management, and internal controls.

3. Effective governance activities consider risk when setting strategy. Conversely, risk management relies on effective governance (e.g., tone at the top, risk appetite and tolerance, risk culture, and the oversight of risk management).

4. Effective governance relies on internal controls and communication to the board on the effectiveness of those controls.

5. Control and risk also are related, as "control" is defined as "any action taken by management, the board, and other parties to manage risk and increase the likelihood that established goals will be achieved."

6. The CAE should consider these relationships in planning assessments of governance processes:

☐ An audit should address those controls in governance processes that are designed to prevent or detect events that could have a negative impact on the achievement of organizational strategies, goals, and objectives; operational efficiency and effectiveness; financial reporting; or compliance with applicable laws and regulations. (See Practice Advisory 2110-3.)

☐ Controls within governance processes are often significant in managing multiple risks across the organization. For example, controls around the code of conduct may be relied on to manage compliance risks, fraud risks, and so on. This aggregation effect should be considered when developing the scope of an audit of governance processes.

☐ If other audits assess controls in governance processes (e.g., audits of controls over financial reporting, risk management processes, or compliance), the auditor should consider relying on the results of those audits.

Practice Advisory 2110-3: Governance—Assessments

1. Internal auditors can act in a number of different capacities in assessing and contributing to the improvement of governance practices. Typically, internal auditors provide independent, objective assessments of the design and operating effectiveness of the organization's governance processes. They also may provide consulting services and advice on ways to improve those processes. In some cases, internal auditors may be called on to facilitate board self-assessments of governance practices.

2. As noted in *Practice Advisory 2110-1: Governance: Definition*, the definition of governance for audit purposes should be agreed on with the board and executive management, as appropriate. In addition, the internal auditor should understand the organization's governance processes and the relationships among governance, risk, and control (refer to *Practice Advisory 2110-2: Governance: Relationship with Risk and Control*).

3. The audit plan should be developed based on an assessment of risks to the organization. All governance processes should be considered in the risk assessment. The plan should include the higher-risk governance processes, and inclusion of an assessment of processes or risk areas

where the board or executive management has requested work be performed should be considered. The plan should define the nature of the work to be performed, the governance processes to be addressed, and the nature of the assessments that will be made (i.e., macro—considering the entire governance framework, or micro—considering specific risks, processes, or activities, or some combination of both).

4. When there are known control issues or the governance process is not mature, the CAE could consider different methods for improving the control or governance processes through consulting services instead of, or in addition to, formal assessments.

5. Internal audit assessments regarding governance processes are likely to be based on information obtained from numerous audit assignments over time. The internal auditor should consider:

   - The results of audits of specific governance processes (e.g., the whistleblower process, the strategy management process).

   - Governance issues arising from audits that are not specifically focused on governance (e.g., audits of the risk management process, internal control over financial reporting, fraud risks).

   - The results of other internal and external assurance providers' work (e.g., a firm engaged by the general counsel to review the investigation process). Refer to *Practice Advisory 2050: Coordination.*

   - Other information on governance issues, such as adverse incidents indicating an opportunity to improve governance processes.

6. *During the planning, evaluating, and reporting phases,* the internal auditor should be sensitive to the potential nature and ramifications of the results and ensure appropriate communications with the board and executive management. The internal auditor should consider consulting legal counsel both before initiating the audit and before finalizing the report.

7. The internal audit activity is an essential part of the governance process. The board and executive management should be able to rely on the QAIP of the internal audit activity in conjunction with external quality assessments performed in accordance with the *Standards* for assurance on its effectiveness.

2120–Risk Management

The internal audit activity must evaluate the effectiveness and contribute to the improvement of risk management processes.

Interpretation: *Determining whether risk management processes are effective is a judgment resulting from the internal auditor's assessment that:*

   - *Organizational objectives support and align with the organization's mission.*

   - *Significant risks are identified and assessed.*

   - *Appropriate risk responses are selected that align risks with the organization's risk appetite.*

   - *Relevant risk information is captured and communicated in a timely manner across the organization, enabling staff, management, and the board to carry out their responsibilities.*

The internal audit activity may gather the information to support this assessment during multiple engagements. The results of these engagements, when viewed together, provide an understanding of the organization's risk management processes and their effectiveness.

Risk management processes are monitored through ongoing management activities, separate evaluations, or both.

2120.A1–The internal audit activity must evaluate risk exposures relating to the organization's governance, operations, and information systems regarding the:

☐ Reliability and integrity of financial and operational information.

☐ Effectiveness and efficiency of operations and programs.

☐ Safeguarding of assets.

☐ Compliance with laws, regulations, policies, procedures, and contracts.

2120.A2–The internal audit activity must evaluate the potential for the occurrence of fraud and how the organization manages fraud risk.

2120.C1–During consulting engagements, internal auditors must address risk consistent with the engagement's objectives and be alert to the existence of other significant risks.

2120.C2–Internal auditors must incorporate knowledge of risks gained from consulting engagements into their evaluation of the organization's risk management processes.

2120.C3–When assisting management in establishing or improving risk management processes, internal auditors must refrain from assuming any management responsibility by actually managing risks.

Practice Advisory 2120-1: Assessing the Adequacy of Risk Management Processes

1. Risk management is a key responsibility of senior management and the board. To achieve its business objectives, management ensures that sound risk management processes are in place and functioning. Boards have an oversight role to determine that appropriate risk management processes are in place and that these processes are adequate and effective. In this role, boards may direct the internal audit activity to assist them by examining, evaluating, reporting, and/or recommending improvements to the adequacy and effectiveness of management's risk processes.

2. Management and the board are responsible for their organization's risk management and control processes. However, internal auditors acting in a consulting role can assist the organization in identifying, evaluating, and implementing risk management methodologies and controls to address those risks.

3. In situations where the organization does not have formal risk management processes, the CAE formally discusses with management and the board their obligations to understand, manage, and monitor risks within the organization and the need to satisfy themselves that there are processes operating within the organization, even if informal, that provide the appropriate level of visibility into the key risks and how they are being managed and monitored.

4. The CAE is to obtain an understanding of senior management's and the board's expectations of the internal audit activity in the organization's risk management process. This understanding is then codified in the charters of the internal audit activity and the board. Internal auditing's responsibilities are to be coordinated among all groups and individuals within the organization's risk management process. The role of internal audit in the risk management process of an organization can change over time and may encompass:

☐ No role.

☐ Auditing the risk management process as part of the internal audit plan.

☐ Active, continuous support and involvement in the risk management process such as participation on oversight committees, monitoring activities, and status reporting.

☐ Managing and coordinating the risk management process.

5. Ultimately, senior management and the board are charged with determining the role of internal auditing in the risk management process. Their view on internal auditing's role is likely to be determined by factors such as the culture of the organization, ability of the internal audit staff, and local conditions and customs of the country. However, taking on management's responsibility regarding the risk management process and the potential threat to internal audit's independence requires a full discussion and board approval.

6. The techniques used by various organizations for their risk management practices can vary significantly. Depending on the size and complexity of the organization's business activities, risk management processes can be:

- ☐ Formal or informal.

- ☐ Quantitative or subjective.

- ☐ Embedded in the business units or centralized at a corporate level.

7. The organization designs processes based on its culture, management style, and business objectives. For example, the use of derivatives or other sophisticated capital markets products by the organization could require the use of quantitative risk management tools. Smaller, less complex organizations could use an informal risk committee to discuss the organization's risk profile and to initiate periodic actions. The internal auditor determines that the methodology chosen is sufficiently comprehensive and appropriate for the nature of the organization's activities.

8. Internal auditors need to obtain sufficient and appropriate evidence to determine that the key objectives of the risk management processes are being met to form an opinion on the adequacy of risk management processes. In gathering such evidence, the internal auditor might consider these audit procedures:

- ☐ Research and review current developments, trends, industry information related to the business conducted by the organization, and other appropriate sources of information to determine risks and exposures that may affect the organization and related control procedures used to address, monitor, and reassess those risks.

- ☐ Review corporate policies and board minutes to determine the organization's business strategies, risk management philosophy and methodology, appetite for risk, and acceptance of risks.

- ☐ Review previous risk evaluation reports issued by management, internal auditors, external auditors, and any other sources.

- ☐ Conduct interviews with line and senior management to determine business unit objectives, related risks, and management's risk mitigation and control monitoring activities.

- ☐ Assimilate information to independently evaluate the effectiveness of risk mitigation, monitoring, and communication of risks and associated control activities.

- ☐ Assess the appropriateness of reporting lines for risk monitoring activities.

- ☐ Review the adequacy and timeliness of reporting on risk management results.

- ☐ Review the completeness of management's risk analysis and actions taken to remedy issues raised by risk management processes, and suggest improvements.

- ☐ Determine the effectiveness of management's self-assessment processes through observations, direct tests of control and monitoring procedures, testing the accuracy of information used in monitoring activities, and other appropriate techniques.

- ☐ Review risk-related issues that may indicate weakness in risk management practices and, as appropriate, discuss with senior management and the board. If the auditor believes that management has accepted a level of risk that is inconsistent with the organization's risk management strategy and policies or that he or she deems unacceptable to the organization, the auditor should refer to Standard 2600 and related guidance for additional direction.

Practice Advisory 2120-2: Managing the Risk of the Internal Audit Activity

1. The role and importance of internal auditing has grown tremendously, and the expectations of key stakeholders (e.g., board, executive management) continue to expand. Internal audit activities have broad mandates to cover financial, operational, IT, legal/regulatory, and strategic risks. At the same time, many internal audit activities face challenges related to the availability of qualified personnel in the global labor markets, increased compensation costs, and high demand for specialized resources (e.g., information systems, fraud, derivatives, and taxes). The combination of these factors results in a high level of risk for an internal audit activity. As a result, CAEs need to consider the risks related to their internal audit activities and the achievement of their objectives.

2. The internal audit activity is not immune to risks. It needs to take the necessary steps to ensure that it is managing its own risks.

3. Risks to internal audit activities fall into three broad categories: audit failure, false assurance, and reputation risks. The following discussion highlights the key attributes related to these risks and some steps an internal audit activity may consider to better manage them.

4. Every organization will experience control breakdowns. Often when controls fail or frauds occur, someone will ask: "Where were the internal auditors?" The internal audit activity could be a contributing factor due to:

   □ Not following the *Standards*.

   □ An inappropriate QAIP (Standard 1300), including procedures to monitor auditor independence and objectivity.

   □ Lack of an effective risk assessment process to identify key audit areas during the strategic risk assessment as well as areas of high risk during the planning of individual audits—as a result, failure to do the right audits and/or time wasted on the wrong audits.

   □ Failure to design effective internal audit procedures to test the "real" risks and the right controls.

   □ Failure to evaluate both the design adequacy and the control effectiveness as part of internal audit procedures.

   □ Use of audit teams that do not have the appropriate level of competence based on experience or knowledge of high-risk areas.

   □ Failure to exercise heightened professional skepticism and extended internal audit procedures related to findings or control deficiencies.

   □ Failure of adequate internal audit supervision.

   □ Making the wrong decision when there was some evidence of fraud—for example, "It's probably not material" or "We don't have the time or resources to deal with this issue."

   □ Failure to communicate suspicions to the right people.

   □ Failure to report adequately.

5. Internal audit failures may not only be embarrassing for internal audit activities; they can also expose an organization to significant risk. While there is no absolute assurance that audit

failures will not occur, an internal audit activity can implement the following practices to mitigate such risk:

- □ **QAIP.** It is critical for every internal audit activity to implement an effective QAIP.

- □ **Periodic review of the audit universe.** Review the methodology to determine the completeness of the audit universe by routinely evaluating the organization's dynamic risk profile.

- □ **Periodic review of the audit plan.** Review the current audit plan to assess which assignments may be of higher risk. By flagging the higher-risk assignments, management of the internal audit activity has better visibility and may spend more time understanding the approach to the critical assignments.

- □ **Effective planning.** There is no substitute for effective audit planning. A thorough planning process that includes updating relevant facts about the client and the performance of an effective risk assessment can significantly reduce the risks of audit failure. In addition, understanding the scope of the assignment and the internal audit procedures to be performed are important elements of the planning process, which will reduce the risks of audit failure. Building internal audit activity management checkpoints into the process and obtaining approval of any deviation from the agreed-on plan is also key.

- □ **Effective audit design.** In most cases, a fair amount of time is spent understanding and analyzing the design of the system of internal controls to determine whether it provides adequate control prior to the start of testing for effectiveness. This provides a firm basis for internal audit comments that address root causes, which sometimes can be the result of poor control design, rather than addressing symptoms. It will also reduce the chance for audit failure by identifying missing controls.

- □ **Effective management review and escalation procedures.** Internal audit management's involvement in the internal audit process (i.e., before the report draft) plays an important part in mitigating the risk of audit failure. This involvement might include work paper reviews, real-time discussions related to findings, or a closing meeting. By including management of the internal audit activity in the internal audit process, potential issues may be identified and assessed earlier in the assignment. In addition, an internal audit activity may have guidance procedures outlining when and what types of issues to escalate to which level of internal auditing management.

- □ **Proper resource allocation.** It is important to assign the right staff to each internal audit engagement. It is especially important when planning a higher-risk or a very technical engagement. Making sure the appropriate competencies are available on the team can play a significant role in reducing the risk of audit failure. In addition to the right competencies, it is important to ensure the appropriate level of experience is on the team, including strong project management skills for those leading an internal audit engagement.

6. An internal audit activity may unknowingly provide some level of false assurance. "False assurance" is a level of confidence or assurance based on perceptions or assumptions rather than fact. In many cases, the mere fact that the internal audit activity is involved in a matter may create some level of false assurance.

7. The use of internal audit resources in assisting the organization to identify and evaluate significant exposures to risk needs to be clearly defined for projects other than internal audits. For example, an internal audit activity was asked by a business unit to provide some "resources" to assist with the implementation of a new enterprise-wide computer system. The business unit

deployed these resources to support some of the testing of the new system. Subsequent to the deployment, an error in the design of the system resulted in a restatement of the financial statements. When asked how this happened, the business unit responded by saying that the internal audit activity had been involved in the process and had not identified the matter. Involvement of internal auditors created a level of false assurance that was not consistent with their actual role in the project.

8. While there is no way to mitigate all of the risk of false assurance, an internal audit activity can proactively manage its risk in this area. Frequent and clear communication is a key strategy to manage false assurance. Other leading practices include:

- ☐ Proactively communicate the role and the mandate of the internal audit activity to the audit committee, senior management, and other key stakeholders.

- ☐ Clearly communicate what is covered in the risk assessment, internal audit plan, and internal audit engagement. Also explicitly communicate what is not in the scope of the risk assessment and internal audit plan.

- ☐ Have a "project acceptance" process to assess the level of risk related to each project and internal audit's role in the project. The assessment may consider the scope of the project, the role of the internal audit activity, the reporting expectations, the competencies required, and the independence of internal auditors.

9. If internal auditors are used to augment the staffing of a project or initiative, document their role and scope of their involvement as well as future objectivity and independence issues rather than using internal auditors as "loaned" resources, which may create false assurance. The credible reputation of an internal audit activity is an essential part of its effectiveness. Internal audit activities that are viewed with high regard are able to attract talented professionals and are highly valued by their organizations. Maintaining a strong "brand" is paramount to the internal audit activity's success and ability to contribute to the organization. In most cases, the internal audit activity's brand has been built over several years through consistent, high-quality work. Unfortunately, this brand can be destroyed instantly by one high-profile, adverse event.

10. For example, an internal audit activity could be highly regarded with several of the key financial executives having had rotational assignments as internal auditors, which was viewed as a training ground for future executives. A string of significant restatements and regulatory investigations, however, would impact the reputation of the internal audit activity. The audit committee and the board might ask if the internal audit activity has the right talent and QAIP to support the organization.

11. In another example, during an audit of the human resource function, the internal auditors may discover that background checks were not being reviewed appropriately. The discovery that newly hired internal auditors did not have the appropriate education background, while others had been involved in criminal activity, could seriously impact the credibility of the internal audit activity.

12. Situations like these are not only embarrassing; they also damage the efficacy of the internal audit activity. Protecting the reputation and the brand of the internal audit activity is important not only to the internal audit activity but to the entire organization. It is important that the internal audit activity consider what types of risks it faces that could impact its reputation and develop mitigation strategies to address these risks.

13. Some practices to protect the reputation include:

- ☐ Implement a strong QAIP over all processes in the internal audit activity, including human resources and hiring.

- ☐ Periodically perform a risk assessment for the internal audit activity to identify potential risks that might impact its brand.

□ Reinforce code of conduct and ethical behavior standards, including the IIA's Code of Ethics to internal auditors.

□ Ensure that the internal audit activity is in compliance with all applicable company policies and practices.

14. To the extent that an internal audit activity experiences an event outlined above, the CAE needs to review the nature of the event and gain an understanding of the root causes. This analysis provides insight into the potential changes to be considered in the internal audit process or control environment to mitigate future occurrences.

2130–Control

The internal audit activity must assist the organization in maintaining effective controls by evaluating their effectiveness and efficiency and by promoting continuous improvement.

2130.A1–The internal audit activity must evaluate the adequacy and effectiveness of controls in responding to risks within the organization's governance, operations, and information systems regarding the:

□ Reliability and integrity of financial and operational information.

□ Effectiveness and efficiency of operations and programs.

□ Safeguarding of assets.

□ Compliance with laws, regulations, policies, procedures, and contracts.

2130.C1–Internal auditors must incorporate knowledge of controls gained from consulting engagements into evaluation of the organization's control processes.

Practice Advisory 2130-1: Assessing the Adequacy of Control Processes

1. An organization establishes and maintains effective risk management and control processes. The purpose of control processes is to support the organization in the management of risks and the achievement of its established and communicated objectives. The control processes are expected to ensure, among other things, that:

□ Financial and operational information is reliable and possesses integrity.

□ Operations are performed efficiently and achieve established objectives.

□ Assets are safeguarded.

□ Actions and decisions of the organization are in compliance with laws, regulations, and contracts.

2. Senior management's role is to oversee the establishment, administration, and assessment of the system of risk management and control processes. Among the responsibilities of the organization's line managers is the assessment of the control processes in their respective areas. Internal auditors provide varying degrees of assurance about the effectiveness of the risk management and control processes in select activities and functions of the organization.

3. The CAE forms an overall opinion about the adequacy and effectiveness of the control processes. The expression of such an opinion by the CAE will be based on sufficient audit evidence obtained through the completion of audits and, where appropriate, reliance on the work of other assurance providers. The CAE communicates the opinion to senior management and the board.

4. The CAE develops a proposed internal audit plan to obtain sufficient evidence to evaluate the effectiveness of the control processes. The plan includes audit engagements and/or other procedures to obtain sufficient, appropriate audit evidence about all major operating units and business functions to be assessed as well as a review of the major control processes operating across the organization. The plan should be flexible so that adjustments may be made during the year as a result of changes in management strategies, external conditions, major risk areas, or revised expectations about achieving the organization's objectives.

5. The audit plan gives special consideration to those operations most affected by recent or unexpected changes. Changes in circumstances can result, for example, from marketplace or investment conditions, acquisitions and divestitures, organizational restructuring, new systems, and new ventures.

6. In determining the expected audit coverage for the proposed audit plan, the CAE considers relevant work performed by others who provide assurances to senior management (e.g., reliance by the CAE on the work of corporate compliance officers). The CAE's audit plan also considers audit work completed by the external auditor and management's own assessments of its risk management process, controls, and quality improvement processes.

7. The CAE should evaluate the breadth of coverage of the proposed audit plan to determine whether the scope is sufficient to enable the expression of an opinion about the organization's risk management and control processes. The CAE should inform senior management and the board of any gaps in audit coverage that would prevent the expression of an opinion on all aspects of these processes.

8. A key challenge for the internal audit activity is to evaluate the effectiveness of the organization's control processes based on the aggregation of many individual assessments. Those assessments are largely gained from internal audit engagements, reviews of management's self-assessments, and other assurance providers' work. As the engagements progress, internal auditors communicate, on a timely basis, the findings to the appropriate levels of management so prompt action can be taken to correct or mitigate the consequences of discovered control discrepancies or weaknesses.

9. In evaluating the overall effectiveness of the organization's control processes, the CAE considers whether:

☐ Significant discrepancies or weaknesses were discovered.

☐ Corrections or improvements were made after the discoveries.

☐ The discoveries and their potential consequences lead to a conclusion that a pervasive condition exists resulting in an unacceptable level of risk.

10. The existence of a significant discrepancy or weakness does not necessarily lead to the judgment that it is pervasive and poses an unacceptable risk. The internal auditor considers the nature and extent of risk exposure as well as the level of potential consequences in determining whether the effectiveness of the control processes are jeopardized and unacceptable risks exist.

11. The CAE's report on the organization's control processes is normally presented **once a year** to senior management and the board. The report states the critical role played by the control processes in the achievement of the organization's objectives. The report also describes the nature and extent of the work performed by the internal audit activity and the nature and extent of reliance on other assurance providers in formulating the opinion.

Practice Advisory 2130.A1-1: Information Reliability and Integrity

1. Internal auditors determine whether senior management and the board have a clear understanding that information reliability and integrity is a management responsibility. This responsibility includes all critical information of the organization regardless of how the information is stored. Information reliability and integrity includes accuracy, completeness, and security.

2. The CAE determines whether the internal audit activity possesses, or has access to, competent audit resources to evaluate information reliability and integrity and associated risk exposures. This includes both internal and external risk exposures, and exposures relating to the organization's relationships with outside entities.

3. The CAE determines whether information reliability and integrity breaches and conditions that might represent a threat to the organization will promptly be made known to senior management, the board, and the internal audit activity.

4. Internal auditors assess the effectiveness of preventive, detective, and mitigation measures against past attacks, as appropriate, and future attempts or incidents deemed likely to occur. Internal auditors determine whether the board has been appropriately informed of threats, incidents, vulnerabilities exploited, and corrective measures.

5. Internal auditors periodically assess the organization's information reliability and integrity practices and recommend, as appropriate, enhancements to, or implementation of, new controls and safeguards. Such assessments can be either conducted as separate stand-alone engagements or integrated into other audits or engagements conducted as part of the internal audit plan. The nature of the engagement will determine the most appropriate reporting process to senior management and the board.

Practice Advisory 2130-A1-2: Evaluating an Organization's Privacy Framework

1. The failure to protect personal information with appropriate controls can have significant consequences for an organization. The failure could damage the reputation of individuals and/or the organization and expose an organization to risks that include legal liability and diminished consumer and/or employee trust.

2. Privacy definitions vary widely depending on the culture, political environment, and legislative framework of the countries in which the organization operates. Risks associated with the privacy of information encompass personal privacy (physical and psychological); privacy of space (freedom from surveillance); privacy of communication (freedom from monitoring); and privacy of information (collection, use, and disclosure of personal information by others). "Personal information" generally refers to information associated with a specific individual or that has identifying characteristics that, when combined with other information, can then be associated with a specific individual. It can include any factual or subjective information—recorded or not—in any form of media. Personal information can include:

- Name, address, identification numbers, family relationships.

- Employee files, evaluations, comments, social status, or disciplinary actions.

- Credit records, income, financial status.

- Medical status.

3. Effective control over the protection of personal information is an essential component of the governance, risk management, and control processes of an organization. The board is ultimately accountable for identifying the principal risks to the organization and implementing appropriate control processes to mitigate those risks. Doing so includes establishing the necessary privacy framework for the organization and monitoring its implementation.

4. The internal audit activity can contribute to good governance and risk management by assessing the adequacy of management's identification of risks related to its privacy objectives and the adequacy of the controls established to mitigate those risks to an acceptable level. The internal auditor is well positioned to evaluate the privacy framework in his or her organization and identify the significant risks as well as the appropriate recommendations for mitigation.

5. The internal audit activity identifies the types and appropriateness of information gathered by the organization that is deemed personal or private, the collection methodology used, and

whether the organization's use of that information is in accordance with its intended use and applicable legislation.

6. Given the highly technical and legal nature of privacy issues, the internal audit activity needs appropriate knowledge and competence to conduct an assessment of the risks and controls of the organization's privacy framework.

7. In conducting such an evaluation of the management of the organization's privacy framework, the internal auditor:

- Considers the laws, regulations, and policies relating to privacy in the jurisdictions where the organization operates.

- Liaises with in-house legal counsel to determine the exact nature of laws, regulations, and other standards and practices applicable to the organization and the country/countries in which it operates.

- Liaises with IT specialists to determine that information security and data protection controls are in place and regularly reviewed and assessed for appropriateness.

- Considers the level or maturity of the organization's privacy practices. Depending on the level, the internal auditor may have differing roles. The auditor may facilitate the development and implementation of the privacy program, evaluate management's privacy risk assessment to determine the needs and risk exposures of the organization, or provide assurance on the effectiveness of the privacy policies, practices, and controls across the organization. If the internal auditor assumes any responsibility for developing and implementing a privacy program, his or her independence will be impaired.

2200–Engagement Planning

Internal auditors must develop and document a plan for each engagement, including the engagement's objectives, scope, timing, and resource allocations.

Practice Advisory 2200-1: Engagement Planning

1. The internal auditor plans and conducts the engagement, with supervisory review and approval. Prior to the engagement's commencement, the internal auditor prepares an engagement program that:

- States the objectives of the engagement.

- Identifies technical requirements, objectives, risks, processes, and transactions that are to be examined.

- States the nature and extent of testing required.

- Documents the internal auditor's procedures for collecting, analyzing, interpreting, and documenting information during the engagement.

- Is modified, as appropriate, during the engagement with the approval of the CAE or his or her designee.

2. The CAE should require a level of formality and documentation (e.g., of the results of planning meetings, risk assessment procedures, level of detail in the work program, etc.) that is appropriate to the organization. Factors to consider would include:

- Whether the work performed and/or the results of the engagement will be relied on by others (e.g., external auditors, regulators, or management).

- Whether the work relates to matters that may be involved in potential or current litigation.

- ☐ The experience level of the internal audit staff and the level of direct supervision required.

- ☐ Whether the project is staffed internally, by guest auditors, or by external service providers.

- ☐ The project's complexity and scope.

- ☐ The size of the internal audit activity.

- ☐ The value of documentation (e.g., whether it will be used in subsequent years).

3. The internal auditor determines the other engagement requirements, such as the period covered and estimated completion dates. The internal auditor also considers the final engagement communication format. Planning at this stage facilitates the communication process at the engagement's completion.

4. The internal auditor informs those in management who need to know about the engagement, conducts meetings with management responsible for the activity under review, summarizes and distributes the discussions and any conclusions reached from the meetings, and retains the documentation in the engagement working papers. Topics of discussion may include:

- ☐ Planned engagement objectives and scope of work.

- ☐ The resources and timing of engagement work.

- ☐ Key factors affecting business conditions and operations of the areas being reviewed, including recent changes in internal and external environment.

- ☐ Concerns or requests from management.

5. The CAE determines how, when, and to whom engagement results will be communicated. The internal auditor documents this and communicates it to management, to the extent deemed appropriate, during the planning phase of the engagement. The internal auditor communicates to management subsequent changes that affect the timing or reporting of engagement results.

Practice Advisory 2200-2: Using a Top-Down, Risk-Based Approach to Identify the Controls to Be Assessed in an Internal Audit Engagement

1. Read this practice advisory in conjunction with *Practice Advisories 2010-2: Using the Risk Management Process in Internal Audit Planning, 2210-1: Engagement Objectives*, and *2210.A1-1: Risk Assessment in Engagement Planning* and the Practice Guide *GAIT for Business and IT Risk* (*GAIT-R*).

2. This practice advisory assumes that the objectives for the internal audit engagement have been determined and the risks to be addressed have been identified in the internal audit planning process. It provides guidance on the use of a top-down, risk-based approach to identify and include in the internal audit scope (per Standard 2220) the key controls relied on to manage the risks.

3. "Top-down" refers to basing the scope definition on the more significant risks to the organization. This is in contrast to developing the scope based on the risks at a specific location, which may not be significant to the organization as a whole. A top-down approach ensures that internal auditing is focused, as noted in Practice Advisory 2010-2, on "providing assurance on the management of significant risks."

4. A system of internal control typically includes both manual and automated controls. (Note that this applies to controls at every level—entity, business process, and IT general controls—and in every layer of the control framework; e.g., activities in the control environment, monitoring, or risk assessment layers may also be automated.) Both types of controls need to be assessed to determine whether business risks are effectively managed. In particular, the internal auditor needs to assess whether there is an appropriate combination of controls, including those related to IT, to mitigate business risks within organizational tolerances. The internal auditor

needs to consider including procedures to assess and confirm that risk tolerances are current and appropriate.

5. The internal audit scope needs to include all the controls required to provide reasonable assurance that the risks are effectively managed (subject to the comments in paragraph 9 below). These controls are referred to as key controls—those necessary to manage risk associated with a critical business objective. Only the key controls need to be assessed, although the internal auditor can choose to include an assessment of nonkey controls (e.g., redundant, duplicative controls) if there is value to the business in providing such assurance. The internal auditor may also discuss with management whether the nonkey controls are required.

6. Note that where the organization has a mature and effective risk management program, the key controls relied on to manage each risk will have been identified. In these cases, the internal auditor needs to assess whether management's identification and assessment of the key controls is adequate.

7. The key controls can be in the form of:

☐ Entity-level controls (e.g., employees are trained and take a test to confirm their understanding of the code of conduct). The entity-level controls may be manual, fully automated, or partly automated.

☐ Manual controls within a business process (e.g., the performance of a physical inventory).

☐ Fully automated controls within a business process (e.g., matching or updating accounts in the general ledger).

☐ Partly automated controls within a business process (also called hybrid or IT-dependent controls), where an otherwise manual control relies on application functionality, such as an exception report. If an error in that functionality would not be detected, the entire control could be ineffective. For example, a key control to detect duplicate payments might include the review of a system-generated report. The manual part of the control would not ensure that the report is complete. Therefore, the application functionality that generated the report should be in scope.

The internal auditor may use other methods or frameworks, as long as all the key controls relied on to manage the risks are identified and assessed, including manual controls, automated controls, and controls within IT general control processes.

8. Fully and partly automated controls—whether at the entity level or within a business process—generally rely on the proper design and effective operation of IT general controls. *GAIT-R* discusses the recommended process for identifying key IT general controls.

9. The assessment of key controls may be performed in a single, integrated internal audit engagement or in a combination of internal audit engagements. For example, one internal audit engagement may address the key controls performed by business process users, while another covers the key IT general controls, and a third assesses related controls that operate at the entity level. This is common where the same controls (especially those at the entity level or within IT general controls) are relied on for more than one risk area.

10. As noted in paragraph 5, before providing an opinion on the effective management of the risks covered by the internal audit scope, it is necessary to assess the combination of all key controls. Even if multiple internal audit engagements are performed, each addressing some key controls, the internal auditor needs to include in the scope of at least one internal audit engagement an assessment of the design of the key controls as a whole (i.e., across all the related internal audit engagements) and whether it is sufficient to manage risks within organizational tolerances.

11. If the internal audit scope (considering other internal audit engagements as discussed in paragraph 9) includes some, but not all, key controls required to manage the targeted risks, a scope limitation should be considered and clearly communicated in the internal audit notification and final report.

2201–Planning Considerations

In planning the engagement, internal auditors must consider:

- ☐ The objectives of the activity being reviewed and the means by which the activity controls its performance.

- ☐ The significant risks to the activity, its objectives, resources, and operations, and the means by which the potential impact of risk is kept to an acceptable level.

- ☐ The adequacy and effectiveness of the activity's risk management and control processes compared to a relevant control framework or model.

- ☐ The opportunities for making significant improvements to the activity's risk management and control processes.

2201.A1–When planning an engagement for parties outside the organization, internal auditors must establish a written understanding with them about objectives, scope, respective responsibilities, and other expectations, including restrictions on distribution of the results of the engagement and access to engagement records.

2201.C1–Internal auditors must establish an understanding with consulting engagement clients about objectives, scope, respective responsibilities, and other client expectations. For significant engagements, this understanding must be documented.

> No Practice Advisory for Standard 2201

2210–Engagement Objectives

Objectives must be established for each engagement.

2210.A1–Internal auditors must conduct a preliminary assessment of the risks relevant to the activity under review. Engagement objectives must reflect the results of this assessment.

2210.A2–Internal auditors must consider the probability of significant errors, fraud, noncompliance, and other exposures when developing the engagement objectives.

2210.A3–Adequate criteria are needed to evaluate controls. Internal auditors must ascertain the extent to which management has established adequate criteria to determine whether objectives and goals have been accomplished. If adequate, internal auditors must use such criteria in their evaluation. If inadequate, internal auditors must work with management to develop appropriate evaluation criteria.

2210.C1–Consulting engagement objectives must address governance, risk management, and control processes to the extent agreed on with the client.

2210.C2–Consulting engagement objectives must be consistent with the organization's values, strategies, and objectives.

Practice Advisory 2210-1: Engagement Objectives

1. Internal auditors establish engagement objectives to address the risks associated with the activity under review. For planned engagements, the objectives proceed and align to those initially identified during the risk assessment process from which the internal audit plan is derived. For unplanned engagements, the objectives are established prior to the start of the engagement and are designed to address the specific issue that prompted the engagement.

2. The risk assessment during the engagement's planning phase is used to further define the initial objectives and identify other significant areas of concern.

3. After identifying the risks, the auditor determines the procedures to be performed and the scope (nature, timing, and extent) of those procedures. Engagement procedures performed in appropriate scope are the means to derive conclusions related to the engagement objectives.

Practice Advisory 2210.A1-1: Risk Assessment in Engagement Planning

1. Internal auditors consider management's assessment of risks relevant to the activity under review. The internal auditor also considers:

☐ The reliability of management's assessment of risk.

☐ Management's process for monitoring, reporting, and resolving risk and control issues.

☐ Management's reporting of events that exceeded the limits of the organization's risk appetite and management's response to those reports.

☐ Risks in related activities relevant to the activity under review.

2. Internal auditors obtain or update background information about the activities to be reviewed to determine the impact on the engagement objectives and scope.

3. If appropriate, internal auditors conduct a survey to become familiar with the activities, risks, and controls to identify areas for engagement emphasis and to invite comments and suggestions from engagement clients.

4. Internal auditors summarize the results from the reviews of management's assessment of risk, the background information, and any survey work. The summary includes:

☐ Significant engagement issues and reasons for pursuing them in more depth.

☐ Engagement objectives and procedures.

☐ Methodologies to be used, such as technology-based audit and sampling techniques.

☐ Potential critical control points, control deficiencies, and/or excess controls.

☐ When applicable, reasons for not continuing the engagement or for significantly modifying engagement objectives.

2220–Engagement Scope

The established scope must be sufficient to satisfy the objectives of the engagement.

2220.A1–The scope of the engagement must include consideration of relevant systems, records, personnel, and physical properties, including those under the control of third parties.

2220.A2–If significant consulting opportunities arise during an assurance engagement, a specific written understanding as to the objectives, scope, respective responsibilities, and other expectations should be reached and the results of the consulting engagement communicated in accordance with consulting standards.

2220.C1–In performing consulting engagements, internal auditors must ensure that the scope of the engagement is sufficient to address the agreed-on objectives. If internal auditors develop reservations about the scope during the engagement, these reservations must be discussed with the client to determine whether to continue with the engagement.

2220.C2–During consulting engagements, internal auditors must address controls consistent with the engagement's objectives and be alert to significant control issues.

> No Practice Advisory for Standard 2220

2230–Engagement Resource Allocation

Internal auditors must determine appropriate and sufficient resources to achieve engagement objectives based on an evaluation of the nature and complexity of each engagement, time constraints, and available resources.

Practice Advisory 2230-1: Engagement Resource Allocation

1. Internal auditors consider the following when determining the appropriateness and sufficiency of resources:

- ☐ The number and experience level of the internal audit staff.

- ☐ Knowledge, skills, and other competencies of the internal audit staff when selecting internal auditors for the engagement.

- ☐ Availability of external resources where additional knowledge and competencies are required.

- ☐ Training needs of internal auditors as each engagement assignment serves as a basis for meeting the internal audit activity's developmental needs.

2240–Engagement Work Program

Internal auditors must develop and document work programs that achieve the engagement objectives.

2240.A1–Work programs must include the procedures for identifying, analyzing, evaluating, and documenting information during the engagement. The work program must be approved prior to its implementation, and any adjustments approved promptly.

2240.C1–Work programs for consulting engagements may vary in form and content, depending on the nature of the engagement.

Practice Advisory 2240-1: Engagement Work Program

1. Internal auditors develop and obtain documented approval of work programs before commencing the internal audit engagement. The work program includes methodologies to be used, such as technology-based audit and sampling techniques.

2. The process of collecting, analyzing, interpreting, and documenting information is to be supervised to provide reasonable assurance that engagement objectives are met and that the internal auditor's objectivity is maintained.

2300–Performing the Engagement

Internal auditors must identify, analyze, evaluate, and document sufficient information to achieve the engagement's objectives.

Practice Advisory 2300-1: Use of Personal Information in Conducting Engagements

1. Internal auditors need to consider concerns relating to the protection of personally identifiable information gathered during audit engagements as advances in IT and communications continue to present privacy risks and threats. Privacy controls are legal requirements in many jurisdictions.

2. "Personal information" generally refers to data associated with a specific individual or data that have identifying characteristics that may be combined with other information. It includes any factual or subjective information, recorded or not, in any form or media. Personal information includes:

- ☐ Name, address, identification numbers, income, blood type.

- ☐ Evaluations, social status, disciplinary actions.

- ☐ Employee files and credit and loan records.

- ☐ Employee health and medical data.

3. In many jurisdictions, laws require organizations to identify the purposes for which personal information is collected at or before the time of collection. These laws also prohibit using and disclosing personal information for purposes other than those for which it was collected except with the individual's consent or as required by law.

4. It is important that internal auditors understand and comply with all laws regarding the use of personal information in their jurisdiction and in those jurisdictions where their organizations conduct business.

5. It may be inappropriate, and in some cases illegal, to access, retrieve, review, manipulate, or use personal information in conducting certain internal audit engagements. If the internal auditor accesses personal information, it may be necessary to develop procedures to safeguard this information. For example, the internal auditor may decide not to record personal information in engagement records in some situations.

6. The internal auditor may seek advice from legal counsel before beginning audit work if there are questions or concerns about access to personal information.

2310–Identifying Information

Internal auditors must identify sufficient, reliable, relevant, and useful information to achieve the engagement's objectives.

Interpretation: *Sufficient information is factual, adequate, and convincing so that a prudent, informed person would reach the same conclusions as the auditor. Reliable information is the best attainable information through the use of appropriate engagement techniques. Relevant information supports engagement observations and recommendations and is consistent with the objectives for the engagement. Useful information helps the organization meet its goals.*

No Practice Advisory for Standard 2310

2320–Analysis and Evaluation

Internal auditors must base conclusions and engagement results on appropriate analyses and evaluations.

Practice Advisory 2320-1: Analytical Procedures

1. Internal auditors may use analytical procedures to obtain audit evidence. Analytical procedures involve studying and comparing relationships among both financial and nonfinancial information. The application of analytical procedures is based on the premise that, in the absence of known conditions to the contrary, relationships among information may reasonably be expected to exist and continue. Examples of contrary conditions include unusual or nonrecurring transactions or events; accounting, organizational, operational, environmental, and technological changes; inefficiencies; ineffectiveness; errors; fraud; or illegal acts.

2. Analytical procedures often provide the internal auditor with an efficient and effective means of obtaining evidence. The assessment results from comparing information with expectations identified or developed by the internal auditor. Analytical procedures are useful in identifying:

- Unexpected differences.
- The absence of differences when they are expected.
- Potential errors.
- Potential fraud or illegal acts.
- Other unusual or nonrecurring transactions or events.

3. Analytical audit procedures include:

- Comparing current period information with expectations based on similar information for prior periods as well as budgets or forecasts.
- Studying relationships between financial and appropriate nonfinancial information (e.g., recorded payroll expense compared to changes in average number of employees).
- Studying relationships among elements of information (e.g., fluctuation in recorded interest expense compared to changes in related debt balances).
- Comparing information with expectations based on similar information for other organizational units as well as for the industry in which the organization operates.

4. Internal auditors may perform analytical procedures using monetary amounts, physical quantities, ratios, or percentages. Specific analytical procedures include ratio, trend, and regression analysis; reasonableness tests; period-to-period comparisons; comparisons with budgets; forecasts; and external economic information. Analytical procedures assist internal auditors in identifying conditions that may require additional audit procedures. An internal auditor uses analytical procedures in planning the engagement in accordance with the guidelines contained in Standard 2200.

5. Internal auditors may use analytical procedures to generate evidence during the audit engagement. When determining the extent of analytical procedures, the internal auditor considers the:

- Significance of the area being audited.
- Assessment of risk management in the area being audited.
- Adequacy of the internal control system.
- Availability and reliability of financial and nonfinancial information.

☐ Precision with which the results of analytical audit procedures can be predicted.

☐ Availability and comparability of information regarding the industry in which the organization operates.

☐ Extent to which other procedures provide evidence.

6. When analytical audit procedures identify unexpected results or relationships, the internal auditor evaluates such results or relationships. This evaluation includes determining whether the difference from expectations could be a result of fraud, error, or a change in conditions. The auditor may ask management about the reasons for the difference and would corroborate management's explanation, for example, by modifying expectations and recalculating the difference or by applying other audit procedures. In particular, the internal auditor needs to be satisfied that the explanation considers both the direction of the change (e.g., sales decreased) and the amount of the difference (e.g., sales decreased by 10%). Unexplained results or relationships from applying analytical procedures may be indicative of a significant problem (e.g., a potential error, fraud, or illegal act). Results or relationships that are not adequately explained may indicate a situation to be communicated to senior management and the board in accordance with Standard 2060. Depending on the circumstances, the internal auditor may recommend appropriate action.

2330–Documenting Information

Internal auditors must document relevant information to support the conclusions and engagement results.

2330.A1–The CAE must control access to engagement records. The CAE must obtain the approval of senior management and/or legal counsel prior to releasing such records to external parties, as appropriate.

2330.A2–The CAE must develop retention requirements for engagement records, regardless of the medium in which each record is stored. These retention requirements must be consistent with the organization's guidelines and any pertinent regulatory or other requirements.

2330.C1–The CAE must develop policies governing the custody and retention of consulting engagement records as well as their release to internal and external parties. These policies must be consistent with the organization's guidelines and any pertinent regulatory or other requirements.

Practice Advisory 2330-1: Documenting Information

1. Internal auditors prepare working papers. Working papers document the information obtained, the analyses made, and the support for the conclusions and engagement results. Internal audit management reviews the prepared working papers.

2. Engagement working papers generally:

☐ Aid in the planning, performance, and review of engagements.

☐ Provide the principal support for engagement results.

☐ Document whether engagement objectives were achieved.

☐ Support the accuracy and completeness of the work performed.

☐ Provide a basis for the internal audit activity's QAIP.

☐ Facilitate third-party reviews.

3. The organization, design, and content of engagement working papers depend on the engagement's nature and objectives and the organization's needs. Engagement working papers document all aspects of the engagement process from planning to communicating results. The internal audit activity determines the media used to document and store working papers.

4. The CAE establishes working paper policies for the various types of engagements performed. Standardized engagement working papers, such as questionnaires and audit programs, may improve the engagement's efficiency and facilitate the delegation of engagement work. Engagement working papers may be categorized as permanent or carry-forward engagement files that contain information of continuing importance.

Practice Advisory 2330.A1-1: Control of Engagement Records

1. Internal audit engagement records include reports, supporting documentation, review notes, and correspondence, regardless of storage media. Engagement records or working papers are the property of the organization. The internal audit activity controls engagement working papers and provides access to authorized personnel only.

2. Internal auditors may educate management and the board about access to engagement records by external parties. Policies relating to access to engagement records, handling of access requests, and procedures to be followed when an engagement warrants an investigation need to be reviewed by the board.

3. Internal audit policies explain who in the organization is responsible for ensuring the control and security of the activity's records, which internal or external parties can be granted access to engagement records, and how requests for access to those records need to be handled. These policies will vary depending on the nature of the organization, practices followed in the industry, and access privileges established by law.

4. Management and other members of the organization may request access to all or specific engagement working papers. Such access may be necessary to substantiate or explain engagement observations and recommendations or for other business purposes. The CAE approves these requests.

5. The CAE approves access to engagement working papers by external auditors.

6. There are circumstances in which parties outside the organization, other than external auditors, request access to engagement working papers and reports. Prior to releasing the documentation, the CAE obtains the approval of senior management and/or legal counsel, as appropriate.

7. Potentially, internal audit records that are not specifically protected may be accessed in legal proceedings. Legal requirements vary significantly in different jurisdictions. When there is a specific request for engagement records in relation to a legal proceeding, the CAE works closely with legal counsel in deciding what to provide.

Practice Advisory 2330.A1-2: Granting Access to Engagement Records

Caution: Internal auditors are encouraged to consult legal counsel in matters involving legal issues as requirements may vary significantly in different jurisdictions. The guidance contained in this Practice Advisory is based primarily on the legal systems that protect information and work performed for, or communicated to, an engaged attorney (i.e., attorney–client privilege), such as the legal system in the United States of America. Practice Advisory 2400-1 discusses attorney–client privilege.

1. Internal audit engagement records include reports, supporting documentation, review notes, and correspondence, regardless of storage media. Engagement records are generally produced under the presumption that their contents are confidential and may contain a mix of facts and opinions. However, those who are not familiar with the organization or its internal audit process may misunderstand those facts and opinions. Outside parties may seek access to engagement

records in different types of proceedings, including criminal prosecutions, civil litigation, tax audits, regulatory reviews, government contract reviews, and reviews by self-regulatory organizations. Most of an organization's records that are not protected by the attorney–client privilege may be accessible in criminal proceedings. In noncriminal proceedings, the issue of access is less clear and may vary according to the jurisdiction of the organization.

2. Explicit practices of the internal audit activity may increase the control of access to engagement records.

3. The internal audit activity may address access to, and control of, internal audit records regardless of the media used for storage.

4. The internal audit activity's policies should cover what to include in engagement records and specify the content and format of the engagement records and how internal auditors handle resolved review notes. The policies also should specify how long internal audit records are to be retained. The CAE, when specifying the length of retention for engagement records, should consider the organization's needs as well as legal requirements.

5. The internal audit activity's policies may document who in the organization is responsible for the control and security of internal audit records, who can be granted access to engagement records, and how requests for access to those records are to be handled. These policies depend on the practices followed in the organization's industry or legal jurisdiction. The CAE should be aware of changing practices in the industry and changing legal precedents. When developing policies, the CAE should consider who may seek access to internal audit records.

6. The policy granting access to engagement records may also address processes:

- For resolving access issues.

- For educating the internal audit staff concerning the risks and issues regarding access to their work products.

- To determine who may seek access to the work product in the future.

7. The CAE also may educate senior management and the board about the risks of access to engagement records. The board may review policies relating to who can be granted access to engagement records and how those requests are to be handled. The specific policies will vary depending on the nature of the organization and the access privileges that have been established by law.

8. When furnishing engagement records, the CAE usually:

- Provides only the specific documents as directed by legal counsel or policies. These usually exclude documents covered by attorney–client privilege. Documents that reveal attorneys' thought processes or strategies will usually be privileged and not subject to forced disclosure.

- Releases documents in a form where they cannot be changed (e.g., as an image rather than in word processing format). For paper documents, the CAE releases copies and keeps the originals.

- Labels each document as confidential and places a notation that secondary distribution is not permitted without permission.

Practice Advisory 2330.A2-1: Retention of Records

1. Engagement record retention requirements vary among jurisdictions and legal environments.

2. The CAE develops a written retention policy that meets organizational needs and legal requirements of the jurisdictions within which the organization operates.

3. The record retention policy needs to include appropriate arrangements for the retention of records related to engagements performed by external service providers.

2340–Engagement Supervision

Engagements must be properly supervised to ensure objectives are achieved, quality is assured, and staff is developed.

Interpretation: *The extent of supervision required will depend on the proficiency and experience of internal auditors and the complexity of the engagement. The CAE has overall responsibility for supervising the engagement, whether performed by or for the internal audit activity, but may designate appropriately experienced members of the internal audit activity to perform the review. Appropriate evidence of supervision is documented and retained.*

Practice Advisory 2340-1: Engagement Supervision

1. The CAE or designee provides appropriate engagement supervision. Supervision is a process that begins with planning and continues throughout the engagement. The process includes:

- Ensuring that designated auditors collectively possess the required knowledge, skills, and other competencies to perform the engagement.

- Providing appropriate instructions during the planning of the engagement and approving the engagement program.

- Ensuring that the approved engagement program is completed unless changes are justified and authorized.

- Determining that engagement working papers adequately support engagement observations, conclusions, and recommendations.

- Ensuring that engagement communications are accurate, objective, clear, concise, constructive, and timely.

- Ensuring that engagement objectives are met.

- Providing opportunities for developing internal auditors' knowledge, skills, and other competencies.

2. The CAE is responsible for all internal audit engagements, whether performed by or for the internal audit activity, and all significant professional judgments made throughout the engagement. The CAE also adopts suitable means to ensure this responsibility is met. "Suitable" means include policies and procedures designed to:

- Minimize the risk that internal auditors or others performing work for the internal audit activity make professional judgments or take other actions that are inconsistent with the CAE's professional judgment such that the engagement is impacted adversely.

- Resolve differences in professional judgment between the CAE and internal audit staff over significant issues relating to the engagement. Such means may include discussion of pertinent facts, further inquiry or research, and documentation and disposition of the differing viewpoints in engagement working papers. In instances of a difference in professional judgment over an ethical issue, suitable means may include referral of the issue to those individuals in the organization having responsibility over ethical matters.

3. All engagement working papers are reviewed to ensure they support engagement communications and necessary audit procedures are performed. Evidence of supervisory review consists of the reviewer initialing and dating each working paper after it is reviewed. Other techniques that

provide evidence of supervisory review include completing an engagement working paper review checklist; preparing a memorandum specifying the nature, extent, and results of the review; or evaluating and accepting reviews within the working paper software.

4. Reviewers can make a written record (i.e., review notes) of questions arising from the review process. When clearing review notes, care needs to be taken to ensure working papers provide adequate evidence that questions raised during the review are resolved. Alternatives with respect to disposition of review notes are to:

- □ Retain the review notes as a record of the reviewer's questions raised, the steps taken in their resolution, and the results of those steps.

- □ Discard the review notes after the questions raised are resolved and the appropriate engagement working papers are amended to provide the information requested.

5. Engagement supervision also allows for training and development of staff and performance evaluation.

2400–Communicating Results

Internal auditors must communicate the results of engagements.

Practice Advisory 2400-1: Legal Considerations in Communicating Results

Caution: Internal auditors are encouraged to consult legal counsel in matters involving legal issues as requirements may vary significantly in different jurisdictions. The guidance contained in this Practice Advisory is based primarily on the legal systems that protect information and work performed for, or communicated to, an engaged attorney (i.e., attorney–client privilege), such as the legal system in the United States of America. Practice Advisory 2400-1 discusses attorney–client privilege.

1. The internal auditor needs to exercise caution when communicating noncompliance with laws, regulations, and other legal issues. Developing policies and procedures regarding the handling of those matters as well as a close working relationship with other appropriate areas (e.g., legal counsel and compliance) is strongly encouraged.

2. The internal auditor gathers evidence, makes analytical judgments, reports results, and determines whether management has taken appropriate corrective action. The internal auditor's need to prepare engagement records may conflict with legal counsel's desire to not leave discoverable evidence that could harm the organization's position in legal matters. For example, even if an internal auditor gathers and evaluates information properly, the facts and analyses disclosed may negatively impact the organization from a legal perspective. Proper planning and policy making—including role definition and methods of communication—are essential so that a sudden revelation does not place the internal auditor and legal counsel at odds with one another. Both parties need to foster an ethical and preventive perspective throughout the organization by sensitizing and educating management about the established policies.

3. A communication made between "privileged persons"—in confidence and for the purpose of seeking, obtaining, or providing legal assistance for the client—is necessary to protect the attorney–client privilege. This privilege, which is primarily used to protect communications with attorneys, can also apply to communications with third parties working with an attorney.

4. Some courts have recognized a privilege of critical self-analysis that shields self-critical materials (e.g., audit work products) from discovery. In general, the recognition of this privilege is premised on the belief that the confidentiality of the self-analysis in these instances outweighs the valued public interest.

5. Privilege usually applies when:

- ☐ The information results from a self-critical analysis undertaken by the party asserting the privilege.

- ☐ The public has a strong interest in preserving the free flow of the information contained in the critical analysis.

- ☐ The information is of the type whose flow would be curtailed if discovery were allowed.

6. Self-evaluative privileges are less likely to be available when a government agency—rather than a party involved in a private legal matter—seeks out the documents. Presumably this reluctance results from recognition of the government's stronger interest in enforcing the law.

7. Documents intended to be protected under the work-product doctrine usually need to be:

- ☐ Some type of work product (e.g., memo and computer program).

- ☐ Prepared in anticipation of litigation.

- ☐ Completed by someone working at the direction of an attorney.

8. Documents prepared and delivered to the attorney before the attorney–client relationship is established are not generally protected by the attorney–client privilege.

2410–Criteria for Communicating

Communications must include the engagement's objectives and scope as well as applicable conclusions, recommendations, and action plans.

2410.A1–Final communication of engagement results must, where appropriate, contain the internal auditors' opinion and/or conclusions. When issued, an opinion or conclusion must take account of the expectations of senior management, the board, and other stakeholders and must be supported by sufficient, reliable, relevant, and useful information.

Interpretation: *Opinions at the engagement level may be ratings, conclusions, or other descriptions of the results. Such an engagement may be in relation to controls around a specific process, risk, or business unit. The formulation of such opinions requires consideration of the engagement results and their significance.*

2410.A2–Internal auditors are encouraged to acknowledge satisfactory performance in engagement communications.

2410.A3–When releasing engagement results to parties outside the organization, the communication must include limitations on distribution and use of the results.

2410.C1–Communication of the progress and results of consulting engagements will vary in form and content depending on the nature of the engagement and the needs of the client.

Practice Advisory 2410-1: Communication Criteria

1. Although the format and content of the final engagement communications varies by organization or type of engagement, they are to contain, at a minimum, the purpose, scope, and results of the engagement.

2. Final engagement communications may include background information and summaries. Background information may identify the organizational units and activities reviewed and

provide explanatory information. It may also include the status of observations, conclusions, and recommendations from prior reports and an indication of whether the report covers a scheduled engagement or is responding to a request. Summaries are balanced representations of the communication's content.

3. Purpose statements describe the engagement objectives and may inform the reader why the engagement was conducted and what it was expected to achieve.

4. Scope statements identify the audited activities and may include supportive information such as time period reviewed and related activities not reviewed to delineate the boundaries of the engagement. They may describe the nature and extent of engagement work performed.

5. Results include observations, conclusions, opinions, recommendations, and action plans.

6. Observations are pertinent statements of fact. The internal auditor communicates those observations necessary to support or prevent misunderstanding of his or her conclusions and recommendations. The internal auditor may communicate less significant observations or recommendations informally.

7. Engagement observations and recommendations emerge by a process of comparing criteria (the correct state) with condition (the current state). Whether there is a difference or not, the internal auditor has a foundation on which to build the report. When conditions meet the criteria, communication of satisfactory performance may be appropriate. Observations and recommendations are based on the following attributes:

☐ **Criteria.** The standards, measures, or expectations used in making an evaluation and/or verification (the correct state).

☐ **Condition.** The factual evidence that the internal auditor found in the course of the examination (the current state).

☐ **Cause.** The reason for the difference between expected and actual conditions.

☐ **Effect.** The risk or exposure the organization and/or others encounter because the condition is not consistent with the criteria (the impact of the difference). In determining the degree of risk or exposure, internal auditors consider the effect their engagement observations and recommendations may have on the organization's operations and financial statements.

Observations and recommendations can include engagement client accomplishments, related issues, and supportive information.

8. Conclusions and opinions are the internal auditor's evaluations of the effects of the observations and recommendations on the activities reviewed. They usually put the observations and recommendations in perspective based on their overall implications. Clearly identify any engagement conclusions in the engagement report. Conclusions may encompass the entire scope of an engagement or specific aspects. They may cover, but are not limited to, whether operating or program objectives and goals conform to those of the organization, whether the organization's objectives and goals are being met, and whether the activity under review is functioning as intended. An opinion may include an overall assessment of controls or may be limited to specific controls or aspects of the engagement.

9. The internal auditor may communicate recommendations for improvements, acknowledgments of satisfactory performance, and corrective actions. Recommendations are based on the internal auditor's observations and conclusions. They call for action to correct existing conditions or improve operations and may suggest approaches to correcting or enhancing performance as a guide for management in achieving desired results. Recommendations can be general or specific. For example, under some circumstances, the internal auditor may recommend a general course of

action and specific suggestions for implementation. In other circumstances, the internal auditor may suggest further investigation or study.

10. The internal auditor may communicate engagement client accomplishments, in terms of improvements since the last engagement or the establishment of a well-controlled operation. This information may be necessary to fairly present the existing conditions and to provide perspective and balance to the engagement final communications.

11. The internal auditor may communicate the engagement client's views about the internal auditor's conclusions, opinions, or recommendations.

12. As part of the internal auditor's discussions with the engagement client, the internal auditor obtains agreement on the results of the engagement and on any necessary plan of action to improve operations. If the internal auditor and engagement client disagree about the engagement results, the engagement communications state both positions and the reasons for the disagreement. The engagement client's written comments may be included as an appendix to the engagement report, in the body of the report, or in a cover letter.

13. Certain information is not appropriate for disclosure to all report recipients because it is privileged, proprietary, or related to improper or illegal acts. Disclose such information in a separate report. Distribute the report to the board if the conditions being reported involve senior management.

14. Interim reports are written or oral and may be transmitted formally or informally. Use interim reports to communicate information that requires immediate attention, to communicate a change in engagement scope for the activity under review, or to keep management informed of engagement progress when engagements extend over a long period. The use of interim reports does not diminish or eliminate the need for a final report.

15. A signed report is issued after the engagement's completion. Summary reports highlighting engagement results are appropriate for levels of management above the engagement client and can be issued separately from or in conjunction with the final report. The term "signed" means the authorized internal auditor's name is manually or electronically signed in the report or on a cover letter. The CAE determines which internal auditor is authorized to sign the report. If engagement reports are distributed by electronic means, a signed version of the report is kept on file by the internal audit activity.

2420–Quality of Communications

Communications must be accurate, objective, clear, concise, constructive, complete, and timely.

Interpretation: *Accurate communications are free from errors and distortions and are faithful to the underlying facts. Objective communications are fair, impartial, and unbiased and are the result of a fair-minded and balanced assessment of all relevant facts and circumstances. Clear communications are easily understood and logical, avoiding unnecessary technical language and providing all significant and relevant information. Concise communications are to the point and avoid unnecessary elaboration, superfluous detail, redundancy, and wordiness. Constructive communications are helpful to the engagement client and the organization and lead to improvements where needed. Complete communications lack nothing that is essential to the target audience and include all significant and relevant information and observations to support recommendations and conclusions. Timely communications are opportune and expedient, depending on the significance of the issue, allowing management to take appropriate corrective action.*

Practice Advisory 2420-1: Quality of Communications
1. Gather, evaluate, and summarize data and evidence with care and precision.

2. Derive and express observations, conclusions, and recommendations without prejudice, partisanship, personal interests, and the undue influence of others.

3. Improve clarity by avoiding unnecessary technical language and providing all significant and relevant information in context.

4. Develop communications with the objective of making each element meaningful but succinct.

5. Adopt a useful, positive, and well-meaning content and tone that focuses on the organization's objectives.

6. Ensure communication is consistent with the organization's style and culture.

7. Plan the timing of the presentation of engagement results to avoid undue delay.

2421–Errors and Omissions

If a final communication contains a significant error or omission, the CAE must communicate corrected information to all parties who received the original communication.

> No Practice Advisory for Standard 2421

2430–Use of "Conducted in Conformance with the *International Standards for the Professional Practice of Internal Auditing*"

Internal auditors may report that their engagements are "conducted in conformance with the *International Standards for the Professional Practice of Internal Auditing*" only if the results of the QAIP support the statement.

> No Practice Advisory for Standard 2430

2431–Engagement Disclosure of Nonconformance

When nonconformance with the definition of internal auditing, the Code of Ethics, or the *Standards* impacts a specific engagement, communication of the results must disclose the:

- Principle or rule of conduct of the Code of Ethics or *Standard(s)* with which full conformance was not achieved.

- Reason(s) for nonconformance.

- Impact of nonconformance on the engagement and the communicated engagement results.

> No Practice Advisory for Standard 2431

2440–Disseminating Results

The CAE must communicate results to the appropriate parties.

Interpretation: *The CAE or designee reviews and approves the final engagement communication before issuance and decides to whom and how it will be disseminated.*

2440.A1–The CAE is responsible for communicating the final results to parties who can ensure that the results are given due consideration.

2440.A2–If not otherwise mandated by legal, statutory, or regulatory requirements, prior to releasing results to parties outside the organization, the CAE must:

☐ Assess the potential risk to the organization.

☐ Consult with senior management and/or legal counsel as appropriate.

☐ Control dissemination by restricting the use of the results.

2440.C1–The CAE is responsible for communicating the final results of consulting engagements to clients.

2440.C2–During consulting engagements, governance, risk management, and control issues may be identified. Whenever these issues are significant to the organization, they must be communicated to senior management and the board.

Practice Advisory 2440-1: Disseminating Results

1. Internal auditors discuss conclusions and recommendations with appropriate levels of management before the CAE issues the final engagement communications. This is usually accomplished during the course of the engagement and/or at postengagement meetings (i.e., exit meetings).

2. Another technique is for the management of the audited activity to review draft engagement issues, observations, and recommendations. These discussions and reviews help avoid misunderstandings or misinterpretations of fact by providing the opportunity for the engagement client to clarify specific items and express views about the observations, conclusions, and recommendations.

3. The level of participants in the discussions and reviews varies by organization and nature of the report; they generally include those individuals who are knowledgeable regarding detailed operations and those who can authorize the implementation of corrective action.

4. The CAE distributes the final engagement communication to the management of the audited activity and to those members of the organization who can ensure engagement results are given due consideration and take corrective action or ensure that corrective action is taken. Where appropriate, the CAE may send a summary communication to higher-level members in the organization. Where required by the internal audit charter or organizational policy, the CAE also communicates to other interested or affected parties such as external auditors and the board.

Practice Advisory 2440-2: Communicating Sensitive Information Within and Outside the Chain of Command

1. Internal auditors often come into possession of critically sensitive information that is substantial to the organization and poses significant potential consequences. This information may relate to exposures, threats, uncertainties, fraud, waste and mismanagement, illegal activities, abuse of power, misconduct that endangers public health or safety, or other wrongdoings. Furthermore, these matters may adversely impact the organization's reputation, image, competitiveness, success, viability, market values, investments and intangible assets, or earnings.

2. Once the internal auditor has deemed the new information substantial and credible, he or she would normally communicate the information—in a timely manner—to senior management and the board in accordance with Standard 2060 and Practice Advisory 2060-1. This communication typically would follow the normal chain of command for the internal auditor.

3. If the CAE, after those discussions, concludes that senior management is exposing the organization to an unacceptable risk and is not taking appropriate action, he or she needs to present the information and the differences of opinion to the board in accordance with Standard 2600.

4. The typical chain-of-command communication scenario may be accelerated for certain types of sensitive occurrences because of laws, regulations, or common practices. For example, in the case of evidence of fraudulent financial reporting by an organization with publicly traded securities, local regulations may prescribe that the board be immediately informed of the circumstances surrounding the possibility of misleading financial reports even though senior management and the CAE may agree on which actions need to be taken. Laws and regulations in some jurisdictions specify that the board should be informed of discoveries of criminal, securities, food, drugs, or pollution laws violations as well as other illegal acts, such as bribery or improper payments to government officials or to suppliers or customers.

5. In some situations, an internal auditor may face the dilemma of considering whether to communicate the information to persons outside the normal chain of command or even outside the organization. This communication is commonly referred to as whistleblowing. The act of disclosing adverse information to someone within the organization but outside the internal auditor's normal chain of command is considered internal whistleblowing, while disclosing adverse information to a government agency or other authority outside the organization is considered external whistleblowing.

6. Most whistleblowers disclose sensitive information internally, even if outside the normal chain of command, if they trust the organization's policies and mechanisms to investigate allegations of illegal or other improper activity and to take appropriate action. However, some persons possessing sensitive information may decide to take the information outside the organization if they fear retribution from their employer or fellow employees, doubt that the issue will be properly investigated, believe that it will be concealed, or possess evidence about an illegal or improper activity that jeopardizes the health, safety, or well-being of people in the organization or community.

7. In a case where internal whistleblowing is elected as an option, an internal auditor must evaluate alternative ways of communicating the risk he or she sees to persons or groups outside the normal chain of command. Because of risks and ramifications associated with these approaches, the internal auditor needs to proceed with caution in evaluating the evidence and reasonableness of his or her conclusions as well as in examining the merits and disadvantages of each potential action. Taking this action may be appropriate if it will result in responsible action by persons in senior management or the board.

8. Many jurisdictions have laws or regulations requiring public servants with knowledge of illegal or unethical acts to inform an inspector general, other public official, or ombudsman. Some laws pertaining to whistleblowing actions protect citizens if they come forward to disclose specific types of improper activities. The activities listed in these laws and regulations include:

- ☐ Criminal offenses and other failures to comply with legal obligations.

- ☐ Acts that are considered miscarriages of justice.

- ☐ Acts that endanger the health, safety, or well-being of individuals.

- ☐ Acts that damage the environment.

- ☐ Activities that conceal or cover up any of the above activities.

Some jurisdictions offer no guidance or protection or offer protection only to public (i.e., government) employees.

9. The internal auditor should be aware of the laws and regulations of the various jurisdictions in which the organization operates. Legal counsel familiar with the legal aspects of whistleblowing can assist internal auditors confronted with this issue. The internal auditor should always obtain legal advice if he or she is uncertain of the legal requirements or consequences of engaging in internal or external whistleblowing.

10. Many professional associations hold their members accountable for disclosing illegal or unethical activities. A distinguishing mark of a profession is its acceptance of broad responsibilities to the public and its protection of the general welfare. In addition to examining the legal requirements, IIA members and all certified internal auditors must follow the requirements presented in the IIA's Code of Ethics.

11. An internal auditor has a professional duty and an ethical responsibility to carefully evaluate all evidence and the reasonableness of his or her conclusions and decide whether further actions are needed to protect the organization's interests and stakeholders, the outside community, or the institutions of society. Also, the auditor will need to consider the duty of confidentiality imposed by the IIA's Code of Ethics to respect the value and ownership of information and avoid disclosing it without appropriate authority unless there is a legal or professional obligation to do so. During this evaluation process, the auditor may seek the advice of legal counsel and, if appropriate, other experts. Those discussions may be helpful in providing a different perspective on the circumstances as well as offering opinions about the potential impact and consequences of possible actions. The manner in which the internal auditor seeks to resolve this type of complex and sensitive situation may lead to reprisals and potential liability.

12. Ultimately, the internal auditor makes a professional decision about his or her obligations to the employer. The decision to communicate outside the normal chain of command needs to be based on a well-informed opinion that the wrongdoing is supported by substantial, credible evidence and that a legal or regulatory imperative, or a professional or ethical obligation, requires further action.

Practice Advisory 2440.A2-1: Communications Outside the Organization

1. The internal audit activity's charter, the board's charter, organizational policies, or the engagement agreement may contain guidance related to reporting information outside the organization. If such guidance does not exist, the CAE may facilitate adoption of appropriate policies that may include:

- Authorization required for reporting information outside the organization.

- Process for seeking approval to report information outside the organization.

- Guidelines for permissible and nonpermissible information that may be reported.

- Outside persons authorized to receive information and the types of information they may receive.

- Related privacy regulations, regulatory requirements, and legal considerations for reporting information outside the organization.

- Nature of assurances, advice, recommendations, opinions, guidance, and other information that may be included in communicating information outside the organization.

2. Requests can relate to information that already exists (e.g., a previously issued internal audit report) as well as for information to be created or determined, which results in a new internal audit engagement or report. If the request relates to information or a report that already exists, the internal auditor needs to determine whether it is suitable for dissemination outside the organization.

3. In certain situations, it may be possible to create a special-purpose report based on an existing report or information to make the report suitable for dissemination outside the organization.

4. Some matters to consider when reporting information outside the organization include:

- Usefulness of a written agreement with the intended recipient concerning the information to be reported and the internal auditor's responsibilities.

☐ Identification of information providers, sources, report signers, recipients, and related persons to the disseminated report or information.

☐ Identification of objectives, scope, and procedures to be performed in generating applicable information.

☐ Nature of report or other communication, including opinions, inclusion or exclusion of recommendations, disclaimers, limitations, and type of assurance or assertions to be provided.

☐ Copyright issues, intended use of the information, and limitations on further distribution or sharing of the information.

5. If the internal auditor discovers information reportable to senior management or the board while conducting engagements that require dissemination of information outside the organization, the CAE needs to provide suitable communication to the board.

2450–Overall Opinions. When an overall opinion is issued, it must take into account the expectations of senior management, the board, and other stakeholders and must be supported by sufficient, reliable, relevant, and useful information.

Interpretation: *The communication will identify:*

- *The scope, including the time period to which the opinion pertains.*

- *Scope limitations.*

- *Consideration of all related projects including the reliance on other assurance providers.*

- *The risk or control framework or other criteria used as a basis for the overall opinion.*

- *The overall opinion, judgment, or conclusion reached.*

The reasons for an unfavorable overall opinion must be stated.

No Practice Advisory for Standard 2450

2500–Monitoring Progress

The CAE must establish and maintain a system to monitor the disposition of results communicated to management.

2500.A1–The CAE must establish a follow-up process to monitor and ensure that management actions have been effectively implemented or that senior management has accepted the risk of not taking action.

2500.C1–The internal audit activity must monitor the disposition of results of consulting engagements to the extent agreed upon with the client.

Practice Advisory 2500-1: Monitoring Progress

1. To effectively monitor the disposition of results, the CAE establishes procedures to include:

☐ The time frame within which management's response to the engagement observations and recommendations is required.

☐ Evaluation of management's response.

- ☐ Verification of the response (if appropriate).

- ☐ Performance of a follow-up engagement (if appropriate).

- ☐ A communications process that escalates unsatisfactory responses/actions, including the assumption of risk, to the appropriate levels of senior management or the board.

2. If certain reported observations and recommendations are significant enough to require immediate action by management or the board, the internal audit activity monitors actions taken until the observation is corrected or the recommendation implemented.

3. The internal audit activity may effectively monitor progress by:

- ☐ Addressing engagement observations and recommendations to appropriate levels of management responsible for taking action.

- ☐ Receiving and evaluating management responses and proposed action plan to engagement observations and recommendations during the engagement or within a reasonable time period after the engagement results are communicated. Responses are more useful if they include sufficient information for the CAE to evaluate the adequacy and timeliness of proposed actions.

- ☐ Receiving periodic updates from management to evaluate the status of its efforts to correct observations and/or implement recommendations.

- ☐ Receiving and evaluating information from other organizational units assigned responsibility for follow-up or corrective actions.

- ☐ Reporting to senior management and/or the board on the status of responses to engagement observations and recommendations.

Practice Advisory 2500.A1-1: Follow-up Process

1. Internal auditors determine whether management has taken action or implemented the recommendation. The internal auditor determines whether the desired results were achieved or if senior management or the board has assumed the risk of not taking action or implementing the recommendation.

2. Follow-up is a process by which internal auditors evaluate the adequacy, effectiveness, and timeliness of actions taken by management on reported observations and recommendations, including those made by external auditors and others. This process also includes determining whether senior management and/or the board have assumed the risk of not taking corrective action on reported observations.

3. The internal audit activity's charter should define the responsibility for follow-up. The CAE determines the nature, timing, and extent of follow-up, considering the following factors:

- ☐ Significance of the reported observation or recommendation.

- ☐ Degree of effort and cost needed to correct the reported condition.

- ☐ Impact that may result should the corrective action fail.

- ☐ Complexity of the corrective action.

- ☐ Time period involved.

4. The CAE is responsible for scheduling follow-up activities as part of developing engagement work schedules. Scheduling of follow-up is based on the risk and exposure involved as well as the degree of difficulty and the significance of timing in implementing corrective action.

5. Where the CAE judges that management's oral or written response indicates that action taken is sufficient when weighed against the relative importance of the observation or recommendation, internal auditors may follow up as part of the next engagement.

6. Internal auditors ascertain whether actions taken on observations and recommendations remedy the underlying conditions. Follow-up activities should be appropriately documented.

2600–Resolution of Senior Management's Acceptance of Risks

When the CAE believes that senior management has accepted a level of residual risk that may be unacceptable to the organization, the CAE must discuss the matter with senior management. If the decision regarding residual risk is not resolved, the CAE must report the matter to the board for resolution.

> No Practice Advisory for Standard 2600

1.3 Code of Ethics

(a) Introduction to the Code of Ethics

The purpose of the Institute's Code of Ethics is to promote an ethical culture in the profession of internal auditing.

> Internal auditing is an independent, objective assurance and consulting activity designed to add value and improve an organization's operations. It helps an organization accomplish its objectives by bringing a systematic, disciplined approach to evaluate and improve the effectiveness of risk management, control, and governance processes.

A code of ethics is necessary and appropriate for the profession of internal auditing, founded as it is on the trust placed in its objective assurance about governance, risk management, and control.

The Institute's Code of Ethics extends beyond the definition of internal auditing to include two essential components:

1. Principles that are relevant to the profession and practice of internal auditing.
2. Rules of conduct that describe behavior norms expected of internal auditors. These rules are an aid to interpreting the Principles into practical applications and are intended to guide the ethical conduct of internal auditors.

"Internal auditors" refers to Institute members, recipients of or candidates for IIA professional certifications, and those who perform internal audit services within the definition of internal auditing.

(b) Applicability and Enforcement of the Code of Ethics

This Code of Ethics applies to both entities and individuals that perform internal audit services.

For IIA members and recipients of or candidates for IIA professional certifications, breaches of the Code of Ethics will be evaluated and administered according to the Institute's Bylaws and

Administrative Directives. The fact that a particular conduct is not mentioned in the Rules of Conduct does not prevent it from being unacceptable or discreditable, and therefore, the member, certification holder, or candidate can be liable for disciplinary action.

(c) Code of Ethics

(i) Principles

Internal auditors are expected to apply and uphold the following principles:

1. **Integrity.** The integrity of internal auditors establishes trust and thus provides the basis for reliance on their judgment.

2. **Objectivity.** Internal auditors exhibit the highest level of professional objectivity in gathering, evaluating, and communicating information about the activity or process being examined. Internal auditors make a balanced assessment of all the relevant circumstances and are not unduly influenced by their own interests or by others in forming judgments

3. **Confidentiality.** Internal auditors respect the value and ownership of information they receive and do not disclose information without appropriate authority unless there is a legal or professional obligation to do so.

4. **Competency.** Internal auditors apply the knowledge, skills, and experience needed in the performance of internal audit services.

(ii) Rules of Conduct

1. **Integrity.** Internal auditors:

    1.1. Shall perform their work with honesty, diligence, and responsibility.

    1.2. Shall observe the law and make disclosures expected by the law and the profession.

    1.3. Shall not knowingly be a party to any illegal activity, or engage in acts that are discreditable to the profession of internal auditing or to the organization.

    1.4. Shall respect and contribute to the legitimate and ethical objectives of the organization.

2. **Objectivity.** Internal auditors:

    2.1. Shall not participate in any activity or relationship that may impair or be presumed to impair their unbiased assessment. This participation includes those activities or relationships that may be in conflict with the interests of the organization.

    2.2. Shall not accept anything that may impair or be presumed to impair their professional judgment.

    2.3. Shall disclose all material facts known to them that, if not disclosed, may distort the reporting of activities under review.

3. **Confidentiality.** Internal auditors:

    3.1. Shall be prudent in the use and protection of information acquired in the course of their duties.

    3.2. Shall not use information for any personal gain or in any manner that would be contrary to the law or detrimental to the legitimate and ethical objectives of the organization.

4. **Competency.** Internal auditors:

   4.1.   Shall engage only in those services for which they have the necessary knowledge, skills, and experience.

   4.2.   Shall perform internal audit services in accordance with the *International Standards for the Professional Practice of Internal Auditing.*

   4.3.   Shall continually improve their proficiency and the effectiveness and quality of their services.

1.4 Sample Practice Questions

As mentioned in the Preface of this book, a small batch of sample practice questions is included here to show the flavor of questions and to create a quiz-like environment. The answers and explanations for these questions are shown in a separate section at the end of this book just before the Glossary. If there is a need to practice more questions to obtain a greater confidence, refer to the section "CIA Exam Study Preparation Resources" presented in the front matter of this book.

1. The IIA's definition of internal auditing emphasizes the effectiveness of which of the following?
   a. Value, cost, and benefit propositions.
   b. Inherent risk, residual risk, and total risk.
   c. Risk management, control, and governance processes.
   d. Purpose, nature, and scope of work.

2. Which of the following adds value to the others?
   a. Governance processes.
   b. Risk management processes.
   c. Internal audit activities.
   d. Control processes.

3. All of the following are examples of assurance services **except:**
   a. Financial engagement.
   b. Compliance engagement.
   c. Due diligence engagement.
   d. Training engagement.

4. All of the following are examples of consulting services **except:**
   a. Legal counsel engagement.
   b. System security engagement.
   c. Advice engagement.
   d. Facilitation engagement.

5. The IIA's Practice Advisories do **not** contain which of the following?
   a. Approaches.
   b. Considerations.
   c. Processes or procedures.
   d. Methodologies.

6. The IIA's Practice Guides do **not** contain which of the following?
   a. Good practices.
   b. Tools and techniques.
   c. Programs.
   d. Deliverables.

7. According to the IIA's Organizational Independence *Standard*, which of the following is **not** a part of functional reporting to the board?
   a. Audit charter.
   b. Audit risk assessment.
   c. Audit budgets.
   d. Audit plan.

8. Which of the following differs between assurance services and consulting services when exercising due professional care?
   a. Costs and benefits.
   b. Complexity of work.
   c. Extent of work.
   d. Materiality.

9. Which of the following is driving the need for assurance maps?
   a. Risk managers.
   b. Board members.
   c. Internal auditors.
   d. Compliance practitioners.

10. Risk registers describe direct links between which of the following?
    a. Risk acceptance and risk avoidance.
    b. Risk categories and risk aspects.
    c. Risk assignment and risk sharing.
    d. Risk limitation and risk spreading.

11. The chief audit executive establishes a method for prioritizing all of the following **except:**

a. Business units with low risk levels.

b. Branch or field office with low risk levels.

c. Outstanding risk areas.

d. Low inherent risk areas.

12. All of the following provide effective relationship in the organization's governance framework **except:**

a. Organizational processes.

b. Governance.

c. Risk management.

d. Internal controls.

13. Which of the following internal audit assessments belong to specific governance processes?

a. Whistleblower process.

b. Risk management audit process.

c. Internal control over financial reporting.

d. Fraud risks.

14. Ensuring internal audit teams have the right competencies with right level of work experience and designing effective internal audit procedures can reduce the risk of which of the following?

a. Business risk.

b. Audit failures.

c. Audit false assurance.

d. Audit reputation risk.

15. Consulting engagement objectives must be consistent with all of the following **except:**

a. Organization's goals.

b. Organization's values.

c. Organization's strategies.

d. Organization's objectives.

16. Which of the following is the **major** purpose of performing analytical procedures in internal audits?

a. To perform additional audit procedures.

b. To plan the audit engagement.

c. To obtain audit evidence.

d. To study relationships among elements of information.

17. According to the IIA *Standards*, which of the following is **not** included in the scope of the internal audit function?

a. Appraising the effectiveness and efficiency of operations and programs.

b. Reviewing the strategic management process, assessing the quality of management decision making both quantitatively and qualitatively and reporting the results to the audit committee.

c. Reviewing the means of safeguarding assets.

d. Complying with the laws, regulations, policies, procedures, and contracts.

18. An internal auditor is auditing the financial operations of an organization. Which of the following is **not** specified by the IIA *Standards* for inclusion in the scope of the audit?

a. Reviewing the reliability and integrity of financial and operational information.

b. Reviewing the compliance with laws, regulations, policies, procedures, and contracts.

c. Appraising the effectiveness and efficiency of operations and programs.

d. Reviewing the financial decision-making process.

19. The audit committee of an organization has charged the chief audit executive (CAE) with bringing the department into full compliance with the *IIA Standards*. The CAE's first task is to develop a charter. Identify the item that should be included in the statement of objectives:

a. Report all audit findings to the audit committee every quarter.

b. Notify governmental regulatory agencies of unethical business practices by organization management.

c. Determine the adequacy and effectiveness of the organization's systems of internal controls.

d. Submit departmental budget variance reports to management every month.

20. If an auditee's operating standards are vague and thus subject to interpretation, the auditor should:

 a. Seek agreement with the auditee as to the standards to be used to measure operating performance.

 b. Determine best practices in this area and use them as the standard.

 c. Interpret the standards in their strictest sense because standards are otherwise only minimum measures of acceptance.

 d. Omit any comments on standards and the auditee's performance in relationship to those standards, because such an analysis would be meaningless.

21. In which of the following situations does the auditor potentially lack objectivity?

 a. An auditor reviews the procedures for a new electronic data interchange connection to a major customer before it is implemented.

 b. A former purchasing assistant performs a review of internal controls over purchasing four months after being transferred to the internal auditing department.

 c. An auditor recommends standards of control and performance measures for a contract with a service organization for the processing of payroll and employee benefits.

 d. A payroll accounting employee assists an auditor in verifying the physical inventory of small motors.

22. Which of the following actions would be a violation of auditor independence?

 a. Continuing on an audit assignment at a division for which the auditor will soon be responsible as the result of a promotion.

 b. Reducing the scope of an audit due to budget restrictions.

 c. Participating on a task force which recommends standards for control of a new distribution system.

 d. Reviewing a purchasing agent's contract drafts prior to their execution.

23. The IIA's Code of Ethics includes which of the following two essential components?

 a. Definition of internal auditing and administrative directives.

 b. Principles and Rules of Conduct.

 c. Integrity and objectivity.

 d. Confidentiality and competency.

24. A Certified Internal Auditor (CIA) is working in a non–internal audit position as the director of purchasing. The CIA signs a contract to procure a large order from the supplier with the best price, quality, and performance. Shortly after signing the contract, the supplier presents the CIA with a gift of significant monetary value. Which of the following statements regarding the acceptance of the gift is correct?

 a. Acceptance of the gift would be prohibited only if it were noncustomary.

 b. Acceptance of the gift would violate the IIA Code of Ethics and would be prohibited for a CIA.

 c. Since the CIA is no longer acting as an internal auditor, acceptance of the gift would be governed only by the organization's code of conduct.

 d. Since the contract was signed before the gift was offered, acceptance of the gift would not violate either the IIA Code of Ethics or the organization's code of conduct.

25. An auditor, nearly finished with an audit, discovers that the director of marketing has a gambling habit. The gambling issue is not directly related to the existing audit, and there is pressure to complete the current audit. The auditor notes the problem and passes the information on to the chief audit executive but does no further follow-up. The auditor's actions would:

 a. Be in violation of the IIA Code of Ethics for withholding meaningful information.

 b. Be in violation of the *Standards* because the auditor did not properly follow-up on a red flag that might indicate the existence of fraud.

 c. Not be in violation of either the IIA Code of Ethics or the *Standards*.

 d. Both a and b.

26. As used by the internal auditing profession, the *IIA Standards* refer to all of the following **except:**

 a. Criteria by which the operations of an internal audit department are evaluated and measured.

 b. Criteria which dictate the minimum level of ethical actions to be taken by internal auditors.

 c. Statements intended to represent the practice of internal auditing, as it should be.

 d. Criteria that is applicable to all types of internal audit departments.

27. Which of the following situations would be a violation of the IIA Code of Ethics?

a. An auditor was subpoenaed in a court case in which a merger partner claimed to have been defrauded by the auditor's company. The auditor divulged confidential audit information to the court.

b. An auditor for a manufacturer of office products recently completed an audit of the corporate marketing function. Based on this experience, the auditor spent several hours one Saturday working as a paid consultant to a hospital in the local area, which intended to conduct an audit of its marketing function.

c. An auditor gave a speech at a local IIA chapter meeting outlining the contents of a program the auditor had developed for auditing electronic data interchange connections. Several auditors from major competitors were in the audience.

d. During an audit, an auditor learned that the company was about to introduce a new product that would revolutionize the industry. Because of the probable success of the new product, the product manager suggested that the auditor buy additional stock in the company, which the auditor did.

28. In applying the standards of conduct set forth in the Code of Ethics, internal auditors are expected to:

a. Exercise their individual judgment.

b. Compare them to standards in other professions.

c. Be guided by the desires of the auditee.

d. Use discretion in deciding whether to use them or not.

29. Reinforcing the Code of Conduct and ethical behavior standards for all internal auditors can protect which of the following?

a. Business risk.

b. Audit failures.

c. Audit false assurance.

d. Audit reputation risk.

Internal Control and Risk (25–35%)

2.1 Types of Controls

Topics covered in this section include: control characteristics; control requirements; combination, complementary, compensating, and contradictory controls; control assessment; cost/benefit analysis; cost versus controls versus convenience; controls by dimension; specific types of controls by function and by objectives; controls in business application systems; inventory of controls in business application systems; and summary of controls.

(a) Control Characteristics

Control is any positive and negative action taken by management that would result in the accomplishment of the organization's goals, objectives, and mission. Controls should not lead to compulsion or become a constraint on employees. Controls should be natural and should be embedded in organizational functions and operations. In addition, controls should be accepted by employees using or affected by them. Use and implementation of controls should be inviting, not inhibiting. Controls should be seen as beneficial from the employee's personal and professional viewpoints. Ideally, controls should facilitate the achievement of employees' and organizational goals and objectives. In other words, any control that does not help to achieve or promote the achievement of the goals and objectives should not be implemented. Controls should be effective and efficient. Controls should not cost more than the benefits derived.

(b) Control Requirements

The auditor needs to understand the control requirements of an application system or a business operation before assessing control strengths and weaknesses. In other words, there should be a basis or baseline in place (i.e., standards, guidelines, and benchmarks) prior to control measurement and assessment. In the absence of a baseline of standards, the auditee will question and will not accept the auditor's findings, conclusions, and recommendations. The next list cites what the basis usually includes.

- Internal control principles
- Operating standards for manual and automated operations in both system-user areas and information systems (IS) areas
- Application system development or maintenance methodology standards
- Technical standards
- Operations standards
- Administrative standards
- Industry standards
- Auditee's operating standards
- Generally accepted accounting principles
- Generally accepted information technology (IT) standards
- Generally accepted auditing standards
- Generally accepted government auditing standards
- Generally accepted IS control objectives and techniques
- Generally accepted system security principles
- Organization's policies and procedures
- Control philosophy of management
- Risk and exposure levels of the system or operation under consideration
- Management's tolerance to risk levels
- Nature and type of industry (i.e., financial, regulated)
- Government, tax, legal, accounting, and regulatory requirements
- Management's directives and circulars
- Good business and management practices

(c) Combination, Complementary, Compensating, and Contradictory Controls

Controls or control measures should prevent, reduce, or even eliminate potential risks and exposures. Controls should also prevent and detect errors, omissions, and irregularities. Controls are needed within and around a computer-based application system as well as in computer operations. Controls are additive.

(i) Combination Controls

Rarely does a single control suffice to meet control objectives. Rather, a combination of controls or complementary controls is needed to make up a whole and to provide a synergistic effect.

Some examples of combination controls are listed next.

- Supervisory reviews and approvals combined with organization's policies, procedures, and standards

- A combination of controls from the five types of controls (i.e., directive, preventive, detective, corrective, and recovery)

- A specific general control (e.g., full-volume backups) combined with another specific general control (e.g., incremental backups)

- A specific general control combined with one or more application system controls

- A specific application system control combined with one or more general controls

- System-user controls in one user department combined with controls in other system-user departments

- IS controls in one IS section or department combined with controls in other IS sections or departments

- System-user controls combined with IS controls

- Manual controls combined with automated controls

- One-application system controls combined with other and related application system controls

- Application system controls combined with:
  - Operating systems software controls
  - Database system controls
  - Automated program library management system controls
  - Automated access-control security system controls
  - Automated data file management system (e.g., tapes and disks) controls
  - Automated documentation system controls
  - Automated report balancing system controls
  - Data communication system controls
  - Data dictionary system controls
  - Telecommunication system controls
  - General data processing controls

- Physical-access security controls combined with logical-access security controls

- A user identification code combined with a password code to make user authentication more assured

An example of a combination of controls is a situation where fire-resistant materials are used in the computer center (a preventive control) to prevent a fire, while smoke and fire detectors are used to detect smoke and fire (a detective control), and fire extinguishers are used to put out the fire (a corrective control). Here a single preventive control would not be sufficient. All three controls are needed to be effective.

(ii) Complementary Controls

Complementary controls (hand-in-hand controls) have an important place in both the manual and the automated control environment. Complementary controls are different from compensating controls in that, in the latter category, weak controls in one area are balanced by strong controls in other areas, and vice versa. An area need not be weak to use complementary controls. Complementary controls can enhance the effectiveness of two or more controls when applied to a function, program, or operation. These individual, complementary controls are effective as stand-alones and are maximized when combined or integrated with each other. In other words, complementary controls have a synergistic effect.

Some examples of complementary controls are listed next.

- External security software functions can complement:
  - Security features available in applications software and vice versa.
  - Security features available in these systems software products:
    - Tape/disk management system
    - Report distribution system
    - Operator console automation system
    - Job-control validation system
    - Job-scheduling system
    - Problem/change management system
    - Online program development facilities
    - Online teleprocessing monitors
    - Database management systems
    - Job rerun software
  - Security features available in hardware devices (access keys, smart cards, access cards) and biometrics devices.
- Security features within a database management system can complement the security functions available in the applications software.
- Data editing and validation routines operating during data entry into the computer system can complement the same routines operating during data updating into the master files.
- Manual controls can complement automated controls and vice versa.

These areas can complement each other:

- Administrative controls, physical security controls, personnel security controls, technical security controls, emanations security controls, operations controls, applications controls, procedural controls, environmental controls (heat, humidity, air-conditioning), and telecommunications security controls

(iii) Compensating Controls

Normally the auditor will find more control-related problems if it is a first-time audit of an area. In general, the more frequently an area is audited, the lower the probability of many control weaknesses. Therefore, determining the nature of efficient and effective operations needs both audit instinct and business judgment. During the control evaluation process, the auditor should consider the availability of compensating controls as a way to mitigate or minimize the impact of inadequate or incomplete controls. In essence, the concept of compensating controls deals with balancing weak internal controls in one area with strong internal controls in other areas of the organization. Here the word "area" can include a section within a user or IS department.

An example of a weak control is a situation where data control employees in the IS department are not reconciling data-input control totals to data-output control totals in an application system. This control weakness in the IS department can be compensated for by strong controls in the user department where end users reconcile their own control totals with those produced by the application system. Sometimes automated compensating controls and procedures are needed to shorten the lengthy manual controls and procedures (e.g., replacing a manual report balancing system with an automated report balancing system).

Compensating controls are needed whenever:

- Manual controls are weak.

  Solution: Look for strong computer controls.

- Computer controls are weak.

  Solution: Look for strong manual controls.

- Interface controls between manual and automated systems are weak.

  Solution: Look for strong controls in either the receiving or the sending system.

- Functional (system) user controls are weak.

  Solution: Look for strong IT controls.

- IS controls are weak.

  Solution: Look for strong controls in system-user departments or other IT departments.

- Third-party manual controls are weak.

  Solution: Look for strong controls in the in-house system in either the manual or the automated part.

- Third-party computer controls are weak.

  Solution: Look for strong controls in the in-house system in either the manual or the automated part.

- Physical-access security controls are weak.

  Solution: Look for strong logical-access security controls.

- Logical-access security controls are weak.

  Solution: Look for strong physical-access security controls, supervisory reviews, or more substantive testing.

- A specific general control is weak.

  Solution: Look for a strong and related application control(s).

- An application system control is weak.

  Solution: Look for a strong and related general control(s).

- Employee performance is weak.

  Solution: Look for strong supervisory reviews and more substantive testing.

(iv) Contradictory Controls

With contradictory controls, two or more controls are in conflict with each other. One control does not fit well with the other controls due to incompatibility. This means that implementation of one control can affect another, related control(s) negatively. Some examples follow.

- Installation of a new software patch can undo or break another related, existing software patch in either the same system or other related systems. This incompatibility can be due to errors in the current patch(es) or previous patch(es) or because the new patches and the previous patches were not fully tested by the software vendor or the user organization.

- Telecommuting work and organization's software piracy policies could be in conflict with each other if a noncompliant telecommuter implements such policies improperly and in an unauthorized manner when he or she purchases and loads unauthorized software on the home/work personal computer.

(d) Control Assessment

During an assessment of control strengths and weaknesses, the auditor might run into situations where a business function, system, or manual/automated procedure is overcontrolled or undercontrolled. This means that there may be too many controls in one area and not enough controls in other areas. Also, there may be duplication or overlapping of controls between two or more areas. Under these conditions, the auditor should recommend the elimination either of some user controls, some IS controls, some manual controls, some automated controls, or a combination of them. The same may be true of situations where a system or operation is oversecured or undersecured and where an application system is overdesigned or underdesigned. This assessment requires differentiating between relevant and irrelevant information; considering compensating controls, which is discussed later; considering interrelationships of controls, which is also discussed later; and judging materiality and significance of audit findings taken separately and as a whole.

> **CONTROL ASSESSMENT CHALLENGE**
>
> The key issues are to know how much control is needed, how to measure it, how to evaluate whether a control is deficient or sufficient, and how to balance it.

Rarely can a single finding lead to the conclusion of an unacceptable audit or uncontrolled area. Usually a combination of control weaknesses is required to call an area unacceptable. For example, a finding such as "housekeeping is poor in the data center" alone or in combination with "there are no no-smoking or eating signs in the data center" will not qualify for an auditor giving an unacceptable or uncontrolled audit rating. Audit findings must be significant and meaningful. The nature of the operation (e.g., automated or manual and sensitive or routine), criticality of the system (high risk versus low risk), costs to develop and maintain controls, and the materiality (significance) of the finding are more important criteria to consider than merely observing control weaknesses. Note that materiality is relative, not absolute. What is material to one organization may not be material to another. Audit judgment plays an important role in deciding what is material, what is a significant control weakness, what is an efficient operation, what is an effective system, and what should be considered separately and as a whole. In other words, the auditor needs to focus on the entire environment of the audited operation or system and take a big-picture approach instead of taking a finding-by-finding approach. A cost/benefit analysis might help the auditor in the process of evaluating controls.

(e) Cost/Benefit Analysis

A cost/benefit analysis is advised during the process of designing each type of control into an application system during its development and maintenance as well as during its operation. Ideally, costs should never exceed the benefits to be derived from installing controls. However, cost should not always be the sole determining factor because it may be difficult or impractical to quantify benefits such as timeliness, improved quality and relevance of data and information, and improved customer service and system response time. When controls are properly planned, designed, developed, tested, implemented, and followed, they should meet one or more of the next 12 attributes. The controls are:

1. Practical
2. Reliable
3. Simple
4. Complete
5. Operational
6. Usable
7. Appropriate
8. Cost effective
9. Timely
10. Meaningful
11. Reasonable
12. Consistent

(f) Costs versus Controls versus Convenience

Costs of controls vary with their implementation time and the complexity of the system or operation. Control implementation time is important to realize benefits from installing appropriate controls. For example, it costs significantly more to correct a design problem in the implementation phase of an application system under development than it does to address the problem in the early planning and design phases.

There are **trade-offs** among costs, controls, and convenience factors. The same is true between system usability, maintainability, auditability, controllability, and securability attributes of systems. For example:

- High-risk systems and complex systems and operations require more controls.

- Excessive use of tight security features and control functions can be costly and may complicate procedures, degrade system performance, and impair system functionality, which ultimately could inhibit the system's usability.

- System users prefer as few integrity and security controls as possible, just those needed to make the system really usable.

- The greater the maintainability of the system, the easier it is for a programmer to modify it. Similarly, the greater the maintainability of the system, the less expensive it is to operate in the long run.

(g) Controls by Dimension

Control can be viewed through three different dimensions of timing: precontrol, concurrent control, and postcontrol (see Exhibit 2.1).

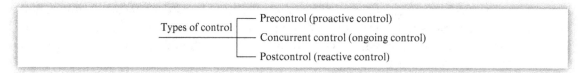

EXHIBIT 2.1 Types of Control

Precontrol (e.g., policy) anticipates problems and is proactive in nature. Concurrent control is exercised through supervision and monitoring. Postcontrol identifies deviations from standards or budgets and calls for corrective action and is similar to feedback control. Precontrol and feed-forward control are interrelated since they deal with future-directed actions. Forecasting, budgeting, and real-time computer systems are examples of feed-forward controls. Precontrol is the most preferred action; the least preferred action is postcontrol. The difference is when a corrective action is taken—the sooner the better.

A feedback control is used to evaluate past activity in order to improve future performance. It measures actual performance against a standard to ensure that a desired result is achieved. Feedback control has been criticized because corrective action takes place after the fact (reactive).

Feedback control can allow costs to build up due to their back-end position. An example is human resource managers holding exit interviews with employees who have resigned to go to work for competitors. Management tabulates the interviewee's responses and uses the information to identify problems with training, compensation, working conditions, or other factors that have caused increased turnover. Other examples include customer surveys, increased finished goods inspections, increased work-in-process (WIP) inspections, variance analysis, postaction controls, monitoring product returns, and evaluating customer complaints.

A feed-forward control attempts to anticipate problems and effect timely solutions (proactive), and hence this control is important to management. An example is when a key auditee employee will not be available for a few weeks for audit work due to illness, and the audit supervisor reschedules the audit work to be done in this auditable area. Other examples include defect prevention by quality control inspection of raw materials and WIP, quality control training programs, budgeting, forecasting inventory needs, and advance notice of a purchase.

(h) Specific Types of Controls

Controls prevent the adverse effects of risks. Many different types of control activities have been described, including directive controls, preventive controls, detective controls, corrective controls, manual controls, computer controls, and management controls.

The complexity of an entity and the nature and scope of activities affect its control activities. Complex organizations with diverse activities may face more difficult control issues than simple organizations with less varied activities. An entity with decentralized operations and an emphasis on local autonomy and innovation presents different control circumstances than a highly centralized one. Other factors that influence an entity's complexity and, therefore, the nature of its controls include location and geographical dispersion, the extensiveness and sophistication of operations, and information processing methods. All these factors affect an entity's control activities, which need to be designed accordingly to contribute to the achievement of the entity's objectives.

Control activities can also be classified by specified control objectives, such as ensuring completeness, timeliness, accuracy, and authorization of transactions, which are applicable to both manual and computer processing environments (see Exhibit 2.2).

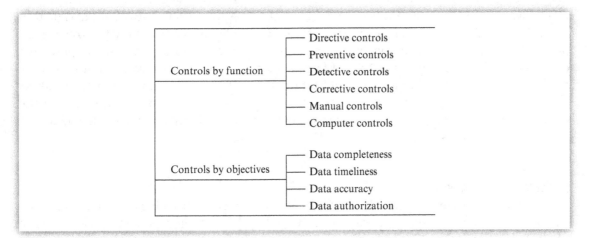

EXHIBIT 2.2   Control Categories by Function and Objective

(i) Controls by Function

Controls can be classified according to the function they are intended to perform. **Directive controls** ensure the occurrence of a desirable event. Examples of directive controls include requiring all members of the internal auditing department to be Certified Internal Auditors and providing management with assurance of the realization of specified minimum gross margins on sales. Other examples include policies, directives, guidance, and circulars.

Preventive controls are needed to avoid the occurrence of an unwanted event. Examples include segregation of duties, use of checklists, use of systems development methodology, competent staff, use of passwords, authorization procedures, and documentation. "Segregation of duties" means duties are divided among different people to reduce the risk of error or inappropriate actions. For example, it includes dividing the responsibilities for authorizing transactions, recording them, and handling the related asset. A manager authorizing credit sales would not be responsible for maintaining accounts receivable records or handling cash receipts. Similarly, salespersons would not have the ability to modify product price files or commission rates. It calls for a separation of the functional responsibilities of custodianship, record keeping, operations, and authorization. Other examples include separating threats from assets to minimize risks and separating resource allocation from resource use to prevent resource misuse.

Detective controls are needed to discover the occurrence of an unwanted event. The installation of detective controls is necessary to provide feedback on the effectiveness of the preventive controls. Examples include reviews and comparisons, bank reconciliations, account reconciliations, and physical counts.

Corrective controls are needed to correct after an unwanted event has occurred. They fix both detected and reported errors. Examples include correction procedures, documentation, and control and exception reports.

Manual controls include budgets, forecasts, policies and procedures; reporting; physical controls over equipment, inventories, securities, cash, and other assets; and periodically counted and compared with amounts shown on control records.

Computer controls include general controls and application controls. General controls include data center operations controls, system software controls, access security controls, and application system development and maintenance controls. Application controls are designed to control application processing, helping to ensure the completeness and accuracy of transaction processing, authorization, and validity. Many application controls depend on computerized edit checks. These edit checks consist of format, existence, reasonableness, and other checks on the data, which are built into each application during its development. When these checks are designed properly, they can help provide control over the data being entered into the computer system. Computer controls are performed to check accuracy, completeness, and authorization of transactions.

(ii) Controls by Objectives

Data completeness controls include use of prenumbered forms, obtaining transaction authorization, and system logging of transactions. Examples of data timeliness controls include use of electronic mail to send urgent messages instead of phone and use of facsimiles to send urgent letters instead of regular mail. Examples of data accuracy controls include use of batch and hash totals, check digits, balance controls, and system-assigned numbers to documents. Examples of data authorization controls include management approvals, two-person controls, and overrides.

KEY CONCEPTS TO REMEMBER: How Many Controls Are There?

- Accounting controls are well defined with a body of professional standards published. They help ensure that there is full accountability for physical assets and that all financial transactions are recorded and reported timely and accurately.

- Administrative controls help ensure resources are safeguarded against waste, loss or fraud, and misappropriation, and support the accomplishment of that organization's goals and objectives. These controls include accurate and timely management information and effective and efficient processes for planning, productivity improvement, quality control, legal and regulatory compliance, and improving economy and efficiency.

- Auditing controls are the system of checks and balances in effect throughout the organization.

- Operating controls include segregation of duties, dual controls, joint custody, rotation of duties, adherence to prescribed policies and procedures, and employees taking vacations.

- Operational controls include controls that are not clearly defined and completely communicated due to constant changes and several functional departments involved in the operating chain. They are not supported by clear standards and are subject to greater misinterpretation.

- Input controls prevent or detect the entry of inaccurate or incomplete data into a computer system.

- Output controls ensure that computer outputs (reports, files, and listings) are distributed only to authorized people.

- Hardware controls must have existing rigid and clear standards in order to operate in different operating environments.

- Physical security controls are rigid, well defined, and subject to less misinterpretation.

- An organizational control system's components include objectives, standards, and an evaluation-reward system.

- A financial control system's components include budgeting, financial ratio analysis, and cash management.

- A managerial control is the result of proper planning, organizing, and directing. Its ultimate objective is to promote organizational effectiveness, which is the degree to which the organization achieves its short-term and long-term objectives. Components of managerial controls include forestalling management fraud and protecting assets. Components do not include implementing plans.

(i) Controls in Business Application Systems

The scope of business application system controls include controls over data origination, preparation, and data input; data processing; system-related file maintenance; data output; application system documentation; spreadsheet work; data integrity; and user satisfaction assessment. Each area is discussed next.

(i) Data Origination, Preparation, and Data Input Controls

There are several approaches to data preparation and data entry into the application system. In some cases, the data are captured on a paper (source) document, such as a sales or purchase order. The source documents are batched into small groups and entered into the system by either functional users or central data-entry operators through the use of terminals. In other cases, there is no externally generated source document; instead, the customer calls in and places an order with the organization.

Other approaches include use of factory data collection devices for factories; automated teller machine recorders for banks; point-of-sale recorders for the retail business with or without bar codes; magnetic ink character recognition devices for the banking industry for customer checks and deposit tickets; optical character recognition devices to read credit card statements, insurance premium notices, and utility company billings; optical mark reading devices to read pencil marks made in specific locations on preprinted forms to be used in grading structured examination questions; scanners for document image processing; and voice recognition input devices used to recognize the human voice in airline and parcel industries to route packages.

Regardless of the method used to capture the data, the entered data are edited and validated to prevent or detect errors and omissions. Therefore, access controls and data editing and validation controls are important to ensure that quality data are entering into the application system.

WHAT CAN GO WRONG IN DATA PREPARATION AND ENTRY?

- Adequate separation of duties may not be maintained over data origination, data preparation, data input, data update, and data output activities between and among system users and data processors.

- Design of forms and documents used for data input preparation and the design of input terminal screens may not match or may be too complex for the skill level of system users. Consequently, data are entered incorrectly and improperly.

- Source transactions may be inaccurate, unauthorized, or lost during movement from department to department, during data entry, and/or during data processing.

- Transaction errors may not be properly prevented, detected, or corrected and resubmitted in a timely manner.

- Data input errors, irregularities, omissions, and alterations are the most common computer-related problems leading to fraud, crime, and abuse.

These red flags suggest vulnerability to data errors: old application system with high program maintenance; large volume of data for processing; frequent processing and updating activity; numerous transaction types and sources; large number of coded data elements; high employee turnover (e.g., data entry clerks, operators, programmers, system analysts); inadequate training; complex data structures; and lack of standards related to security, access, and program-change control.

(ii) Data Processing Controls

Although there are some common data processing controls, controls are different between batch and online processing. Similar to data input, data editing and validation controls are important during computer processing. Therefore program-based processing controls should be used more to ensure data integrity and security. These controls include limit check, range test, validity check, table lookup, reasonableness test, sequence check, comparison test, check digit test, ratio test, and relationship test.

WHAT CAN GO WRONG IN PROCESS VALIDATION AND EDITING?

- Transactions may be processed in the wrong fiscal period.

- Transactions may be improperly classified, valued, summarized, or reported.

- Adequate data editing and validation controls may not be available in application program processing logic to prevent or detect errors, omissions, or irregularities.

- Application program processing jobs may take longer due to inefficient data file structures, poor choice of design techniques, poor selection of data file access methods, poorly structured program logic, and/or ineffective program statements.

- Backout or fallback procedures may not be available for programs, causing abnormal termination or other operational problems during computer-job processing.

(iii) System-Related File Maintenance Controls

The auditor will encounter many system-related files during an audit of the application system. These files contain valuable data for audit analysis and reporting purposes. Major concerns for the auditor should be who can access and update these files. Some examples of these files are listed next.

- **Master files.** Examples of master files are customer files, vendor files, employee files, account files.

- **Transaction files.** Transaction files are detail files used with the master files. Routine and repeat transactions are collected into transaction files and then used to update the master data files.

- **Backup files.** Backup files contain program or data files.

- **Program files.** Program files contain source, object, or executable code.

- **Table files.** Table files contain data such as office codes, state codes, postal zip codes, department codes, tax codes, and plant codes. These tables are used during program execution for data editing, validation, and referencing purposes.

- **Summary/history files.** Summary files contain a history of transactions such as month-to-date, quarter-end, year-end, or last five years' data. These transactions are maintained in a summary form.

- **Archive files.** Archive files contain data or programs that are infrequently used and yet important to store for many reasons.

- **Control files.** Control files contain parameter-related information, such as dates, cycles, and reports. These parameters are used in processing computer jobs.

- **Print files.** Print files contain data and program files waiting to be printed. These files are stored in a spool area and until the current print job is completed. When their turn comes up, these files are printed.

- **Report files.** Report files contain report records for each application system–generated output.

- **Command files.** Command files contain certain key commands (e.g., execute, copy, delete, write) required by an application program, operating system, or other support systems software. Commands are supplied to various programs during their execution.

- **Work files.** Work files are any files that are created, used, and then deleted at the end of one job step. Work files are also called scratch files. Normally work files are used to sort data files. Application programs create these files as needed. Work files are temporary in nature.

- **Temporary files.** A temporary file is one that lasts for the duration of the job regardless of the successful completion or termination of the job. The operating system automatically deletes all such files when the job terminates. Sometimes programmers have the application program create a temporary cross-reference file from an input file and then use it in the downstream (subsequent job) processing.

- **Log files.** A log file is a data file or command file that contains data and commands that are logged during computer job and program processing. Log files can be created by an operating system, application system, database system, telecommunication system, or security system. For example, a database system may create before-and-after images of records during an update process in a database log file. Log files are also temporary in nature.

- **Document image files.** An image file is created out of a document such as a loan, credit, or employment application; payment invoice; and purchase order. These documents are then stored and retrieved as needed. An image file can be downloaded or uploaded to and from the host computer and the personal computer.

- **User files.** User files are created by each user of the system for the user's personal library and use.

- **Transmission files.** Transmission files are the ones waiting to be transmitted from one location to the other, from one computer system to the other, from one entity to the other, or from one time zone to the other.

WHAT CAN GO WRONG IN FILE MAINTENANCE?

- A computer file may be lost or damaged due to bad write/read head error or disk failure on an input/output device.

- Both the original and backup file may be stored on the same magnetic media (e.g., disk, tape, cartridge) or physical area, thus losing both.

- System files may be erased, destroyed, or unlogged intentionally or accidentally.

- Before (from) and after (to) image record reporting may not be available when database or data files are updated, thus losing accountability.

- Identification of production data files could be difficult because file names may not consistently indicate whether files are related to production application systems.

(iv) Data Output Controls

There are many output devices in use. Some examples are terminals, printers, plotters, microfilm, microfiche, and voice recognition units. System output documents are photographed onto a roll of film and stored on microfilm, microfiche, and optical disk. Audio response systems will help people inquire about a customer's bank balance, get time and temperature readings, and obtain a telephone number from a directory. Usually system outputs are in the form of hard-copy reports. Trends indicate that paper will be replaced by online viewing of reports on a terminal.

WHAT CAN GO WRONG IN SYSTEM OUTPUT ACTIVITIES?

- Exception reporting may not be available to focus on deviations.

- Report balancing rules may not be documented or may be changed without authorization.

- Unneeded reports may be sent to system users.

- System output reports may be delivered to wrong users.

- System outputs (i.e., reports, lists, screens) may be lost, delayed, or truncated due to incorrect sizes between receiving and sending data fields.

- System users may not clearly understand the system outputs.

- System outputs may not be accurate or complete.

Balancing, distribution, and retention of system outputs are of major concern to the auditor since they affect the quality and timeliness of data and usefulness of the system.

(v) Application System Documentation Controls

System documentation is a key element of audit evidence. Without correct and complete documentation, new users cannot be trained properly, programmers cannot maintain the system correctly, users of the system cannot make any meaningful references to the system functions and features, management or anyone cannot understand the system functions and features, and reviewers of the systems (e.g., auditors) cannot make an objective evaluation of the system functions and controls.

Six types of documentation manuals (systems, program, computer operations, user, help-desk, and network control) can be expected in a well-run IT organization. Each type of documentation is targeted for a specific individual or department, sometimes more than one department. For example, help-desk and network control manuals are very much needed by both end users and help-desk staff for an online system or one that is connected to outside third-party data-processing services for access during in-house processing. See Exhibit 2.3 for details of these six types of documentation manuals that would be developed during system development work.

WHAT CAN GO WRONG IN APPLICATION DOCUMENTATION?

- User manuals/guides or documentation may not be available to users to understand how the system works, or the material may not be current.

- System/program documentation may not be available to programmers to facilitate system/program maintenance, or it may not be current.

- Help-desk/network documentation may not be available to help-desk staff to facilitate system/network diagnosis and troubleshooting, and it may not be current.

- Operations documentation may not be available to computer operators to facilitate operations and troubleshooting of operational problems, and it may not be current.

Documentation type	Documentation contents
Systems manual	System flowchart; systems requirements; system functions; design specifications; screen layouts; sample reports
Program manual	Program flowcharts; program functions; file layouts; program specifications
Computer operations manual	Job setup procedures; job narratives; job rerun and restart procedures; file backup procedures; report distribution procedures
User manual	System functions; sample screen and report layouts; report balancing procedures; file maintenance procedures; error correction procedures
Help-desk manual	Contact names and phone numbers of users and IS staff; problem diagnostic and reporting procedures; problem escalation procedures; problem logging, tracking, and closing procedures
Network control manual	Information about circuits, nodes, line, modems; problem diagnostic procedures; problem reporting and resolution procedures; network backup and contingency procedures

EXHIBIT 2.3 Application System Documentation Types and Contents

(vi) Spreadsheet Controls

Spreadsheet software is getting more powerful and simpler to use. Some applications include financial budgeting, project/product costing, payroll, word processing, analytical comparison, and others. Problems can arise: (1) through improper usage of spreadsheet software; (2) due to inadequate planning, design, and documentation of spreadsheet application; and (3) due to human errors. The consequences of these problems and errors are significant as the outputs of spreadsheet are used in decision making.

WHAT CAN GO WRONG IN SPREADSHEET SOFTWARE AND ITS USE?

- Applicable quality control techniques such as author verification (desk checking) and supervisory review may not be available over spreadsheets to ensure that they are error-free.

- Spreadsheet work may not be documented clearly and completely.

- Formulas and key data may not be protected from writing over.

- The most frequent errors in spreadsheets occur during data entry and formulation.

- Errors or mistakes during data entry may not have been noticed or corrected in a timely manner.

- Assumptions and instructions related to the planning, operation, and interpretation of the spreadsheet application may not be documented clearly and adequately.

(vii) Data Integrity Controls

Data integrity is the heart of any application. Data integrity controls ensure the reliability and usability of data and information in making management decisions. The higher the integrity of controls, the greater the credibility and reliability of the application system. Here the term "data integrity" refers to five control attributes: completeness, authorization, accuracy, consistency, and timeliness. The interrelationships of the five control attributes are shown in Exhibit 2.4.

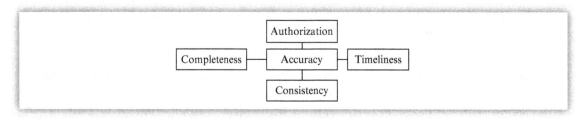

EXHIBIT 2.4 Interrelationships of Control Attributes

The objectives of a data integrity review are to ensure that basic internal controls, such as documented procedures, access controls, management reviews, audit trails, and automated program-processing controls, are established and to verify that they are functioning properly and effectively. Directive, preventive, detective, corrective, and recovery controls should be established in each application system during system development, system maintenance, and system operations activities to achieve the five control attributes of data integrity.

DATA INTEGRITY RULES AND CONTROLS

- A directive control will ensure that people follow data integrity rules consistently.

- A preventive control will stop a data integrity violation from happening.

- A detective control will recognize a data integrity violation.

- A corrective control will fix or repair the damage done by a data integrity violation.

- A recovery control will help in recovering or restoring from a disaster caused by a data integrity violation.

Specifically:

1. **Data completeness** refers to the presence or absence of information. All required data elements must be present for a transaction or record to be complete. For example, all numeric places should be filled, and a check cannot be issued unless all fields have a valid value.

2. **Data accuracy** asks whether data values have been entered into the system correctly and whether data values have been distorted during processing. The sources of the data in terms of where they came from and incorruptibility of data are also important here. This means that the received data are unchanged (no additions, changes, and deletions from the original order, without repetition and omission) with positive assurance and an acceptable degree of confidence. Examples include checking for numeric ranges, spelling errors, data duplication, and data omission.

3. **Data authorization** looks at whether transactions are authorized by appropriate personnel for proper accountability. The person who is approving the transactions is also important here. Moreover, authorization function should be tailored or responsive to the requirements of the application system.

4. **Data consistency** asks whether policies, procedures, and standards have been uniformly applied. It refers to the relation between intradata elements and intra- and inter-records and files. Examples: A requestor's name cannot equal an approver's name, and an approver's name cannot equal a signatory's name in a check-approval scenario. The causes of data inconsistencies can be invalid, untimely, incomplete, and inaccurate data.

5. **Data timeliness** means that data are not stale for intended use and that they are current. Management needs to understand the need for establishing controls to ensure data integrity. This understanding makes the system more effective and useful.

(viii) User Satisfaction Assessment

Assessment of system user satisfaction is a very important part of the audit of an application system. This is because it is the system user who paid for the system, owns the system, and uses the system.

In fact, the system is not successful and useful if the system user is not satisfied with system functions and results. One way to assess user satisfaction is to conduct user surveys periodically. System usability should be a major concern for the user and the auditor.

ISSUES IN USER SATISFACTION

- The application system may not be user friendly—that is, it may not be easy to use.

- System users may not be satisfied with the performance of the system—that is, online system response time may be too slow or batch job turnaround time may be too long.

- The application system may not be available to system users for use when it is needed and where it is needed.

- The application system may not be providing the right kind of information needed to run business operations.

- The application system may not be giving users control reports, exception reports, summary reports, aging reports, error reports, productivity reports, and audit trail reports.

- Functional users may not have documented and tested plans and procedures for operating their application systems during a power outage, natural disaster, or system failure.

- Access to an application system may take longer due to too many screens, menus, submenus, or steps to get into programs. Usually the greater the number of screens, the longer it takes to move from one screen to the other.

(j) Inventory of Controls in Business Application Systems

Application controls are designed to control computerized application systems, helping to ensure the completeness and accuracy of transaction processing, authorization, and validity. The next list provides the nature of each control (preventive, detective, and corrective); the type of control (completeness, accuracy, continuity, authorization, consistency, and security) is indicated where necessary.

Preventive Controls

- **Brevity codes.** Shortened forms of standardized messages that reduce the amount of input required by valid users while often hiding the message type or other information obtained from the user interface, from unauthorized users. This control increases data accuracy.

- **Data attribute checks.** Verification that data have particular attributes (e.g., length, type, content).

- **Validity checks.** These are tests for the validity of codes such as state, tax rates, Social Security number, customer number, vendor number, or employee number. Usually table lookups are performed for data comparison. This accuracy control is a preventive and a detective control.

- **Compatibility tests.** These tests are used to determine whether an acceptable user is allowed to proceed in the system. They focus on passwords, access rules, and system privileges. Compatibility tests are a type of security control.

- **Processing parameters.** The flexible use of parameters facilitates operation. Customized reporting features can be used to specify dates (beginning and ending), processing frequency and cycles (daily, weekly, monthly), report numbers, computer-job numbers, and locations (plant numbers, office numbers, or store numbers). Processing parameters are a type of continuity control.

- **Prenumbered forms.** Sequential numbers on individual source documents or input forms (i.e., purchase orders or invoices) are preprinted to allow subsequent detection of loss or misplacement of documents and forms. Prenumbered forms are a type of completeness control.

- **System-assigned numbers.** These are the same as prenumbered forms except that the system automatically assigns the sequential numbers. System-assigned numbers are a type of accuracy control.

- **Precoded forms/screens.** Fixed data elements or fields are entered or printed on input forms, source documents, terminal screen menus, or report listings to prevent errors in data coding and data entry, for example, on turnaround documents, such as utility bills. A variation of this is called **preformatting,** where a document is displayed with blanks for data items to be entered by the system user or the data entry operator. Precoded forms/screens are a type of accuracy control.

- **Turnaround documents.** Source documents and input forms can be designed in such a way that they serve as a bill, invoice, or notice to a customer or a user and can be used when returned as an input document for entering the necessary data into the computer system. Turnaround documents are a type of accuracy control.

- **Reference values or codes kept outside the program.** For ease of system or program maintenance, it is better to keep frequently used or changing values or codes (i.e., Social Security numbers, tax rates, pay classes) outside the program as an external table or other means (LEVEL 88 values in COBOL programs), not embedded in the programming statements. Table lookups are provided. This type of control is a continuity control.

- **Transaction cancellation.** The system can be designed in such a way as to cancel each transaction record after it is used in order to prevent its repeated use. Examples are purchase orders, receiving reports, invoices, sales returns, and the like. The system flags repeated use of the same document number; this is analogous to manual stamping of "paid" or "processed." Cancellation also can be used to reverse or back-out previous transactions for any reason. Transaction cancellations are a type of completeness control.

- **Management approvals**. Supervisors or managers should be required to approve sensitive and important transactions that others enter into the system or calculated using the system. This is achieved by entering a secret keyword or number as a means of authorization. Management approvals are a type of authorization control.

- **Concurrent access controls.** For database systems, concurrent access (updates) to the same record or file by multiple users is a concern as it affects data integrity. Usually automatic file/record locking facilities are used to prevent concurrent accesses. These controls are required to minimize the possibility of destroying data records. They are a type of security control.

- **Two-person controls.** Two individuals review or approve the work of each other. Examples are: one person initiates a transaction and the other person approves it; one person counts inventory or cash while other person observes it. The purpose is to provide accountability or accuracy in dealing with sensitive or high-risk transactions or activities to minimize fraud or other irregularities. Two-person controls are a type of accuracy control.

- **Overrides.** Overrides can include manual and system-based overrides. The system should prevent unauthorized individuals overriding exceptions or errors. A report should be produced showing who did what. Overrides are a type of security and authorization control.

Detective Controls

- **Summary integrity check.** This is a method for checking the correctness of data by comparing data with a "summary" of the data. It is similar to a batch-control technique.

- **Batch totals.** To ensure accuracy in data entry and processing, control totals can be compared by the system with manually calculated and entered control totals using the data fields such as quantities, line items, documents, or dollars. Batch totals are a type of completeness control.

- **Hash totals.** This is a technique for improving data accuracy, whereby totals are obtained on identifier (meaningless) data fields, such as account number, Social Security number, part number, or employee number. These totals have no significance other than for internal system control purposes. Hash totals are a type of accuracy control.

- **Limit check.** The program tests specified data fields against defined high- or low-value limits (e.g., quantities or dollars) for acceptability before further processing. The limits can be based on transaction values and times. Limit checks are a type of accuracy control. Examples of error messages: Transaction is over $30,000. Purchase order is over $50,000, or multiple price change number cannot be higher than 9999.

- **Reasonableness test.** This test can be used to determine whether input data, updated data, calculated data, or output data are reasonable. Ascending/descending checks for numeric and alphabetic data can be performed. Tolerance tests measuring dollar or percentage deviation of vendor invoice from purchase-order amount can be designed. This test is specific to an application-system function. Reasonableness tests are a type of accuracy control. Examples of error messages: Airline passenger departure flight time is not reasonable with arrival flight time for the same day. Customer order quantity is not reasonable with historical order.

- **Check digit.** A check digit is a digit, derived by a mathematical formula, that is a function of the other digits within a word or number. It is a checksum calculated on each digit of a numeric string. It is used for testing accuracy of transcription, transposition, data entry, and data processing, and detects such errors. Part numbers, stock-keeping numbers, credit card numbers, employee numbers, and account numbers can be check-digited. Check digits can be operated on any part of the number as long as they are applied consistently. They are a type of accuracy control. Examples of error messages: Invalid check-digit must be zero through six. Invalid check digit on transfer number.

- **Overflow check.** This is a limit check based on the capacity of a computer memory or data file area to accept data. This programming technique can be used to detect the truncation of a financial or quantity data-field value after computation (e.g., addition, multiplication, and division). Usually the first digit is lost. Overflow checks are a type of accuracy control.

- **Format checks.** These are used to determine that data are entered in the proper mode, as numeric or alphabetical characters, within designated fields of information. The proper mode in each case depends on the data record definition. Format checks are accuracy controls. Examples of error messages: Invalid transaction format. Invalid date format, date must be mm-dd-yy.

- **Date checks.** These can be used to record transactions falling in the proper accounting (fiscal) month; they relate to logical consistencies between transaction dates and events. Date checks are continuity controls. Examples of error messages: Merchandise date received should be after the date shipped. Budget transaction date out of range. Control card "to" date is less than "from" date the job canceled.

- **Label check.** This is a processing control whereby a computer application program verifies internal file labels for tapes to ensure that the correct data file is used in the processing. Label checks are also a type of continuity control. Example of error message: Wrong file is mounted.

- **Completeness test.** This is a programming test to determine whether data entries have been made in data fields that should be left blank. It can be used to detect missing data fields or records. This test is a completeness control.

- **Range test.** This is the same as "limit check," but this term is used when both high and low values are used for testing. It can also define include and exclude values. Range tests are a type of accuracy control. Examples of error messages: Percentage must be between 10 and 75 inclusive. Price change number must be in range 1000 through 1999.

- **Range check.** This is a verification that data are within a certain range of values.

- **Discrete value check.** This is verification that data have either certain permissible values or do not have other restricted values, out of a wider set of possible values.

- **Record count.** This is a processing control whereby information such as maximum, active, inactive, and available record counts will ensure proper size of the file and avoid loss of records. Record counts are also a type of continuity control. Example of error message: Transaction counts and actual record counts do not agree.

- **Sign test.** This is a test for a numeric data field containing a designation of an algebraic sign such as + or −, which can be used to denote, for example, debits or credits for financial data fields. Sign tests are a type of accuracy control. Example of error message: Sign is inconsistent with transaction type.

- **Size test.** This test can be used to test the full size of the data field. For example, a Social Security number in the United States should have nine digits. Size tests are a type of completeness control. Examples of error messages: Line quantity or total may not be more than five digits long. Numeric postal zip code must be either five or nine digits.

- **Sequence check.** This is a way of testing for a certain sequence of record types or transaction numbers during computer processing. It can also be used to test the sequence of purchase orders, receiving reports, invoices, and the like. It is also called anticipation control and depends on the system and its design logic. Sequence checks are a type of completeness control. Examples of error messages: Missing transaction No. 06. Missing record type 09.

- **Duplicate checks.** These are the same as sequence checks but look for duplication. Duplicate checks are completeness controls. Examples of error messages: Multiple tax records. Multiple account records.

- **Cross-field editing.** Cross-field editing tests for the validity of multiple data fields simultaneously with a logical and predefined relationship to each other in the same record. It is a consistency control. Examples of error messages: No tax on taxable department. Tax amount received or paid on a nontaxable item or department. Incorrect telephone area code compared to postal zip code.

- **Cross-record editing.** This is the same as cross-field editing, but the tests are performed among multiple records. It is a consistency control. Examples of error messages: Account number in a transaction record does not match with the master file. Department number not on file for the store/plant/office.

- **System matching.** The system matches certain transactions, such as purchase order numbers to receiving report numbers to vendor invoices or shipping advices to billing numbers, and lists unmatched transactions for review and follow-up. System matching is a type of completeness control. Examples of error messages: Account number does not match with the recording code. Tax percentage calculated does not match with tax tables.

- **Field combination tests.** One or more data fields are tested for the right combination. These tests are a type of accuracy control. Examples of error messages: Invalid plant number for the business division. City and/or state cannot have city code. No price found for the given item/style. If the style number is entered, then the house number must also be entered. Invalid employee number for the location. Invalid payclass for the given subclass.

- **Run-to-run totals.** These are processing controls whereby output control totals resulting from one process (cycle, program, or module) are used as input control totals over subsequent processing. The control totals are used as a verification mechanism (automatically or manually) and link one process or cycle to another in a sequence. The control totals can be grouped by dollars or records or in some other way. Run-to-run totals ensure program-processing accuracy. They are also a type of continuity controls. Examples of error messages: Database-beginning records total plus transaction activity records total is not equal to ending-records total. Net amount is not equal to total cost plus transportation cost minus discount.

- **Suspense file.** In this technique, computer files are designed to contain unprocessed or partially processed transactions awaiting further action. All pending or rejected transactions (errors) can be maintained in a suspense file for later review and correction. This will ensure that all errors are corrected. Suspense files are a type of completeness control. Examples of error messages: Transaction is rejected. Transaction is incomplete or suspended.

- **Header and trailer record verification.** This is a processing-control technique used to verify the accuracy of header information in a first record of a file and to verify the accuracy of a control total in the trailer or last record for comparison with accumulated counts or values of records processed. This verification is an accuracy control. Examples of error messages: Wrong file entered for processing. Trailer record counts do not equal accumulated counts.

- **Balance controls.** The system can be designed to balance transactions using a system- or function-dependent technique whereby an out-of-balance condition is automatically detected and reported. Balance controls are a type of accuracy control. Examples of error messages: The total sum of units or dollars must equal the sum of units or dollars for each location.

- **System logging of transactions.** This is a processing control whereby the system maintains a log to record user ID, password, transaction number, department number, terminal ID, date, and time to provide an electronic audit trail. System logging is also a security control

- **Comparison controls.** The program is designed to compare certain values in the same or different records to determine accuracy and reasonableness. This technique is dependent on the application system's function. Comparison controls are a type of consistency control. Examples are: listing of differences between prices on purchase orders and purchase invoices, listing of differences between stock-status dollar values and general-ledger amounts, listing of shipment values and billed amounts, comparison of merchandise total plus freight plus tax amount with purchase-invoice total, comparison of quantities of product sold in the last quarter with quantities in inventory and reports of slow-moving inventory based on criteria built into the program, and comparison of debit-dollar totals with credit-dollar totals for financial accounting journal entry transactions.

- **Computation controls.** The program logic includes columnar footing and cross-footing, extensions, and postings to ensure mathematical and processing accuracy. Most techniques described here are dependent on the application system's functions. Computation controls are a type of accuracy control. Examples of error messages: Total quantity must be the sum of all line quantities.

- **Ratio test.** This is a mathematical calculation whereby one data element is divided into another to yield a ratio value. The ratio test is a consistency control. An example is: Return on investment/assets (ROI/ROA) is calculated as dividing the data element "operating or net income" in the numerator by the data element "investment or assets" in the denominator.

- **Rounding technique.** For financial and accounting calculations such as multiplication and division, the system analyst or programmer should decide how to handle rounding calculations and decimal-point rounding rules consistently across and within all programs and systems. The rounding technique is an accuracy control.

- **Relationship test.** This is a comparison of values to validate a logical or defined correlation; it is also referred to as a conditional test. For example, an invoice date must be the same as or earlier than the related payment date. Relationship tests are a type of consistency control.

- **Descriptive read-back.** This is a design technique whereby a code or number is converted to its description and appears on the computer terminal screen for human inspection to determine its accuracy and completeness. Descriptive read-backs are a type of accuracy control. An example is when a customer number is entered, the customer's name and address will appear on the screen to ensure that the right customer record is accessed.

- **Data checks.** The system analyst or programmer should test for the presence of blank spaces when numeric data are expected to be received in a numeric data field or should test for division by zero when a division is expected with a nonzero value. This prevents program failure during processing as a result of missing or improper data. Data checks are a type of accuracy control.

- **Key verification.** Important data elements or fields need to be key verified by rekeying to verify data entry accuracy. This is an accuracy control. Example of error message: Incorrect account number, check it.

- **One-for-one checking.** Critical reports or input documents should be compared one for one with subsequent outputs to ensure accuracy and completeness of data entry and computer processing. One-for-one checking is an accuracy control.

- **Cross footing.** Cross footing compares horizontal (rows) and vertical (columns) totals in a table or report to be equal. Cross footing is an accuracy control.

Corrective Controls

- **Program comments.** The consistent inclusion of English comments in the program will help programmers understand the program's functions and features during its maintenance. Use of program comments is a consistency control.

- **Job control comments.** The consistent inclusion of English comments in the job control language will help the maintenance programmer and the data control analyst understands the purpose of job control language. Use of job control comments is a consistency control.

- **Automatic error correction.** The system is designed to correct errors automatically on the basis of predefined criteria and in cases where human intervention is not immediately needed. Automatic error correction is a continuity control.

- **Overrides by supervisors.** The system should be designed so that the ability to override certain critical and sensitive errors is limited to supervisors and managers using a password control. Such overrides are both continuity controls and authorization controls.

- **Audit trail report.** The system should provide a clear and complete listing of audit trail reports for tracing and verification purposes. Audit trail reports are a type of accuracy control.

- **Control report.** The system should provide a clear and complete listing of batch control and system logging reports for user balancing and verification purposes. Control reports are a type of accuracy control.

- **Exception report.** This is a report produced on request or in response to certain specified conditions and highlights exceptions or deviations from the anticipated situation. The type of report and its details depend on the application system's function. Exception reports are a type of accuracy control.

- **Error report.** This is a report showing all rejected transactions in error, indicating the severity level of the error and the required action to correct the error. An error report is an accuracy control.

- **Before/after image record reporting for file maintenance.** To ensure data integrity, the system must report the data field values both before and after the changes so functional users can detect data entry and update errors. This type of record reporting is an accuracy control.

- **Clear and complete error messages.** To facilitate error correction, all error messages should be easy to understand and meaningful. They should not be cryptic or negative and should not use code numbers. Use of clear and complete error messages is a continuity control.

- **Error totals.** To facilitate error correction and increase employee productivity, error totals should be provided by error type, department, position, transaction, plant, store, or company. Errors can be totaled as dollars, quantities, or records. Error totals are a type of accuracy control.

- **Documentation.** Correct, up-to-date system, programming, computer operations, network control, help desk, and user manuals (documented procedures) will help system analysts, programmers, computer operators, network control analysts, and functional users correct errors, answer questions, and resolve problems during maintenance, operation, and use of the system. Documentation is a continuity control.

- **Automatic backup and recovery.** The system is designed to provide automated periodic backup of all required disk files rather than needing human intervention to ensure timely recovery from a disaster. In some systems, file restoration and recovery are automatic. This is a continuity control.

- **Journaling.** All application system transactions should be captured on a journal file so that recovery can be made should a system failure occur. Journaling is a continuity control.

- **Checkpoint control.** All application system batch jobs requiring more than one hour of CPU processing time need to be designed with a checkpoint control so that automatic backup of files is made at every 15 or 30 minutes to facilitate a recovery should a disaster occur. Checkpoint control is a continuity control.

- **Transaction back-out.** All application systems (database or not) should have the ability to back-out or reverse invalid or improper transaction data should a processing problem or error occur. Transaction back-out is a continuity control.

- **Recovery logging.** For database systems, a recovery log can be used to record system status information as well as information describing the changes made to the database. Both before images and after images of the database pages affected by an update can be stored in the recovery log, which can be accessed by means of rollback and roll-forward techniques. Recovery logging is a continuity control.

- **Fallback procedure.** In the event of a failure of transactions or the system, the program has the ability to fall back to the original or alternate method for continuation of processing. A fallback procedure is a continuity control.

(k) Summary of Controls

(i) Operational Application System Controls
Exhibit 2.5 provides a summary of preventive, detective, and corrective controls as they relate to IS in operation. Implementation of these controls would help IT management in strengthening overall controls.

(ii) Information Technology Management
Operating management has the ultimate responsibility for the implementation of cost-effective controls in manual or automated systems. Management activities range from strategic planning to operational control. Strategic planning requires external, very broad, future-oriented data whereas operational control requires information that is largely internal, narrow, and current.

Feed-forward controls help management in anticipating problems. Exhibit 2.6 presents a summary of preventive, detective, and corrective controls as they relate to the IS environment. Implementation of these controls would help IT management in strengthening overall controls.

(iii) Information Technology Operation
Exhibit 2.7 presents a summary of preventive, detective, and corrective controls as they relate to functional areas of IT operations. Implementation of these controls would help IT management in strengthening overall controls.

(iv) Data and Network Communications
Exhibit 2.8 presents a summary of preventive, detective, and corrective controls as they relate to data and network communications. Implementation of these controls would help IT management in strengthening overall controls.

(v) System Security and Information Protection
Privacy of information is important and is protected by logging and analyzing system usage, implementing program change controls, and separating personal/personnel data from operating or statistical data. Both management and auditors can be equally liable for security breaches that occur in the

Preventive controls	Detective controls	Corrective controls
Data dictionary	Batch control totals	Program comments
Structured techniques	Hash totals	Job control comments
Programming and documentation standards	Limit checks	Automatic error correction
	Reasonableness checks	Overrides by supervisors
Processing parameters	Check digits	Audit trail reports
Online prompting	Overflow checks	Control reports
Self-help features	Format checks	Exception reports
Default options	Date checks	Productivity reports
Good screen design	Label checks	Aging reports
Field highlighting	Completeness tests	Error reports
Screen diagnostic messages	Range tests	Before/after image reporting
	Record counts	Clear and complete error messages
Prenumbered forms	Sign test	Error totals
System-assigned numbers	Size test	Documentation
Precoded forms and screens	Sequence checks	Automated backup and recovery mechanisms
	Duplicate checks	
Turnaround documents	Cross-field checking	Journaling
Data ownership	Cross-record checking	Data retention
Data classification	System matching	Checkpoint controls
Table lookups	Field combination tests	Transaction backout
Passwords	Validity checks	Recovery logging
Transaction cancellation	Run-to-run totals	Fallback procedures
Data encryption	Suspense files	
Management approvals	Header/trailer record verifications	
Concurrent access controls	Balance controls	
Two-person controls	System logs	
Fault-tolerant controls	Comparison controls	
System or manual overrides	Computation controls	
	Ratio tests	
	Rounding techniques	
	Descriptive readback	
	System walk-throughs	
	Data checks	
	Key verification	
	One-for-one checking	
	Crossfooting	

EXHIBIT 2.5 Operational Application System Preventive, Detective, and Corrective Controls Summary

organization. Situational pressures (e.g., gambling, drugs), opportunities to commit for fraud (e.g., weak system of controls), and personal characteristics (e.g., lack of integrity or honesty) are major causes of fraud, whether computer-related or not. There is nothing new about the act of committing fraud. There is no new way to commit fraud because someone somewhere has already tried it.

Exhibit 2.9 presents a summary of preventive, detective, and corrective controls as they relate to the security function. Implementation of these controls would help IT management in strengthening overall controls.

Preventive controls	Detective controls	Corrective controls
Policies, procedures, standards	Project management tools	Exception reports
Separation of duties	Control parameters	Progress reports
Job (position) descriptions	Operating/capital budgets	Control reports
Short-range plans	Tolerance limits	Error reports
Long-range plans		Special reports
System access rules		

EXHIBIT 2.6 Information Systems Environment Preventive, Detective, and Corrective Controls Summary

(vi) Contingency Planning

Exhibit 2.10 presents a summary of preventive, detective, and corrective controls as they relate to contingency planning. Implementation of these controls would help IT management in strengthening overall controls.

(vii) Application Development

Exhibit 2.11 presents a summary of preventive, detective, and corrective controls as they relate to IS acquisition, development, and maintenance. Implementation of these controls would help IT management in strengthening overall controls.

Preventive controls	Detective controls	Corrective controls
Establish IT steering committee	Install smoke and fire detectors and fire alarms	Automate the report balancing procedures
Establish service-level agreements	Require system logging of transactions	Use comments in job execution language
Establish and enforce computer center policies, procedures, and standards	Reduce computer operator intervention by installing console management system	Provide periodic backup of data and programs, and rotate them through off-site storage
Establish a problem, change, and configuration management function	Review system activity logs, journals, and exception reports	Facilitate system recovery and restart procedures
Install help-desk function to support system users	Rotate key employees in the computer center	Install automated job recovery software
Establish a separate and centralized network control function	Require employees to take vacations	Develop fall-back systems and procedures
Require periodic audits of the computer center	Acquire or develop an automated job accounting information system	Install fault-tolerant devices and software to recover from a system failure
Establish a chargeback system	Ensure running of correct version of production programs	
Eliminate manual job scheduling practices	Compare production resource usage	
Discourage printing of hardcopy reports	Install water detection measures and environmental control devices	
Install automated tape and disk management systems		
Install computer capacity management function		

EXHIBIT 2.7 Functional Areas of IT Operations Preventive, Detective, and Corrective Controls Summary

Preventive controls	Detective controls	Corrective controls
Policies, procedures, and standards	Contingency plan testing	Contingency plan maintenance and update
Encryption techniques	Network line utilization statistics	Network diagnostic data collection tools with automatic corrective action
Transborder data transmission laws	Network diagnostic tools	
Training and education plans	Network testing capabilities	Network routing capabilities
Problem and change management system	Test cables and connectors prior to power-up for each node	Networking monitoring tools
Fault-tolerance network design practices	Periodic inventory of network equipment	Recovery mechanisms such as checkpoints, roll-back and roll-forward features in the database
Resilient network design principles such as redundant equipment and components; alternate paths, routes, nodes, and circuits and lines; and parallel links	Install physical security devices	Recovery techniques from computer viruses
	Implement logical security mechanisms	
	Message sequence numbers	
Contingency plan development	Checksum techniques	
Network management tools	Computer malware detection tools	
Install quality cables for local area network (LAN)		

EXHIBIT 2.8 Network Communications Preventive, Detective, and Corrective Controls Summary

(viii) End-User Computing

Lack of adequate separation of duties is a potential control weakness in a personal computer or desktop computer environment. Direct supervision and frequent work reviews should be conducted to balance the control weaknesses.

When uploading data to a host computer, the data conversion programs residing on the host computer should reject inaccurate or incomplete data before updating any host-resident data files. Control totals should be developed between the personal computer and the host computer and reconciled automatically by the program. Uploading is one source of computer viruses, and its effects on other programs and data files are unknown.

Exhibit 2.12 presents a summary of preventive, detective, and recovery controls as they relate to small computers and end-user computing. Implementation of these controls would help IT management in strengthening overall controls.

(ix) Third-Party Services

Almost every IT department uses third-party service providers, such as outsourcers. Management should be cautious about knowing what to outsource and when.

Exhibit 2.13 presents a summary of preventive, detective, and corrective controls as they relate to third-party services. Implementation of these controls would help IT management in strengthening overall controls.

Preventive controls	Detective controls	Corrective controls
Establish a computer security management (steering) committee	Require all employees to wear badges	Provide application system–generated error reports to users for review
Establish a computer security function	Provide last activity/sign-on data on computer terminals	
Assign asset responsibility to employees and exact accountability	Inform the user of any unauthorized attempts to guess his password	Provide periodic backup of data and programs, and rotate through off-site storage
Distribute job descriptions with security responsibility	Install continuous area surveillance mechanisms	
Generate a security awareness among employees	Review system activity logs, journals, and exception reports to detect security violations	Establish system recovery/restart guidelines in applications and systems software
Encourage legal ownership of software and protection of copyrighted (intellectual) property	Conduct periodic security audits	Implement vital records retention programs
Provide guidelines to protect confidentiality of data and information	Require that employees take vacations	
Establish a quality control technique for computer security function	Insert dummy names and known addresses as decoys into financially related mailing lists to detect their unauthorized use	
Require audits of data processing systems and operations by auditors	Provide dummy data files for intruders to trap while reviewing the data	
Issue guidelines for software development and maintenance methodology focusing on computer security design	Control program changes to ensure that only authorized changes are made	

EXHIBIT 2.9 Security Function Preventive, Detective, and Corrective Controls Summary

Preventive controls	Detective controls	Corrective controls
Conduct risk analysis	Establish recovery organization with clearly defined responsibilities	Provide periodic backup of data and programs, and rotate through off-site storage
Establish the planning committee		
Prioritize application systems	Establish recovery logging procedures	Test the disaster recovery plan
Revisit the data storage and retention practices	Conduct disaster recovery training	Install automated job recovery software
Install electronic vaulting	Conduct recovery testing	Test the emergency procedures
Purge data and program files periodically	Conduct periodic fire drills	Obtain sufficient insurance coverage
Issue guidelines on how to discard/dispose of used paper records, mechanical records, and electronic records	Maintain a problem log during plan testing	Implement vital records retention programs
Develop disaster awareness among employees		Develop fallback systems and procedures
Establish system recovery/restart guidelines in applications and systems software		Update the planning document
		Issue a report of lessons learned from testing

EXHIBIT 2.10 Contingency Planning Preventive, Detective, and Corrective Controls Summary

Preventive controls	Detective controls	Corrective controls
Establish a software development management (steering) committee	Practice peer reviews	Design automated error correction features into applications software
Establish a software quality assurance function	Use program tracing tools and techniques	Produce before and after image (from and to) reports for correction errors during data file maintenance activities
Issue software development methodology guidelines	Practice structure walk-throughs	
Establish a data administration and database administration function	Use automated documentation aids	
Encourage auditor and management participation and reviews	Practice software verification and validation techniques	Design audit trail reports, control reports, aging reports, and exception reports for user and auditor review
Require active user participation and receiver user sign-off letters	Use software debugging tools during testing	Use preprocessors to make programs more readable
Issue guidelines for software usability, maintainability, securability, auditability, and controllability criteria	Design data-editing and validation control routines into the software	Use interactive program debugging tools
Implement good project management techniques	Inspect and test software independently	Use comments in computer programs and job execution language
Use structured techniques for analysis, design, programming, and testing		Design checkpoint, recovery/restart procedures into the software
Inspect and test software independently		

EXHIBIT 2.11 Information Systems Acquisition, Development, and Maintenance Preventive, Detective, and Corrective Controls Summary

2.2 Management Control Techniques

Management controls, in the broadest sense, include the plan of organization, methods, and procedures adopted by management to ensure that its goals and objectives are met. Management controls, also known as internal controls, include accounting and administrative controls.

Management control systems must be integrated with ongoing management practices and, where appropriate and effective, with other management initiatives, such as productivity improvement, quality improvement, business process improvement, reengineering, and performance measures and standards. Examples of management practices include periodic staff meetings, quarterly management reviews, budget planning and execution, and variance analysis.

Management control systems must be effective and efficient—balancing the costs of control mechanisms and processes with the benefits the systems are intended to provide or control. They should identify who is accountable and provide accountability for all activities.

Preventive controls	Detective controls	Corrective controls
Establish a PC or personal computer support function	Install physical security devices	Develop control reports
Issue policies, procedures, and standards	Implement logical security mechanisms	Develop audit trail reports
Establish controls in application programs used for mini and midrange computers (e.g., label checking, recovery procedures, batch and file balancing, audit trails)	Test end user–developed software	Develop exception reports
Require a user ID and a password prior to accessing the PC system		
Initiate a preventive maintenance program for the PCs		
Install program change controls for end user–developed systems		
Require documentation for end user–developed and maintained systems		

EXHIBIT 2.12 Small Computer and End-User Computing Preventive, Detective, and Corrective Controls Summary

(a) Traditional Management Controls

Management controls include the process for planning, organizing, directing, and controlling the entity's operations. They include the management control systems for measuring, reporting, and monitoring operations. Specifically, they include automated and manual systems, policies and procedures, and other ongoing management activities that help ensure that risks are managed and controlled. Internal auditing is an important part of management control.

Preventive controls	Detective controls	Corrective controls
Legal contracts with right to audit clauses	Periodic review and modification of contracts	Periodic progress reporting
Nondisclosure agreements	Logical access and physical access security controls	Exit interviews
Noncompeting agreements	Time reporting	Ad hoc or regular reports to monitor third-party vendor's work
Work proposals with clear and measurable deliverables	Review of work products and deliverables	
Copyright protection awareness		

EXHIBIT 2.13 Summary of Controls Related to Third-Party Services

Managerial control can be divided into feed-forward and feedback controls. A feed-forward control is a proactive control such as defect prevention, inspection, training, and budgeting. A feedback control is used to evaluate past activity to improve future performance. It measures actual performance against a standard to ensure that a defined result is achieved. Examples of feedback controls include surveys and variance analysis.

(b) Contemporary Management Controls

Many new management controls have evolved over the years, including economic value added (EVA), market value added (MVA), activity-based costing (ABC), open-book management, and the balanced scorecard system.

EVA is a financial control technique that is defined as a company's net (after-tax) operating profit minus the cost of capital invested in the company's tangible assets. It captures all the things a company can do to add value from its activities, such as running the business more efficiently, satisfying customers, and rewarding shareholders. Each job, department, or process in the organization is measured by the value added.

MVA measures the stock market's estimate of the value of a company's past and projected capital investment projects. For example, when a company's market value (the value of all outstanding stock plus the company's debt) is greater than all the capital invested in it from shareholders, bondholders, and retained earnings, the company has a positive MVA, an indication that it has created wealth. A positive MVA usually goes hand in hand with a high EVA measurement.

ABC attempts to identify all the various activities needed to provide a product or service and allocate costs accordingly. Because ABC allocates costs across business processes, it provides a more accurate picture of the cost of various products and services. In addition, it enables managers to evaluate whether more costs go to activities that add value or to activities that do not add value. They can then focus on reducing costs associated with non-value-added activities.

Open-book management allows employees to see for themselves—through charts, computer printouts, meetings, and reports—the financial condition of the company. It also shows individual employees how their job fits into the big picture and affects the financial future of the organization. Finally, it ties employee rewards to the company's overall success. The goal of open-book management is to get every employee thinking like a business owner rather than like a hired hand—what money is coming in and where it is going. Open-book management helps employees appreciate why efficiency is important to the organization's success. It turns the traditional control on its head.

The **balanced scorecard system** is a comprehensive management control system that balances traditional financial measures with measures of customer service, internal business processes, and the organization's capacity for learning and growth. The financial perspective reflects a concern that the organization's activities contribute to improving short- and long-term financial performance (e.g., net income and return on investment). Customer service indicators measure such things as how customers view the organization as well as customer retention and satisfaction. Internal business process indicators focus on production and operating statistics, such as order fulfillment or cost per order. The learning and growth indicator focuses on how well resources and human capital are being managed for the company's future. Metrics may include employee retention and the introduction of new products.

2.3 Internal Control and Alternative Control Frameworks

Seven control frameworks or models are discussed in this section:

1. Committee of Sponsoring Organizations (COSO) of the Treadway Commission, in the United States
2. The Criteria of Control (CoCo) in Canada
3. The Control Self-Assessment (CSA) in the United States
4. The Cadbury Report in the United Kingdom
5. The Turnbull model in the United Kingdom
6. The King model in South Africa
7. The KonTraG model in Germany

(a) COSO's Definition of Internal Control

Internal controls have objectives, concepts, and components. According to the Committee of Sponsoring Organizations (COSO) of the Treadway Commission report, internal control is a process affected by an entity's board of directors, management, and other personnel that is designed to provide reasonable assurance regarding the achievement of objectives in three categories:

1. Effectiveness and efficiency of operations
2. Reliability of financial reporting
3. Compliance with applicable laws and regulations

This definition reflects four fundamental concepts.

1. Internal control is a process. It is a means to an end, not an end in itself.
2. Internal control is affected by people. It is not merely a policy manual and forms but people at every level of an organization.
3. Internal control can be expected to provide only reasonable assurance, not absolute assurance, to an entity's management and board.
4. Internal control is geared to the achievement of objectives in one or more separate but overlapping categories.

The three objectives and the four fundamental concepts of internal controls are shown in Exhibit 2.14.

(i) Process
Internal control is not one event or circumstance but a series of actions that permeate an entity's activities. These actions are pervasive and are inherent in the way management runs the business.

Business processes, which are conducted within or across organization units or functions, are managed through the basic management processes of planning, executing, and monitoring.

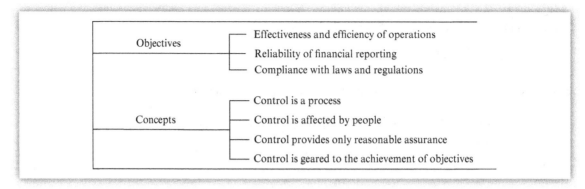

EXHIBIT 2.14 Internal Control Objectives and Concepts

Internal control is a part of these processes and is integrated with them. It enables the processes to function and monitors their conduct and continued relevancy. It is a tool used by management, not a substitute for management.

This conceptualization of internal control is very different from the perspective of some observers who view internal control as something added on to an entity's activities, or as a necessary burden imposed by regulators or by the dictates of overzealous bureaucrats, or unnecessarily dependent on a person's attitude.

The internal control system is intertwined with an entity's operating activities and exists for fundamental business reasons. Internal controls are most effective when they are built into the entity's infrastructure and are part of the essence of the enterprise. They should be built *in* rather than built *on*.

Building in controls can directly affect an entity's ability to reach its goals and supports quality initiatives of businesses. The quest for quality is directly linked to how businesses are run and how they are controlled. Quality initiatives become part of the operating fabric of an enterprise, as evidenced by

- Senior executive leadership ensuring that quality values are built into the way a company does business.

- Establishing quality objectives linked to the entity's information collection and analysis and other processes.

- Using the knowledge of competitive practices and customer expectations to drive continuous quality improvement.

These quality factors parallel those in effective internal control systems. In fact, internal control is not only integrated with quality programs but usually critical to their success.

Building in controls also has important implications to cost containment and response time.

- Most enterprises are faced with highly competitive marketplaces and a need to contain costs. Adding new procedures separate from existing ones adds costs. By focusing on existing operations and their contribution to effective internal control and building controls into basic operating activities, an enterprise often can avoid unnecessary procedures and costs.

- A practice of building controls into the fabric of operations helps trigger development of new control necessary to new business activities. Such automatic reactions makes entities more nimble and competitive.

(ii) People
The board of directors, management, and other personnel in an entity affect internal control. The people of an organization accomplish internal control by what they do and say. People establish the entity's objectives and put control mechanisms in place.

Similarly, internal control affects people's actions. Internal control recognizes that people do not always understand, communicate, or perform consistently. Each individual brings to the workplace a unique background and technical ability and has different personal needs and priorities.

The realities affect, and are affected by, internal control. People must know their responsibilities and limits of authority. Accordingly, a clear and close linkage needs to exist between people's duties and the way in which those duties are carried out to align with the entity's objectives.

The organization's people include the board of directors as well as management and other personnel. Although directors might be viewed as primarily providing oversight, they also provide direction and approve certain transactions or policies. As such, the board of directors is an important element of internal control.

(iii) Reasonable Assurance
Internal control, no matter how well designed and operated, can provide only reasonable assurance to management and the board of directors regarding achievement of an entity's objectives. The likelihood of achievement of objectives is affected by limitations inherent in all internal control systems.

These limitations include the realities that human judgment in decision making can be faulty, persons responsible for establishing controls need to consider their relative costs and benefits, and breakdowns can occur because of human failures, such as a simple errors or mistakes. Additionally, controls can be circumvented by collusion of two or more people. Finally, management has the ability to override the internal control system.

(iv) Objectives
Every entity sets out on a mission, establishing objectives it wants to achieve and strategies for achieving them. Objectives may be set for an entity as a whole or be targeted to specific activities within the entity. Although many objectives are specific to a particular entity, some are widely shared. For example, objectives common to virtually all entities are achieving and maintaining a positive reputation within the business and consumer communities, providing reliable financial statements to stakeholders, and operating in compliance with laws and regulations.

An internal control system can be expected to provide reasonable assurance of achieving objectives relating to the reliability of financial reporting and compliance with laws and regulations. Achievement of those objectives, which are based largely on standards imposed by external parties, depends on how activities within the entity's control are performed.

However, achievement of operations objectives—such as a particular return on investment, market share, or entry into new product lines—is not always within the entity's control. Internal control cannot prevent bad judgment or decisions or external events that can cause a business to fail to achieve operations goals. For these objectives, the internal control system can provide reasonable assurance only that management and, in its oversight role, the board are made aware, in a timely manner, of the extent to which the entity is moving toward those objectives.

(v) Internal Control Components

Internal control consists of five interrelated components. These are derived from the way management runs a business and are integrated with the management process. The components presented by the COSO study are shown in Exhibit 2.15 and discussed next.

1. **Control environment.** The core of any business is its people—their individual attributes, including integrity, ethical values, and competence—and the environment in which they operate. They are the engine that drives the entity and the foundation on which everything rests.

2. **Risk assessment.** The entity must be aware of and deal with the risks it faces. It must set objectives, integrated with sales, production, marketing, financial, and other activities, so that the organization is operating in concert. It must also establish mechanisms to identify, analyze, and manage the related risks.

3. **Control activities.** Control policies and procedures must be established and executed to help ensure that the actions identified by management as necessary to address risks to achievement of the entity's objectives are effectively carried out. Examples of control activities include approvals, authorizations, verifications, reconciliations, reviews of operating performance, security of assets, and segregation of duties. Types of control activities can include preventive controls, detective controls, manual controls, computer controls, and management controls. The policy, whether written or not, it must be implemented thoughtfully, conscientiously, and consistently. Controls are also classified into two categories: (a) hard controls and (b) soft controls. Hard controls are formal, tangible, and easier to measure and evaluate than soft controls. Examples of hard controls include budgets, dual controls, written approvals, reconciliations, authorization levels, verifications, and segregation of duties. Soft controls are informal, intangible, subjective, and difficult to measure and evaluate. Examples of soft controls include an organization's ethical climate, integrity, values, culture, vision, people's behaviors and attitudes, commitment to competence, tone at the top, management philosophy and operating style, level of understanding and commitment, and communication. Tools to evaluate hard controls include flowcharts, system narratives, testing, and counting. Tools to evaluate soft controls include self-assessments, questionnaires, interviews, and workshops. Generally speaking, senior managers most often use soft skills and soft controls to achieve their objectives; other managers most often use hard skills and hard controls. Soft skills include people skills such as interpersonal skills, motivation, leadership, and communications skills. Hard skills include technical skills such as functional skills, problem identification and solving skills, and decision-making skills.

4. **Information and communication.** Activities include information and communication systems. These systems enable the entity's people to capture and exchange the information needed to conduct, manage, and control its operations.

5. **Monitoring.** The entire process must be monitored, and modifications must be made as necessary. In this way, the system can react dynamically, changing as conditions warrant.

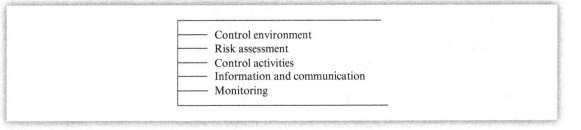

Control environment
Risk assessment
Control activities
Information and communication
Monitoring

EXHIBIT 2.15 Five Components of Internal Control

(vi) Tiered Approach to Audits

When there is a conflict between the choices, the COSO-based approach should not override the risk-based approach to audits. Self-assessment questionnaires, which are soft controls, can be applied at any organizational level (first tier). The second tier is the activity level (e.g., process, subprocess, function, or department). Hard controls, such as documenting and testing control activities, are evaluated during the second tier. The best approach is analytical, starting from objectives, identifying risks and controls, evaluating the design of the controls, and testing control effectiveness.

(vii) Relationship of Internal Control Objectives and Components

There is a direct relationship between objectives, which are what an entity strives to achieve, and components, which represent what is needed to achieve the objectives. Information is needed for all three objective categories—to manage business operations effectively, to prepare financial statements reliably, and to determine compliance. All five components are applicable and important to achievement of operations objectives. Each component cuts across and applies to all three objectives categories. Examples are listed next.

- Financial and nonfinancial data generated from internal and external sources, which are part of the information and communication component, are needed to manage business operations effectively, develop reliable financial statements, and determine that the entity is complying with applicable laws.

- Also relevant to all three objectives categories is the establishment and execution of control policies and procedures to ensure that management plans, programs, and other directives are carried out—representing the control activities component.

(viii) Responsibility for Internal Controls

Who is responsible for establishing and ensuring an adequate and effective internal control environment within the organization? It is the management, the audit committee, and the board of directors—not the auditors. Auditors are responsible for ensuring an adequate and effective system of internal control in the organization. Here the term *management* refers to senior management, operating management, and department/section management. The term *auditors* refers to both internal and external (independent) auditors. For example, company management is responsible for ensuring the adequacy of disclosures in the financial statements of a publicly held company.

According to the COSO study, everyone in an organization has responsibility for internal control: management, board of directors, internal auditors, and other personnel.

WHAT INTERNAL CONTROLS CAN AND CANNOT DO

What internal controls do. Internal controls can help an entity achieve its performance and profitability targets and can prevent loss of resources. They can help ensure reliable financial reporting. And they can help ensure that the enterprise complies with laws and regulations, avoiding damage to its reputation and other consequences. In sum, internal controls can help an entity get to where it wants to go and avoid pitfalls and surprises along the way.

What internal controls cannot do. Unfortunately, some people have greater, and unrealistic, expectations. They look for absolutes, believing that

- Internal controls can ensure an entity's success—that is, they will ensure achievement of basic objectives or will, at the least, ensure survival.

  Even effective internal controls can only help an entity achieve these objectives. It can provide information to management about the entity's progress, or lack of it, toward the achievement of the objectives. But internal controls cannot transform an inherently poor manager into a good one. And shifts in government policy or programs, competitor's actions, or economic conditions can be beyond management's control. Internal controls cannot ensure success or even survival.

- Internal controls can ensure the reliability of financial reporting and compliance with laws and regulations.

  This belief is also unwarranted. An internal control system, no matter how well conceived and operated, can provide only reasonable—not absolute—assurance to management and the board regarding achievement of an entity's objectives. The likelihood of achievement is affected by limitations inherent in all internal control systems. These limitations include the realities that judgments in decision making can be faulty and control breakdowns can occur because of a simple error or mistake.

  Additionally, controls can be circumvented by the collusion of two or more people, and management has the ability to override the system. Another limiting factor is that the design of an internal control system must reflect the fact that there are resource constraints, and the benefits of controls must be considered relative to their costs.

Thus, while internal controls can help an entity achieve its objectives, they are not panaceas.

(A) Management The chief executive officer (CEO) is ultimately responsible and should assume ownership of the system. More than any other individual, the CEO sets the tone at the top that affects integrity and ethics and other factors of a positive control environment.

In a large company, the CEO fulfills this duty by providing leadership and direction to senior managers and reviewing the way they are controlling the business. Senior managers, in turn, assign responsibility for establishment of more specific internal control policies and procedures to personnel responsible for the unit's functions.

In a smaller entity, the influence of the CEO, often an owner-manager, is usually more direct. In any event, in a cascading responsibility, a manager is effectively a chief executive of his or her sphere of responsibility. Of particular significance are financial officers and their staffs, whose control activities cut across, as well as up and down, the operating and other units of an enterprise.

(B) Board of Directors Management is accountable to the board of directors, which provides governance, guidance, and oversight. Effective board members are objective, capable, and inquisitive. They also have knowledge of the entity's activities and environment and commit

the time necessary to fulfill their board responsibilities. Management may be in a position to override controls and ignore or stifle communications from subordinates, enabling a dishonest management that intentionally misrepresents results to cover its tracks. A strong, active board, particularly when coupled with effective upward communications channels and capable financial, legal, and internal audit functions, is often best able to identify and correct such a problem.

(C) Internal Auditors Internal auditors play an important role in evaluating the effectiveness of a control system and contribute to its ongoing effectiveness. Because of its organizational position and authority in an entity, an internal audit function often plays a significant monitoring role.

(D) Other Personnel Internal controls are, to some degree, the responsibility of everyone in an organization and therefore should be an explicit or implicit part of everyone's job descriptions. Virtually all employees produce information used in the internal control system or take other actions needed to effect control. Also, all personnel should be responsible for communicating upward problems in operation, noncompliance with the code of conduct, or other policy violations or illegal actions.

A number of external parties often contribute to the achievement of an entity's objectives. External auditors, bringing an independent and objective view, contribute directly through the financial statement audit and indirectly by providing information useful to management and the board in carrying out their responsibilities. Others providing information to the entity useful in effecting internal control are legislators and regulators, customers, and others transacting business with the enterprise, financial analysts, bond raters, and the news media. External parties, however, are not responsible for, nor are they a part of, the entity's internal control system.

(ix) Limitations of Internal Controls

Some observers, such as COSO, have viewed internal control systems as ensuring that an entity will not fail—that is, the entity will always achieve its operations, financial reporting, and compliance objectives.[1] In this sense, internal controls sometimes are looked on as a cure-all for all real and potential business ills. This view is misguided. Internal controls are not panaceas.

In considering limitations of internal controls, two distinct concepts must be recognized.

1. Internal controls—even effective internal controls—operate at different levels with respect to different objectives. For objectives related to the effectiveness and efficiency of an entity's operations—achievement of its basic mission, profitability goals, and the like—internal controls can help to ensure that management is aware of the entity's progress, or lack of it. But they cannot provide even reasonable assurance that the objectives themselves will be achieved. The first set of limitations acknowledges that certain events or conditions are simply outside management's control.

2. Internal controls cannot provide absolute assurance with respect to any of the three objectives categories (i.e., effectiveness and efficiency of operations, reliability of financial reporting, and compliance with applicable laws and regulations). The second set of limitations has to do with the reality that no system will always do what it is intended to do. The best that can be expected in any internal control system is that reasonable assurance is obtained.

---

[1] Committee of Sponsoring Organizations of the Treadway Commission (COSO), *Internal Control—Integrated Framework*, 1992.

COSO'S INTERNAL CONTROL STANDARDS SUMMARY

Five component standards include control environment, risk assessment, control activities, information and communication, and monitoring. Each standard is presented next along with its major factors or subcomponents.

Standard 1: Control Environment

1.1 Integrity and ethical values

1.2 Commitment to competence

1.3 Management's philosophy and operating style

1.4 Organizational structure

1.5 Assignment of authority and responsibility

1.6 Human resources policies and practices

1.7 Oversight groups

Standard 2: Risk Assessment

2.1 Risk identification

2.2 Risk analysis

2.3 Managing risk during change

Standard 3: Control Activities

3.1 Types of control activities

3.2 Integration with risk assessment

3.3 Control over information systems

3.4 Entity-specific control activities

Standard 4: Information and Communication

4.1 Information

4.2 Communications

4.3 Means of communicating

Standard 5: Monitoring

5.1 Ongoing monitoring activities

5.2 Separate evaluations

5.3 Internal reporting of deficiencies

(x) Factors to Be Considered When Understanding Limitations of Internal Control

Six factors need to be considered when understanding limitations of internal controls. These factors include reasonable assurance, judgment, control breakdowns, management override, collusion, and costs versus benefits (see Exhibit 2.16).

1. **Reasonable assurance.** Reasonable assurance certainly does not imply that an internal control system will fail frequently. Many factors, individually and collectively, serve to provide strength to the concept of reasonable assurance. The cumulative effect of controls that satisfy multiple objectives and the multipurpose nature of controls reduce the risk that an entity may not achieve its objectives. However, because of the inherent limitations discussed earlier, there is no guarantee that, for example, an uncontrollable event, a mistake, or an improper reporting incident could never occur. In other words,

even an effective internal control system can experience a failure. *Reasonable assurance is not absolute assurance.*

2. **Judgment.** The effectiveness of controls will be limited by the realities of human frailty in the making of business decisions. Such decisions must be made with human judgment in the time available, based on information at hand, and under the pressures of the conduct of business. In hindsight, some decisions based on human judgment may later be found to produce less than desirable results and may need to be changed.

   The nature of internal control–related decisions that must be made based on human judgment is described further in the discussions of control breakdowns, management override, and costs versus benefits.

3. **Control breakdowns.** Even if internal controls are well designed, they can break down. Personnel may misunderstand instructions. They may make judgment mistakes. Or they may commit errors due to carelessness, distraction, or fatigue. Temporary personnel executing control duties for vacationing or sick employees might not perform correctly. System changes may be implemented before personnel have been trained to react appropriately to signs of incorrect functioning.

4. **Management override.** An internal control system can be only as effective as the people who are responsible for its functioning are. Even in effectively controlled entities—those with generally high levels of integrity and control consciousness—a manager might be able to override internal controls.

   The term "management override" is used here to mean overruling prescribed policies or procedures for illegitimate purposes with the intent of personal gain or an enhanced presentation of an entity's financial condition or compliance status. Override practices include deliberate misrepresentations to bankers, lawyers, accountants, and vendors and intentionally issuing false documents, such as purchase orders and sales invoices.

   Management override should not be confused with management intervention, which represents management's action to depart from prescribed policies or procedures for legitimate purposes. Management intervention is necessary to deal with nonrecurring and nonstandard transactions or events that otherwise might be handled inappropriately by the control system.

   Provision for management intervention is necessary in all internal control systems because no system can be designed to anticipate every condition. Management's actions to intervene are generally overt and commonly documented or otherwise disclosed to appropriate personnel, whereas actions to override usually are not documented or disclosed, with an intent to cover up the actions.

———— Reasonable assurance (not absolute assurance)
———— Judgment
———— Control breakdowns
———— Management override of internal controls
———— Collusion
———— Costs versus benefits

EXHIBIT 2.16 Factors to Be Considered When Understanding Limitations of Internal Control

> **MANAGEMENT OVERRIDE VERSUS MANAGEMENT INTERVENTION**
>
> ■ "Management override" means departing from prescribed policies or procedures for illegitimate purposes and is not documented or disclosed.
>
> ■ "Management intervention" means departing from prescribed policies or procedures for legitimate purposes and is documented or disclosed.

5. **Collusion.** The collusive activities of two or more individuals can result in control failures. Individuals acting collectively to perpetrate and conceal an action from detection often can alter financial data or other management information in a manner that cannot be identified by the control system. For example, there may be collusion between an employee performing an important control function and a customer, supplier, or another employee. On a different level, several layers of sales or divisional management might collude in circumventing controls so that reported results meet budgets or incentive targets.

6. **Costs versus benefits.** Resources always have constraints, and entities must consider the relative costs and benefits of establishing controls. In determining whether a particular control should be established, the risk of failure and the potential effect on the entity are considered along with the related costs of establishing a new control.

   Costs and benefit measurements for implementing controls are done with different levels of precision. Generally, it is easier to deal with the cost side of the equation, which, in many cases, can be quantified in a fairly precise manner. The benefit side often requires an even more subjective valuation. Nevertheless, certain factors can be considered in assessing potential benefits: the likelihood of the undesired condition occurring, the nature of the activities, and the potential financial or operating effect the event might have on the entity.

   The complexity of the cost/benefit determination is compounded by the interrelationship of controls with business operations. Where controls are integrated with, or built in to, management and business processes, it is difficult to isolate either their costs or their benefits.

   Similarly, many times a variety of controls may serve, individually or together, to mitigate a particular risk. Cost/benefit determinations also vary considerably depending on the nature of the business. High-risk activities definitely require cost/benefit analysis while low-risk activities might not.

   The challenge is to find the right balance. Excessive control is costly and counterproductive. For example, customers making telephone orders will not tolerate order acceptance procedures that are too cumbersome or time consuming. Too little control, however, presents undue risk of bad debts. An appropriate balance is needed in a highly competitive environment. And, despite the difficulties, cost/benefit decisions will continue to be made.

(b) CoCo Model in Canada

The Canadian Institute of Chartered Accountants (CICA) has issued several "Criteria of Control" (CoCo) as a framework for making judgments about control. The term "control" has a broader meaning than internal control over financial reporting. CoCo defines control as "those elements of an organization (including its resources, systems, processes, culture, structure, and tasks) that, taken together, support people in the achievement of the organization's objectives." It defines three categories of objectives:

1. Effectiveness and efficiency of operations

2. Reliability of internal external reporting

3. Compliance with applicable laws, regulations, and internal policies

CoCo is the basis for understanding control in an organization and for making judgments about its effectiveness. The criteria are formulated to be broadly applicable. The effectiveness of control in any organization, regardless of the objective it serves, can be assessed using these criteria. The criteria are phrased as goals to be worked toward over time; they are not minimum requirements to be passed or failed.

CoCo defines four types of criteria: purpose, commitment, capability, and monitoring and learning. The *purpose* type groups criteria that provide a sense of the organization's direction and address objectives (including mission, vision, and strategy); risks (and opportunities); policies; planning; and performance targets and indicators. The *commitment* type groups criteria that provide a sense of the organization's identity and values and address ethical values, including integrity, human resource policies, authority, responsibility, accountability, and mutual trust. The *capability* type groups criteria that provide a sense of the organization's competence and address knowledge, skills, and tools; communication processes; information; coordination; and control activities. The *monitoring and learning* type groups criteria that provide a sense of the organization's evolution and address monitoring internal and external environment, monitoring performance, challenging assumptions, reassessing information needs and IS, follow-up procedures, and assessing the effectiveness of control.

(c) Control Self-Assessment Model

Control self-assessment (CSA) deals with evaluating the system of internal control in any organization. CSA is a shared responsibility among all employees in the organization, not just internal auditing or senior management. The examination of the internal control environment is conducted within a structured, documented, and repetitive process. The formal assessment approach takes place in workshop sessions with business users as participants (process owners) and internal auditors as facilitators (subject matter experts) and as nonfacilitators (note takers). The purpose of the sessions is conversation and mutual discovery and information sharing.

(i) Elements of CSA
CSA has five elements:

1. Up-front planning and preliminary audit work

2. The gathering of process owners with a meeting facilitator

3. A structured agenda to examine the process's risks and controls

4. A note taker and electronic voting technology to input comments and opinions

5. Reporting the results and the development of corrective action plans

(ii) Scope of CSA
CSA can be done either as a stand-alone project or as a supplement to traditional audit work. CSA is not suitable to situations such as finding fraud or compliance reviews (e.g., regulatory audits), or when participants have conflicting objectives, as in third-party contracts. CSA can be applied

to numerous situations, business issues, and industries, regardless of size. It is a management tool that has equal application to horizontal (organization-wide), vertical (single department), or diagonal (process inquiries) issues.

(iii) Effect on Auditors

CSA can be used to assess business and financial statement risks, control activities, ethical values, and control effectiveness; the controls that mitigate those risks; and overall compliance with policies and procedures.

During the assessment process, there is a constant interactive dialogue between the auditor and the auditee as well as between the auditees. This interaction increases communication and builds trust and confidence between each party. At the same time, it is educational to both parties because there is a knowledge transfer between the auditor and the auditee. The auditors will have a greater knowledge of business functions, while the auditees will have a better understanding of and appreciation for controls and the business process of which they are a part.

The increased communication and the knowledge transfer adds value to the organization in these ways:

- Auditors accomplish control assessment.
- Auditees understand the purpose of controls.
- Management takes responsibility for the development and maintenance of the control environment.
- Process improvement issues are identified and resolved (i.e., implemented or deferred).

(iv) Interrelationships Among CSA, CoCo, and COSO

CSA can be an effective tool for accomplishing the objectives of both CoCo and COSO. CSA acts as a link to the CoCo and COSO.

The CSA audit can address the four elements of the CoCo framework (i.e., purpose, commitment, capability, and monitoring and learning). Both commitment and capability are examples of soft controls (e.g., risk assessment, the achievement of business objectives and goals, and the attitude of people toward controls).

(v) Conclusion

CSA is a dynamic business process improvement and control-enhancing technique. In relation to internal auditing, CSA is like total quality management and continuous process improvement techniques in relation to other parts of the organization. The only difference is how the CSA program is implemented in each organization, but the benefits are real and long lasting.

(d) Cadbury Report in the United Kingdom

The Cadbury Report of the Committee on the Financial Aspects of Corporate Governance issued in December 1992 consists of internal controls, fraud, audit (internal and external), financial reporting practices, audit committees, shareholders, corporate governance, the board of directors, and the code of best practice.

Regarding internal controls, the report says that directors maintain a system of internal controls over the financial management of the company, including procedures designed to minimize the risk of fraud. The directors should make a statement in the report and accounts on the effectiveness of their system of internal control and the auditors should report thereon.

Regarding fraud, the report says that prime responsibility for the prevention and detection of fraud and other illegal acts is that of the board, as part of its fiduciary responsibility for protecting the assets of the company. The auditor's responsibility is to properly plan, perform, and evaluate his or her audit work so as to have a reasonable expectation of detecting material misstatements in the financial statements.

Regarding the internal audit, the report states that the function of internal auditors is complementary to, but different from, that of external (outside) auditors. The committee regards the internal audit as good practice for companies to establish internal audit function to undertake regular monitoring of key controls and procedures. Such regular monitoring is an integral part of a company's system of internal control and helps to ensure its effectiveness. An internal audit function is well placed to undertake investigations on behalf of the audit committee and to follow up any suspicion of fraud. It is essential that heads of internal audit should have unrestricted access to the chairman of the audit committee in order to ensure the independence of their position.

Regarding the external audit, the report says that an essential first step is to be clear about the respective responsibilities of directors and external auditors for preparing and reporting on the financial statements of companies, in order to begin to narrow the expectations gap. This gap is due to lack of understanding of the nature and extent of the external auditors' role. The gap is the difference between what audits do achieve and what it is thought they achieve or should achieve. The expectations gap is damaging not only because it reflects unrealistic expectations of audits but also because it has led various interested parties to become disenchanted with the value of audits.

The external auditors' role is to report whether the financial statements give a true and fair view, and the audit is designed to provide a reasonable assurance that the financial statements are free of material misstatements. The auditors' role is not (to cite a few of the misunderstandings) to prepare the financial statements, or to provide absolute assurance that the figures in the financial statements are correct, or to provide a guarantee that the company will continue to exist.

(e) Turnbull Model in the United Kingdom

In 1998, the London Stock Exchange developed a combined code for corporate governance. The code requires that company directors should, at least annually, conduct a review of the effectiveness of the system of internal control and should report to shareholders that they have reviewed the effectiveness of all three types of controls, including financial, operational, and compliance control.

(f) King Model in South Africa

The Institute of Directors in South Africa has established the King Committee on Corporate Governance that produced the King Report in 1994. The committee has developed a Code of Corporate Practices and Conduct, and compliance with the code is a requirement to be listed in the Johannesburg Securities Exchange in South Africa.

(g) KonTraG Model in Germany

In 1998, the German government proposed changes for the reform of corporate governance. The model affects control and transparency in business. Specifically, it impacts the board of directors, supervisory board, corporate capitalization principles, authorization of no-par-value shares, small nonlisted stock corporations, banks investing in industrial companies, and the acceptance of internationally recognized accounting standards.

2.4 Risk Vocabulary and Concepts

Risk vocabulary as it relates to general risk management and enterprise risk management is presented here from a conceptual viewpoint. Both general risk management and enterprise risk management address loss control, risk financing, and risk control, but in a different way.

Audit risk
The risk that the auditor may unknowingly fail to appropriately modify his or her opinion on financial statements that are materially misstated. It is also defined as the risk that an auditor may fail to detect a significant error or weakness during an examination.
Audit risk is equal to inherent risk multiplied by control risk and by detection risk. Inherent risk is the susceptibility of a management assertion to a material misstatement, assuming that there are no related internal control structure policies or procedures. Control risk is the risk that a material misstatement in a management assertion will not be prevented or detected on a timely basis by the entity's internal control structure policies or procedures. Detection risk is the risk that the auditor will not detect a material misstatement present in a management assertion.

Residual risk
The risk remaining after management takes action to reduce the impact and likelihood of an adverse event, including control activities in responding to a risk. Residual risk is current risk, which, in turn, is called managed risk with existing control systems. Residual risk is calculated as potential risks minus covered risks, resulting in uncovered risk.
Several equations are available to express residual risks:

$$\text{Residual risks} = \text{Total risks} - \text{Mitigated risks}$$
$$\text{Residual risks} = \text{Potential risks} - \text{Covered risks}$$
$$\text{Residual risks} = \text{Total risks} - \text{Control measures applied}$$
$$\text{Residual risks} = \text{Potential risks} - \text{Countermeasures applied}$$
$$\text{Residual risks} = \text{Uncovered or unaddressed risks}$$

Risk
The possibility of an event occurring that will have an impact on the achievement of objectives. Risk is measured in terms of impact and likelihood. Risks can be classified or categorized into three types: static versus dynamic, subjective versus objective, and pure versus speculative. Risk is uncertainty about loss. Risks should be avoided where possible; if not, they should be managed well. There are at least six types of risks, including pure, strategic, operational, financial, hazard, and speculative.

Risk management
The total process of identifying, assessing, controlling, and mitigating risks as it deals with uncertainty. It includes risk assessment (risk analysis); cost/benefit analysis; the selection,

implementation, test, and evaluation of safeguards (risk mitigation); risk financing (risk funding); and risk monitoring (reporting, feedback, and evaluation). It is expressed as:

Risk management = Risk assessment + Risk mitigation + Risk financing + Risk monitoring

The ultimate goal of risk management is to minimize the adverse effects of losses and uncertainty connected with pure risks. Pure risks are those in which there is a chance of loss or no loss only (e.g., default of a debtor or disability). Pure risks are of several types, including personal risks, property risks, liability risks, and performance risks. Risk management is broken down into two major categories: risk control and risk financing.

Risk acceptance

Accepting a potential risk and continuing with operating a process or system. It is like accepting risks as part of doing business (a kind of self-insurance). Risk acceptance is also called risk tolerance and risk appetite in order to achieve a desired result.

Risk retention

Most appropriate for situations in which there is a low probability of occurrence (frequency) with a low potential severity. Such risks seldom occur, and, when they do happen, the financial impact is small or negligible. Severity dictates whether a risk should be retained. If the potential severity is more than the organization can afford, retention is not recommended. Frequency determines whether the risk is economically insurable. The higher the probabilities of loss, the higher the expected value of loss and the higher the cost of transfer.

Risk appetite

The level of risk that an organization is willing to accept.

Risk assessment

Includes identification, analysis, measurement, and prioritization of risks. Risk assessment (or risk analysis) is the process of identifying the risks and determining the probability of occurrence, the resulting impact, and additional safeguards that would mitigate this impact. It includes risk measurement and prioritization.

Risk assignment

Consists of transferring or assigning risk to a third party by using other options to compensate for the loss, such as an insurance company or outsourcing firm.

Risk avoidance

Eliminates the risk causes and/or consequences (e.g., add controls that prevent the risk from occurring, remove certain functions of the system, or shut down the system when risks are identified). It is like reducing, avoiding, or eliminating risks by implementing cost-effective safeguards and controls. Risk situations that have high severity and high frequency of loss should be either avoided or reduced. Risk reduction is appropriate when it is possible to reduce either the severity or the frequency. Otherwise, the risk should be avoided or transferred. Examples of risk avoidance controls include (1) separating threats from assets or assets from threats to minimize risks and (2) separating resource allocation from resource use to prevent resource misuse.

Risk control

Identifies the presence or lack of effective controls in the form of prevention, detection, and correction of risks. Risk control focuses on minimizing the risk of loss to which an organization is exposed. The situation of high frequency and low severity should be managed with additional controls (loss control). Risk control includes risk avoidance and risk reduction.

Risk financing

Concentrates on arranging the availability of internal funds to meet occurring financial losses. It also involves external transfer of risk. Risk financing includes risk retention and risk transfer, a tool used by captive insurers. Risk retention applies to risks that have a low expected frequency and a low potential severity. Risk transfer applies to risks that have a low expected frequency and a high potential severity (e.g., buying insurance). Insurance should be purchased for losses in excess of a firm's risk retention level.

When losses have both high expected frequency and high potential severity, it is likely that risk retention, risk transfer, and loss control all will need to be used in varying degrees. Common methods of loss control include reducing the probability of losses (i.e., frequency and severity reduction) and decreasing the cost of losses that do occur (i.e., cost reduction). Note that "high" and "low" loss frequency and severity rates are defined differently for different firms.

Risk financing includes internal funding for risks (self-insurance and residual risk) and external transfer of risks, such as insurance and hedging. It can be unfunded or funded retention. The unfunded retention is treated as part of the overall cost of doing business. A firm may decide to practice funded retention by making various preloss arrangements to ensure that money is readily available to pay for losses that occur. Examples of funded retention include use of credit, reserve funds, self-insurance, and captive insurers.

Risk limitation

Limiting or containing risks by implementing controls that minimize the adverse impact of a threat's exercising a vulnerability (e.g., use of supporting, preventive, and detective controls) or by authorizing operation for a limited time during which additional risk mitigation efforts by other means is installed.

Risk mapping

Involves profiling risk events to their sources (i.e., threats and vulnerabilities), determining their impact levels (i.e., low, medium, or high), and evaluating the presence of or lack of effective controls to mitigate risks.

Risk mitigation

Involves implementation of preventive, detective, and corrective controls along with management, operational, and technical controls to reduce the effects of risks. Risk mitigation includes designing and implementing controls and control-related procedures to minimize risks.

Risk monitoring

Addresses internal and external reporting and provides feedback into the risk assessment process, continuing the loop.

Risk transfer

Involves payment by one party (the transferor) to another party (the transferee, or risk bearer). Five forms of risk transfer are (1) hold-harmless agreements, (2) incorporation, (3) diversification, (4) hedging, and (5) insurance. Risk transfer is most likely ideal for a risk with a low expected frequency and a high potential severity.

Alternative risk-transfer tools

Five alternative risk-transfer tools, other than traditional insurance, exist. Of the five, multiple-trigger policies and risk securitization tools are more commonly used. The alternative risk-transfer tools include:

1. **Captive insurance methods,** where a noninsurance firm is created for the purpose of accepting the risk of the parent firm who owns an insurer. Here, a parent firm establishes a subsidiary (called captive insurance company) to finance its retained losses. Captives combine risk transfer and risk retention.

2. **Financial insurance contracts,** which are based on spreading risk over time, as opposed to across a pool of similar exposures. These contracts usually involve a sharing of the investment returns between the insurer and the insured.

3. **Multiline/multiyear insurance contracts,** which combine a broad array of risks (multiline) into a contract with a policy period that extends over multiple years (multiyear). For example, a pure risk may be combined with a financial risk.

4. **Multiple-trigger policies,** which reflect the source of the risk, are not as important as the impact of the risk on the earnings of the firm. A pure risk is combined with a financial risk. The policy is triggered, and payment is made, only upon the occurrence of an adverse event.

5. **Risk securitization,** which involves the creation of securities such as bonds, or derivatives contracts, options, swaps, futures, that have a payout or price movement linked to an insurance risk. Examples include catastrophe options, earthquake bonds, catastrophe bonds, and catastrophe equity puts.

Risk registers

Document the risks below the strategic level and include inherent risks (high or higher) and unchanged residual risks, lack of or ineffectiveness of key internal controls, and lack of mitigating factors (e.g., contingency plans and monitoring activities). Risk registers provide direct links among risk categories, risk aspects, audit universe, and internal controls.

Risk spreading or sharing

Involves spreading and sharing risks with other divisions or business units of the same organization. Risk sharing is viewed as a special case of risk transfer, in which the risk is transferred from an individual to a group, from one division to another, or from one business unit to another. Risk sharing is a form of risk retention, depending on the success of the risk sharing arrangement.

Financial risks

Risks arising from volatility in foreign currencies, interest rates, and commodities. They include credit risk, liquidity risk (bankruptcy risk), interest rate risk, and market risk.

Hazard risks

Risks that are insurable, such as natural disasters, various insurable liabilities, impairment of physical assets and property, and terrorism.

Strategic risk

A high-level and corporate-wide risk, which includes strategy risk, political risk, economic risk, regulatory risk, reputation risk, global risk, leadership risk, customer risk, and market brand management risk. It is also related to failure of strategy and changing customer needs and business conditions.

Operational risk

A risk related to the organization's internal systems, products, services, processes, technology, and people.

Hazard

A condition that creates or increases the probability of a loss. Three types of hazards exist: (1) physical hazard, (2) moral hazard, and (3) morale hazard. Physical hazard is a condition of the subject of insurance that creates or increases the chance of loss, such as structural defects, occupancy, or similar conditions. Moral hazard is a dishonest predisposition on the part of an insured that increases the chance of loss. Morale hazard is a careless attitude on the part of an insured that increases the chance of loss or causes losses to be greater than would otherwise be the case.

Hedging

Taking a position opposite to the exposure or risk. This can be done with financial derivatives, such as futures contracts, forward contracts, options, and swaps. A perfect hedge is not possible because financial derivatives used to hedge do not move together, leaving some risk. The goal of hedging is to minimize risk. A value is created for shareholders if corporate hedging does not duplicate the shareholders' "homemade" hedging.

Natural hedges

Hedges created from the relationship between revenues and costs of a business unit or a subsidiary. The more revenues over the cost, the better protection is. The key is the extent to which cash flows adjust naturally to currency changes due to exchange-rate fluctuations. One way to explore the likelihood of a natural hedge is to determine whether a subsidiary's revenue and cost functions are sensitive to domestic or global business conditions.

Many types of risks may be relatively correlated with each other. Consequently, combining these risks produces a form of natural hedging. The traditional silo approach could actually reduce the overall efficiency of the firm's risk management activities by destroying the natural hedging that exists at the enterprise-wide level.

Insurance

An economic device whereby an individual or a corporation substitutes a small certain cost (the premium) for a large uncertain financial loss (the claim, or contingency insured against) that would exist if it were not for the insurance policy (contract). Insurance is most appropriate for situations in where there is a low frequency and a high severity of occurrence. Insurance is a risk transfer mechanism.

Insurable interest

An interest that might be damaged if the peril insured against occurs; the possibility of a financial loss to an individual or a corporation that can be protected against through insurance.

Self-insurance

A risk-retention program that incorporates elements of the insurance mechanism where the self-insured organization pays the claims rather than an insurance company.

Peril

The cause of possible loss, the event insured against. *Open peril* describes a broad form of property insurance in which coverage applies to loss arising from any fortuitous cause other than those perils or causes specifically excluded.

Portfolio risk

A risk that considers risk and return of a firm when it is investing in acquisition or expansion projects. Management needs to find the relationship between the net present values (NPVs) for new projects and the NPVs for existing projects. In a portfolio framework, the trade-off between risk and expected NPV for different combinations of investments can be analyzed.

Pure risk

A condition in which there is the possibility of loss or no loss (e.g., default of a debtor or disability). Risk is a possibility of loss. Many types of risks exist, including pure risk, speculative risk, static risk, dynamic risk, subjective risk, and objective risk. Pure risks are of several types. Including personal risks, property risks, liability risks, and performance risks. Risk management is a scientific approach to the problem of dealing with the pure risks facing an individual or an organization. In risk management, insurance is viewed as simply one of several approaches for dealing with pure risks. The techniques of insurance and self-insurance are commonly limited to the treatment of pure risks, such as fire, product liability, and worker's compensation.

Traditionally, the risk management tools—avoidance, loss control, and transfer—are applied primarily to the pure or hazard risks facing a firm.

Speculative risk

The risk that exists when there is uncertainty about an event that could produce either a profit or a loss. It involves the chance of loss or gain (e.g., hedging, options, and derivatives).

Static risk

A risk, which can be either pure or speculative, that stems from an unchanging society that is in stable equilibrium. Examples of pure static risk include uncertainties due to such random events as lightning, windstorms, and death. Business undertakings in a stable economy illustrate the concept of speculative static risk.

Dynamic risk

Risk that is produced because of changes in society, in contrast to static risks. Dynamic risks also can be either pure or speculative. Examples of sources of dynamic risk include urban unrest, increasingly complex technology, and changing attitude of legislatures and courts about a variety of issues.

Subjective risk

Refers to the mental state of an individual who experiences doubt or worry as to the outcome of a given event. In addition to being subjective, a particular risk may be either pure or speculative and either static or dynamic.

Objective risk

Risk that differs from subjective risk primarily in the sense that it is more precisely observable and therefore measurable. In general, objective risk is the probable variation of actual from expected experience.

2.5 Fraud Risk Awareness

Topics covered in this section include nature of fraud, types of fraud, risk factors, red flags, symptoms of fraud, and acts and profiles of fraud perpetrators.

(a) Nature of Fraud

(i) Overview of Fraud

What is fraud? Here is the legal definition of fraud by most statutes:

> Fraud is a generic term and embraces all the multifarious means that human ingenuity can devise, which are resorted to by one individual, to get an advantage over another by false representations. It includes all surprise, trick, cunning, and unfair ways by which another is cheated.

Fraud is a term of law, applied to certain facts as a conclusion from them, but is not in itself a fact. It has been defined as any cunning deception or artifice used to cheat or deceive another.

Cheat and defraud means every kind of trick and deception, from false representation and intimidation to suppression and concealment of any fact and information by which a party is induced to part with property for less than its value or to give more than it is worth for the property of another. The terms *fraud* and *bad faith* are synonymous when applied to the conduct of public offenders.

(ii) Types of Fraud

There are many varieties of frauds, limited only by the ingenuity of the perpetrators. Fraud can be classified in a number of ways from a discovery point of view. The reason for this classification is that different approaches and procedures are required to discover each type of fraud and to control the occurrence of each type.

Davia and coauthors present four types of fraud: (1) theft of assets, (2) fraud by frequency, (3) fraud by conspiracy, and (4) varieties of fraud (see Exhibit 2.17).[2]

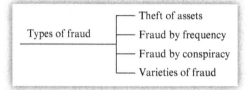

Types of fraud	─ Theft of assets
	─ Fraud by frequency
	─ Fraud by conspiracy
	─ Varieties of fraud

EXHIBIT 2.17 Types of Fraud

(A) Theft of Assets Theft of assets is classified into three categories.

1. Theft of assets that appears openly on the books as distinct accounting entries (fraud open on the books are the least difficult to discover)

2. Theft of assets that appears on the books but is hidden as a part of other, larger otherwise legitimate accounting entries (fraud hidden on the books)

3. Theft of assets that is not on the books and could never be detected by an examination of "booked" accounting transactions (fraud off the books, most difficult to discover)

Fraud open on the books includes criminal acts that involve discrete entries in the accounting records. Here the term *discrete entry* means that the fraud involves the entire transaction; if that transaction is selected by an auditor for examination, this type of fraud offers the best chance for discovery (e.g., a fraudulent duplicate payment that stands by it).

Fraud hidden on the books involves acts of fraud that are included in accounting entries that appear on the books, but are not discrete entries. That is, the amount of the fraud is always buried in a larger, legitimate accounting entry, never appearing as a discrete amount (e.g., kickbacks).

In **fraud off the books,** the amount of the fraud is neither a discrete accounting entry nor a hidden part of an accounting entry. It is the loss of a valuable asset for the victim. Examples include diverting vending machine sales money and conversion of payment on accounts receivable that have been written off.

(B) Fraud by Frequency Another way of classifying fraud is by its frequency of occurrence: nonrepeating or repeating. In nonrepeating fraud, a fraudulent act, even though repeated many times, is singular in nature in that it must be triggered by the perpetrator each time (e.g., a weekly payroll check requires a time card every week in order to generate the fraudulent paycheck).

In repeating fraud, a defrauding act may occur many times; however, it needs to be initiated only once. It then keeps running until it is stopped. It could possibly recur in perpetuity (e.g., a salaried payroll check that does not require input each time in order to generate the paycheck. It continues until a stop order is issued).

---

[2] Howard R. Davia, Patrick C. Coggins, John C. Wideman, and Joseph T. Kastantin, *Management Accountant's Guide to Fraud Discovery and Control* (New York: John Wiley & Sons, 1992).

THREE ELEMENTS OF FRAUD

1. An intent to defraud
2. The commission of a fraudulent act
3. The accomplishment of the fraud

For the auditor, the significance of whether a fraud is nonrepeating or repeating lies in where to look for the evidence. For example, the auditor would have to review a computer application program to obtain evidence of a repeating fraud involving skimming of a few cents off every bank customers' account service charge.

(C) Fraud Involving Conspiracy   Fraud can be classified as that involving conspiracy, that which does not involve conspiracy, and that involving partial (pseudo-) conspiracy. Here the word "conspiracy" is synonymous with "collusion." It has been proven that most frauds involve conspiracy, either bona fide or pseudo. In the bona fide conspiracy, all parties involved are fully aware of the fraudulent intent; in the pseudo-conspiracy, one or more of the parties to the fraud is innocent of fraudulent intent.

(D) Varieties of Fraud   The varieties of fraud can be grouped in two categories: (1) specialized fraud, which is unique to people working in certain kinds of business operations, and (2) the garden varieties of fraud, which all people are likely to encounter in general business operations.

Examples of specialized fraud include: embezzlement of assets entrusted by depositors to financial institutions such as banks, savings and loans, credit unions, pension funds (called custodial fraud); and false insurance claims for life, health, auto, and property coverage.

Examples of garden varieties of fraud include kickbacks, defective pricing, unbalanced contracts or purchase orders, reopening completed contracts, duplicate payments, double payments,

---

RISK FACTORS RELATED TO GENERAL FRAUD (RED FLAGS OF CORPORATE FRAUD)

- There is infighting among top management.
- There is low morale and motivation among employees.
- Accounting departments are understaffed.
- There is a high level of complaints against the organization from customers, suppliers, or regulatory authorities.
- Inconsistent and surprising cash flow deficiencies exist.
- Sales or income is decreasing while accounts payable and receivable are rising.
- The company's line of credit is used to its limit for long periods of time.
- There is a significant excess inventory.
- There is an increasing number of year-end adjusting journal entries.

Source: Association of Certified Fraud Examiners, *The White Paper Journal* 7, no. 5 (October/November 1993). Original source: KPMG Canada, *The Fraud Prevention Primer.*

shell payments, and defective delivery. These eight types of fraud are the more common frauds occurring today.

According to Jack Bologna, corporate fraud can be generated internally (perpetrated by directors, officers, employees, or agents of a corporation for or against it or against others) and externally (perpetrated by others—suppliers, vendors, customers, hackers) against a corporation.[3] Bologna includes as a part of corporate fraud management fraud wherein there is intentional overstatement of corporate or division profits. Management fraud is inspired, perpetrated, or induced by managers who seek to benefit in terms of promotions, job stability, larger bonuses, and status symbols.

(b) Risk Factors, Red Flags, and Symptoms of Fraud

(i) Risk Factors in Fraud
Internal auditors should be aware of risk factors related to general fraud as well as computer fraud.

The degree of fraud can be linked to the environment of an organization, as described next.

- **High fraud environment.** Low management integrity, poor control environment, loose accountability, and high pressure for results.
- **Low fraud environment.** A culture of honesty, management openness, and employee assistance programs, and total quality management.

The user-friendliness of computer systems and the increase in user computer literacy combined with a lack of or inadequate system controls could have significant effect on computer crime and fraud. The rewards of computer crime can be greater than other crimes, and there is less chance of being discovered and convicted. Embarrassment, expense, and time are the reasons given for not prosecuting computer criminals. In addition, it is difficult to prove malicious intent. A computer is used as a tool but is also the means to perpetrate fraud. The motivations for, or causes of, computer abuse or fraud include:

- Situational pressures
- Opportunities
- Personal or financial gain
- Revenge

Situational pressures can include when an honest employee becomes addicted to alcohol or drugs or incurs large debts because of gambling. Opportunities are provided by weak policies and procedures and/or a poor system of controls or lack of audit trails. Given the opportunity, dishonest employees will find a shortcut around certain controls. Some employees will steal given any opportunity. System users can reveal system vulnerabilities due to their close working knowledge of the system, both manual and automated. Other causes include personal or financial gain and revenge against employers and coworkers.

Creating a team environment can help employees feel that they are a part of the decision-making process and be content with their job condition. This in turn motivates employees to behave in a normal manner and be less tempted to commit computer crime and fraud.

---

[3] Jack Bologna, *Handbook on Corporate Fraud* (Stoneham, MA: Butterworth-Heinemann, 1993).

(ii) Red Flags for Fraud

Red flags do not signal that a fraud has occurred but rather that the opportunity for a fraud exists. Some examples of red flags are:

- Concealed assets
- Missing or destroyed records and documents
- Split purchases
- Excessive voids or refunds
- Rapid turnover of financial managers and executives

According to Belden Menkus, all types of frauds, including computer frauds, are characterized by certain contributing factors related to the values and motivations of the fraud perpetrator and the management of the defrauded organization.[4] Understanding how computer fraud can occur will not eliminate the menace; however, auditors must ferret out weaknesses and develop counterstrategies. The eight factors that contribute to computer fraud are:

1. **Inadequate design of the information system.** Inadequate design deals with the flaws and errors in the system. The system's performance does not rest on a reliable foundation and its results are not predictable in any reasonable or consistent fashion. This provides opportunity for fraud.

2. **Aggregation of the information system's transaction processing steps so that a review of what is taking place becomes impossible.** The separation of duties within the system may be reduced or eliminated as a result of this information system design technique called chaining. Verification of the operation becomes difficult if not impossible.

3. **Insufficient discrimination as to the legitimacy of the transactions processed by the information system.** Data editing and validation routines at data entry and update activities may not be available or may be too primitive to be of any use.

4. **Error toleration by the information system, either in data content or in processing results.** Users may establish some arbitrary upper limit on individual errors that would disguise fraudulent activity as apparent error. This means that the fraud perpetrator who does not become either greedy or careless is almost impossible for the auditor to detect, except by accident.

5. **Detachment of the information system's ongoing operation from the physical or functional reality that it is supposed to reflect.** For example, an inventory database does not reflect the actual items. In this situation, it is possible for a set of numbers to look right but for them to be essentially worthless.

6. **Unrestrained, unmediated remote access to an information system that is subject to possible compromise or manipulation.** Sometimes it is difficult to isolate the actual identity or even the location of the individual perpetrating the fraud.

7. **Restricted ability to collect sufficient knowledge about the fraud itself—especially its scope and the extent of the loss that has occurred.** The fraud perpetrator may not leave sufficient evidence of his or her actions or the evidence may have been destroyed. This can occur when the system permits files to be modified without leaving any trace of what was added, changed, or deleted.

---

[4] Belden Menjus, "Eight Factors Contributing to Computer Fraud," *Internal Auditor* (October 1990).

CONTROL/AUDIT RISKS: COMPUTER FRAUD AND CRIME

- Good internal controls do not deter some employees who will always steal. However, good internal controls do detect the fraud early and therefore lessen the loss. Internal controls are there for honest employees.

- Most computer crimes and frauds are committed internally, by employees of the organization.

- More and more frauds are being committed by individuals outside the organization, such as consultants, contractors, and hackers.

- Most people will take advantage of any weakness in the computer system and in company policies and procedures as well as their employment position.

- Application program development and maintenance work are equal targets for computer crime and fraud activities.

- Additions, deletions, and changes made to computer data files are a major source for committing computer crime and fraud.

- Employees may sell computer-based client/customer lists, vendor names and addresses, bid information, or other sensitive and confidential information to competitors and others for money, to take revenge, or for other reasons.

- Employees may walk out the door with the organization's data and programs through disks, flash drives, thumb drives, pen drives, USB drives, and tapes.

- Third-shift service bureau employees may conduct computer work for their own clients without the knowledge of the service bureau management.

- For each irregularity or fraud discovered, there might be hundreds of dead ends.

- One of the weakest links in the security and fraud chain is the reliability of applications software.

- Programmers, systems analysts, tape librarians, database analysts and administrators, and functional users all are capable of committing computer crime and fraud.

- Passwords and other identification codes can be cracked with a brute-force approach.

- Spool area print files can be the targets of fraud in which files are copied before they are printed

BUSINESS RISKS: FRAUD

- Employee hiring efforts could be ineffective since computer criminals usually have the same characteristics as employees that organizations are seeking.

- Employees will not take a code of conduct seriously if it is not consistently enforced.

- Not prosecuting employees caught in committing a computer crime can send a wrong signal to other employees that illegal acts are considered acceptable.

- If organizations quietly fire without prosecuting employees who committed computer crime and fraud, the problem is never solved. The fired employee will find another job, where he or she is more than likely to resume illicit behavior.

- If an employee's rights are violated either by improper search or by lack of evidence when suspected of computer crime, the organization may be legally liable for damages.

- Computer crime will never be completely eliminated because the control elements are themselves subject to human error and manipulation.

8. **Limits in the investigative tools for analyzing the knowledge that auditors may gain about the fraud.** The volume, volatility, and complexity of the data that must be considered in detecting and investigating computer frauds may exceed the auditor's ability to deal with constructively and in a timely manner.

(iii) Symptoms of Fraud

(A) Symptoms of Management Fraud Management fraud tends to involve a number of people with conspiracy in mind. It occurs because senior managers, due to their position of power, circumvent internal controls. According to Jack Bologna, the major symptoms of management fraud are the intentional understatement of losses and liabilities and overstatement of assets or profits.[5] For example:

- Profits can be manipulated by overstating revenues or understating costs.
- Revenues can be overstated by recording fictitious sales, recording unfinalized sales, recording consignments as sales, or recording shipments to storage facilities as sales.
- Costs can be manipulated by deferring them to the next accounting period or understating them in the current period. This is accomplished by such ploys as overstating ending inventories of raw materials, work in process, and finished goods or by understating purchases of raw materials.

In almost every case of management fraud, signs (**red flags**) of the fraud exist for some time before the fraud itself is detected or disclosed by a third party. These signs include:

- Knowledge that the company is having financial difficulties, such as frequent cash flow shortages, declining sales and profits, and loss of market share.
- Signs of management incompetence, such as poor planning, organization, communication, and controls; poor motivation and delegation; management indecision and confusion about corporate mission, goals, and strategies; management ignorance of conditions in the industry and in the general economy.
- Autocratic management, low trust of employees, poor promotion opportunities, high turnover of employees, and poorly defined business ethics.

Some of accounting-related transaction-based **red flags** include:

- Cash flow is diminishing.
- Sales and income are diminishing.
- Payables and receivables are increasing.
- Unusual or second endorsements on checks.
- Inventory and cost of sales are increasing.
- Income and expense items are continually reclassified.
- Suspense items are not reconciled at all or are reconciled in an untimely manner.
- Suspense items are written off without explanation.
- Accounts receivable write-offs are increasing.
- Journal entries are adjusted heavily at year-end.
- Old outstanding checks exist.
- There are heavy customer complaints.

---

[5] Bologna, *Handbook on Corporate Fraud.*

ACCOUNTING FRAUD BY HIGH-LEVEL MANAGERS

- Early booking of sales
- Expense deferrals
- Inventory overstatement
- Expense account padding

In planning and performing inventory procedures, auditors should be aware that reported methods of fraudulently misstating inventory have involved:

- Nonexistent items recorded as inventory
- Goods that have been sold (and recorded as sales) included in inventory
- Goods shipped between two sites and recorded as inventory at both locations
- Scrap materials substituted for genuine inventory for the physical inventory observation
- False invoices or journal entries
- Inflated inventory costs
- Inventory that has been excluded from the physical count because management states it has been sold when, under the terms of the bill-and-hold arrangement, title has not yet passed to the customer
- Inadequate reserves for slow-moving and obsolete inventory.[6]

IIA PROFESSIONAL STANDARDS

According to the IIA's Due Professional Care *Standard*, fraud encompasses an array of irregularities and illegal acts characterized by intentional deception. It can be perpetrated for the benefit of or to the detriment of the organization and by persons outside as well as inside the organization. Management fraud is perpetrated by anyone in an organization with responsibilities for setting and/or achieving objectives. Generally, fraud is perpetrated for the direct or indirect benefit of an employee, outside individual, or another firm.

(B) Symptoms of Employee Fraud Embezzlement and corruption are two major types of employee fraud. The crime of embezzlement consists of the fraudulent misappropriation of the property of an employer by an employee to whom the possession of that property has been entrusted. Here is the difference between embezzlement and larceny: Embezzlement occurs when the embezzler gains initial possession of property lawfully but subsequently misappropriates it. Larceny is committed when property is taken without the owner's consent.

Common Embezzlement Techniques

- Cash disbursement embezzlement involves the creation of fake documents or false expense entries using phony invoices, time cards, and receipts.

---

[6] American Institute of Certified Public Accountants, *Audit of Inventories, Auditing Procedure Study* (New York: Author, 1993).

- Cash receipts fraud involving the lapping of cash or accounts receivable. Here the embezzler "borrows" from today's receipts and replaces them with tomorrow's receipts. Other examples are skimming, where the proceeds of cash sales are intercepted before any entry is made of their receipts, and granting fake credits for discounts, refunds, rebates, returns, and allowances, possibly through collusion with a customer.

- Another technique is theft of property involving assets such as tools, supplies, equipment, finished goods, raw materials, and intellectual property, such as software, data, and proprietary information.

ACCOUNTING FRAUD BY LOWER-LEVEL EMPLOYEES

- Check kiting
- Lapping of receivables
- Phony vendor invoices
- Phony benefit payment claims
- Expense account padding

Corruption is another common type of employee fraud. Vendors, suppliers, service providers, or contractors often corrupt employees of an organization on both a small-scale level (e.g., gifts and free tickets of nominal value) and a large-scale level (e.g., commissions, payoffs, free trips, free airline tickets and hotel accommodations).

(C) Professional Skepticism in Fraud   An auditor is to plan and perform an audit with an attitude of professional skepticism. This means "the auditor neither assumes that management is dishonest nor assumes unquestioned honesty." An objective evaluation of the situation and management integrity are important considerations for the auditor. *The auditor needs to balance between excessive audit costs due to suspicion and time constraints.*

The auditor should use professional skepticism in establishing the audit scope and in gathering audit evidence. The auditor needs to be aware of the inherent limitations of the auditing process, which include flaws in the audit procedures, auditor errors, risks created by management override of controls, collusion, forgeries, and unrecorded transactions.

The audit engagement needs to be planned so as to provide reasonable assurance of determining material errors or irregularities. *Errors are unintentional mistakes. Irregularities are intentional distortions, misrepresentations, and fraud.*

The auditor's understanding of the internal control structure influences the degree of professional skepticism applied in the course of the audit. The auditor gains an understanding of the internal control structure through previous experiences in the auditable area and by reviewing evidence obtained through preliminary audit survey work, which includes inquiry, inspection, and observation. *The more comfortable the auditor is with the internal control structure, the less skeptical he or she would be.*

It is good to remain skeptical throughout the course of an audit even if the preliminary survey results indicate that no irregularities exist. If internal auditors discover significant errors and

KEY CONCEPTS TO REMEMBER: Symptoms of Employee Fraud

- Adjusting journal entries that lack management authorization and supporting details
- Expenditures that lack supporting documents
- False and improper entries in books of accounts
- Destruction, counterfeiting, and forgery of documents that support payments
- Short shipments received
- Overpricing of goods purchased
- Double billing
- Substitution of inferior goods

irregularities during the audit, they are required to inform the audit committee through a quarterly report and by quantifying their effects after obtaining sufficient evidence of their existence. In essence, it is good for internal auditors to maintain professional skepticism at all times.

(D) Management Representations versus Risk The auditor needs to assess the risk of management misrepresentations and to consider the effects of such risks in establishing an overall audit strategy and the scope of the audit. Examples of situations (red flags) that could lead to risk of management representations include:

- Frequent disputes about aggressive application of generally accepted accounting principles.
- Excessive emphasis on meeting targets on which management compensation program is based.
- Evasive responses to audit inquiries.
- Employees who lack necessary knowledge and experience yet develop various estimates, including accounting.
- Supervisors of employees who generate estimates appear careless or inexperienced in reviewing and approving the estimates.
- A history of unreliable or unreasonable estimates.
- The existence of constant crisis conditions in operating and accounting areas of the organization.
- Frequent and excessive back orders, shortages of materials and products, delays, or lack of documentation of major transactions.
- Unrestricted access to computer-based application systems initiating or controlling the movement of assets.
- High levels of transaction processing errors.
- Unusual delays in providing operating results and accounting reports.

VALUE OF AUDITEE REPRESENTATIONS

Auditee representations are not good substitutes for effective auditing procedures.

(E) Review of Accounting Estimates   Many assumptions go into accounting estimates. The internal auditor should understand these assumptions and should evaluate to determine whether the assumptions are subjective and are susceptible to misstatements and bias.

The auditor should show professional skepticism during the review and evaluation of the reasonableness of accounting estimates. These estimates contain both subjective and objective factors. Professional skepticism is important with respect to subjective factors where personal bias could be significant.

Examples of accounting estimates include:

- Uncollectible receivables
- Allowance for loan losses
- Revenues to be earned on contracts
- Subscription income
- Losses on sales contracts
- Professional membership or union dues income
- Valuation of financial securities
- Trading versus investment security classifications
- Compensation in stock option plans and deferred plans
- Probability of loss
- Obsolete inventory
- Net realizable value of inventories
- Losses in purchase commitments
- Property and causality insurance accruals
- Loss reserves
- Warranty claims
- Taxes on real estate and personal property

In addition to review, the auditor should test management's process of developing accounting estimates or develop an independent estimation. The auditor can compare prior estimates with subsequent results to assess the reliability of the process used to develop estimates. The auditor should also review whether the accounting estimates are consistent with the operational plans and programs of the entity.

KEY CONCEPTS TO REMEMBER: Sequence of Audit Activities Related to Professional Skepticism

1. Reviewing internal control structure
2. Performing audit planning work
3. Determining the audit scope
4. Collecting audit evidence
5. Reviewing accounting estimates
6. Issuing an audit opinion

(c) Acts and Profiles of Fraud Perpetrators

(i) Acts of Fraudulent Behavior
A list of fraudulent behavior acts about which an internal auditor must be concerned is presented next.

- Significant changes in the behavior of the defrauder (e.g., easygoing attitude, irregular work habits, and expensive social life)

- Knowledge that the defrauder is undergoing an emotional trauma at home or in the workplace

- Knowledge that the defrauder is betting heavily

- Knowledge that the defrauder is drinking heavily

- Knowledge that the defrauder is heavily in debt

- Audit findings of errors or irregularities that are considered immaterial when discovered

- The defrauder works quietly, works hard, works long hours, often works alone

- Appearance of living beyond means

- Expensive car or clothes

(ii) Profiles of Fraud Perpetrators

(A) Traits of Managers According to Joseph Wells, personality traits of managers associated with frauds include wheeler-dealers and a management that is feared, impulsive, too number-oriented, and insensitive to people (especially to employees).[7] Obviously, the contrast is a management that is friendly, calm, generous with time, self-confident, and goal oriented.

Many frauds occur where an autocratic management arbitrarily sets budgets for lower-level managers to meet. When these budgets are unattainable, the managers have a choice to either cheat or fail. When their jobs, reputations, and careers are at stake, cheating is sometimes easier than failing.

(B) Traits of Employees The next traits are suggested as an indication of fraudulent behavior.

- Managers and executives seem to be the major sources of ethical attitudes within organization. That is, there is pressure from superiors to commit unethical behavior. Superiors pressure subordinates to support incorrect viewpoints, sign false documents, overlook superiors' wrongdoing, and do business with superiors' friends. The CEO sets the ethical tone of the organization.

- Employees never take vacations, live beyond their means, or suffer from mood swings.

- Males arrested for embezzlement outnumber females by about two to one.

- About one-third of both male and female embezzlers are 22 to 29 years of age; they constitute the largest grouping of all.

(C) White-Collar Crime White-collar crime is a breach of trust, confidence, or fiduciary duty. Someone relies on and trusts another, to his or her economic detriment. White-collar crime is

---

[7] Joseph Wells, *Fraud Examination: Investigative and Audit Procedures* (New York; Quorum Books, 1992).

PROFILE OF A CORPORATE FRAUDSTER

- Extravagant purchases or lavish lifestyle

- Unexplained mood swings or compulsive behavior (e.g., workaholics, alcohol, or drug abusers, overeaters, gamblers)

- Unable to deal with pressure

- Able to rationalize their thefts

- Able to exploit internal control weaknesses to cover up their fraud

- Reluctant to take vacations or to stay away from the office

- Chronic job frustration, low morale

- Unusually close ties to vendors or a sudden switch in a long-term vendor

- Suggestions of heavy personal debt

SOURCE: Association of Certified Fraud Examiners, *The White Paper Journal* 7, no. 5 (October/November 1993). Original source: KPMG Canada, *The Fraud Prevention Primer.*

classified as that directed against consumers and that directed against employers. It is caused by greed and by weak internal control mechanisms. Jack Bologna defines white-collar crime as occupational, corporate, economic, or financial.[8]

The common characteristics of each of the so-called white-collar crimes are intentional deception (fraud theft, embezzlement, and corruption), destruction of property (industrial sabotage), gross negligence (product liability), and failure to comply with government regulations on environmental pollution, unfair pricing practices, untrue advertising, unsafe and unhealthy products, stock fraud, tax fraud, and so on. *High-level employee crimes are perceived to be based on economic greed, while low-level employee crimes are perceived as based on economic need.*

In his book *White Collar Crime,* Edwin Sutherland gave examples of violations by larger American corporations.[9] These involved restraints of trade; misrepresentation in advertising; patent, trademark, and copyright infringements; unfair labor practices; illegal rebates; and other types of violations. Sutherland found that many of the corporations were serious repeaters.

Irwin Ross, writing for *Fortune* magazine, compiled statistics on fraud committed by the largest industrial and nonindustrial corporations.[10] Included were five kinds of offenses, all of which were committed for the benefit of the organization rather than for personal profit: bribe-taking or bribe-giving by high-level corporate officials (including kickbacks and illegal rebates), criminal fraud, illegal campaign contributions, tax evasion, and criminal antitrust violations.

(D) Profiles of Organizational Crime   Research by Edwin Sutherland, Marshall B. Clinard, and Peter Yeager found these profiles for organizations committing crime: The oil, pharmaceutical, and motor vehicle industries were the most likely to violate the law; firms that were relatively more prosperous tended more often to pollute illegally; larger corporations in general commit no

---

[8] Bologna, *Handbook on Corporate Fraud.*

[9] Quoted in Gary S. Green, *Occupational Crime* (Chicago: Nelson-Hall, 1990). Originally from Edwin O. Sutherland, *White Collar Crime* (New York: CBS, 1961).

[10] Quoted in Green, *Occupational Crime.* Originally from Irwin Ross, "How Lawless Are Big Companies?" *Fortune,* December 1, 1980.

more violations per unit size than do smaller corporations.[11] In some cases, larger corporations had more infractions generally, but smaller corporations had more violations per unit size. More diversified firms will violate more often. (This is because they are exposed to a greater number of regulations. More diversified firms seem more likely to violate labor and manufacturing laws than those less diversified.) Firms with more market power had slightly fewer violations per unit size than less dominant firms, which suggests that market power may diminish pressures to violate the law. Firms and industries with greater labor concentration tend to have more official censures for labor violations.

---

[11] Cited in Green, *Occupational Crime*, based on research studies conducted by Sutherland, Clinard, and Yeager in 1949, 1980, and 1983.

2.6 Sample Practice Questions

As mentioned in the Preface of this book, a small batch of sample practice questions is included here to show the flavor of questions and to create a quiz-like environment. The answers and explanations for these questions are shown in a separate section at the end of this book just before the Glossary. If there is a need to practice more questions to obtain a greater confidence, refer to the section "CIA Exam Study Preparation Resources" presented in the front matter of this book.

1. An exception report for management is an example of which of the following?
   a. Preventive control.
   b. Detective control.
   c. Corrective control.
   d. Directive control.

2. Organizational procedures allow employees to anticipate problems. This type of control is known as:
   a. Feedback control.
   b. Strategic control.
   c. Feed-forward control.
   d. Performance appraisal.

3. As part of a total quality control program, a firm not only inspects finished goods but also monitors product returns and customer complaints. Which type of control best describes these efforts?
   a. Feedback control.
   b. Feed-forward control.
   c. Production control.
   d. Inventory control.

4. To be successful, large companies must develop means to keep the organization focused in the proper direction. Organization control systems help keep companies focused. These control systems consist of which of the following components?
   a. Budgeting, financial ratio analysis, and cash management.
   b. Objectives, standards, and an evaluation-reward system.
   c. Role analysis, team building, and survey feedback.
   d. Coaching, protection, and challenging assignments.

5. **Control** has been described as a closed system consisting of six elements. Identify one of the six elements.
   a. Setting performance standards.
   b. Adequately securing data files.
   c. Approval of audit charter.
   d. Establishment of independent audit function.

6. The three basic components of all organizational control systems are:
   a. Objectives, standards, and an evaluation-reward system.
   b. Plans, budgets, and organizational policies and procedures.
   c. Statistical reports, audits, and financial controls
   d. Inputs, objectives, and an appraisal system.

7. Which of the following management control systems measures performance in terms of operating profits minus the cost of capital invested in tangible assets?
   a. Open-book management system.
   b. Economic value added system.
   c. Activity-based costing system.
   d. Market value added system.

8. A comprehensive management control system that considers both financial and nonfinancial measures relating to a company's critical success factors is called a(n):
   a. Balanced scorecard system.
   b. Economic value added system.
   c. Activity-based costing system.
   d. Market value added system.

9. According to the IIA Planning Standard, the term "risk appetite" means which of the following?
   a. Risk avoidance.
   b. Risk limitation.
   c. Risk acceptance.
   d. Risk spreading.

10. According to the IIA Planning Standard, residual risk is also known as which of the following?
   a. Audit risk.
   b. Pure risk.
   c. Current risk.
   d. Inherent risk.

11. Residual risk is calculated as which of the following?

    a. Known risks minus unknown risks.

    b. Actual risks minus probable risks.

    c. Probable risks minus possible risks.

    d. Potential risks minus covered risks.

12. Which of the following is closely linked to risk acceptance?

    a. Risk detection.

    b. Risk prevention.

    c. Risk tolerance.

    d. Risk correction.

13. Which of the following risk concepts can be assumed to have **no** mitigating controls?

    a. Business risk.

    b. Residual risk.

    c. Inherent risk.

    d. Current risk.

14. The internal audit charter normally requires the internal audit activity to focus on areas consisting of which of the following?

    a. High inherent risk and high residual risk.

    b. High audit risk and high current risk.

    c. Low inherent risk and low audit risk.

    d. Low inherent risk and high outstanding risk.

15. Internal auditors would be more likely to detect fraud if they developed/strengthened their ability to:

    a. Recognize and question changes which occur in organizations.

    b. Interrogate fraud perpetrators to discover why the fraud was committed.

    c. Develop internal controls to prevent the occurrence of fraud.

    d. Document computerized operating system programs.

16. According to the IIA Standards, which of the following **best** describes the two general categories or types of fraud that concern most internal auditors?

    a. Improper payments (i.e., bribes and kickbacks) and tax fraud.

    b. Fraud designed to benefit the organization and fraud perpetrated to the detriment of the organization.

    c. Acceptance of bribes or kickbacks and improper related-party transactions.

    d. Acceptance of kickbacks or embezzlement and misappropriation of assets.

17. A company hired a highly qualified accounts payable manager who had been terminated from another company for alleged wrongdoing. Six months later, the manager diverted $12,000 by sending duplicate payments of invoices to a relative. A control that might have prevented this situation would be to:

    a. Adequately check prior employment backgrounds for all new employees.

    b. Not hire individuals who appear overqualified for a job.

    c. Verify educational background for all new employees.

    d. Check to see if close relatives work for vendors.

18. Red flags are conditions that indicate a higher likelihood of fraud. Which of the following would **not** be considered a red flag?

    a. Management has delegated the authority to make purchases under a certain dollar limit to subordinates.

    b. An individual has held the same cash-handling job for an extended period without any rotation of duties.

    c. An individual handling marketable securities is responsible for making the purchases, recording the purchases, and reporting any discrepancies and gains/losses to senior management.

    d. The assignment of responsibility and accountability in the accounts receivable department is not clear.

19. Internal auditors and management have become increasingly concerned about computer fraud. Which of the following control procedures would be **least** important in preventing computer fraud?

    a. Program change control that requires a distinction between production programs and test programs.

    b. Testing of new applications by users during the systems development process.

    c. Segregation of duties between the applications programmer and the program librarian function.

    d. Segregation of duties between the programmer and systems analyst.

Conducting Internal Audit Engagements—Audit Tools and Techniques (28–38%)

3.1 Data-Gathering Tools and Techniques

Auditors use several data-gathering tools and techniques to obtain background information on the auditee's operations and to collect audit evidence and pertinent data for the audit purpose. Either statistical or nonstatistical sampling methods can be used to collect audit evidence and to control risk. Specific data-gathering tools and techniques include interviews, questionnaires, checklists, focus groups, observations, unobtrusive measures, and anecdotal records (see Exhibit 3.1).

— Interviews (expensive, require good preparation)

— Questionnaires (popular, inexpensive way of getting information; a benefit-risk analysis is needed)

— Checklists (ensure that all actions are completed)

— Focus groups (good for exploring ideas and opinions)

— Observation (good for direct evidence)

— Unobtrusive measures (techniques not readily noticeable to others)

— Anecdotal records (used to describe a specific situation such as fraud or performance evaluation)

EXHIBIT 3.1 Data-Gathering Tools and Techniques

(a) Interviews

(i) Types of Interviews

Interviews are of two types: structured and unstructured (i.e., less structured). A **structured interview** is one in which auditors ask the same questions of numerous individuals or individuals representing numerous organizations in a precise manner, offering each interviewee the same set of possible responses.[1] In contrast, an **unstructured interview** contains many open-ended questions that are not asked in a structured, precise manner. With unstructured interviews, different auditors interpret questions and often offer different explanations when respondents ask for clarification. The structured interview technique is good to apply in an organization with multiple locations, units, or divisions. The less structured and less guided type of unstructured interview may be more useful to one-of-a-kind interview.

STRUCTURED VERSUS UNSTRUCTURED INTERVIEWS

- Structured interviews are good for repetitive types of interviews.
- Unstructured interviews are good for one-of-a-kind interviews.

The telephone interview and, even more, the face-to-face interview enable the interviewer to establish rapport with respondents. Individuals who would not answer certain questions on their own can be persuaded to provide truthful answers in a telephone or face-to-face interview.

In comparison to the telephone interview, the face-to-face interview gives the interviewer the opportunity to observe as well as listen. More complex questions can be asked in a face-to-face interview than in a telephone interview. More questions can be asked in a face-to-face interview since the interview can last up to an hour (optimum time) while 30 minutes is the usual limit for telephone interviews. In comparison with mail questionnaires, face-to-face and telephone interviews are much faster methods of gathering data.

A good preparation for an interview requires several dimensions, such as making sure that interview questions are appropriate (i.e., relevant to the audit), directed to the proper persons, and easily answered.

- **Relevance** requires that interview questions should have a good probability of yielding data needed for the final audit report. Auditors should not go on fishing expeditions and try to include all sorts of variables that can create an unnecessary burden on the interviewee and distract attention from the central purpose of the interview.

- **Selection of respondents.** Consideration should be given to auditees who can be expected to answer given questions. A question may be relevant to a given audit, but the choice of persons to answer it may be inappropriate.

- **Ease of response.** Interviews are meant to obtain data that otherwise may not be documented or, if documented, may need some interpretation. Questions should be constructed that are relatively easy to answer and do not cause undue burden to the interviewee (auditee).

If sensitive questions must be asked, it is best to use a mail questionnaire where confidentiality or anonymity can be granted. In face-to-face interviews, it is wise to avoid questions that

---

[1] *Using Structured Interviewing Techniques* (Washington, DC: U.S. General Accounting Office, 1991).

could cause unnecessary confrontation, causing the interviewer and interviewee to take sides and do battle.

Also to be avoided are questions that have no answers and questions that, if you attempt to ask them, produce unusable results. These are not to be confused with questions for which the legitimate answer might be "no basis to judge" or "no opinion."

(ii) Organizing Interview Questions

The order in which the questions are presented in an interview is important. Early questions, which set the tone for the data collection procedure and can influence responses to later questions, also help the auditor get to know the interviewee and to establish the rapport essential to a successful interview. Remember that the questions should hold the interviewee's attention; thus, the auditor must begin to introduce some "interesting" questions.

The questions should be presented in a logical manner, keeping the flow of questions in chronological or reverse order, as appropriate. It is good to avoid haphazardly jumping from one topic to another. It is also good to avoid introducing bias in the ordering of questions.

(iii) Interview Design

There are ways to compose good interview questions and to forestall problems with comprehension or bias. The appropriateness and level of language used in the interview, the effects of qualifying language, and the importance of clarity are all important to consider. The auditor needs to be familiar with the various kinds of bias that can creep into the wording of interview questions and their effect on the validity of the audit results (see Exhibit 3.2).

(A) Appropriateness of the Language Whether interviewing language is appropriate or inappropriate may relate to what is said, how it is said, or when it is said. What is said in the interview is basically dictated by the writer's structured data collection instrument. How it is said concerns the speech and mannerisms of the interviewer who controls the presentation and whose delivery of questions may alter their intended meaning. When it is said refers to the context of the interview in which each question is placed. If the interviewee expresses concern or sensitivity to a given question, changing the language of a subsequent question might defuse the concern.

(B) Level of Language When composing interview questions, it is wise to consider the level of the language used. The auditor should seek to communicate at the level the interviewee understands and to create a verbal setting that is conducive to serious data gathering yet one in which the interviewee is comfortable. One problem often encountered is maintaining a level of language that is neither above nor below the interviewee's level of understanding. Speaking over the

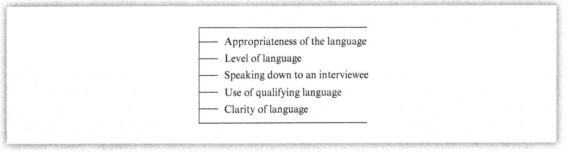

— Appropriateness of the language
— Level of language
— Speaking down to an interviewee
— Use of qualifying language
— Clarity of language

EXHIBIT 3.2 Considerations in Designing Interview Questions

interviewee's head includes the use of complex, rare, and foreign words and expressions; words of many syllables; abbreviations; acronyms; and certain jargon. Such language, while it may seem appropriate to the interviewer or audit team, may not be understood by the interviewee. Thus, speaking over the interviewee's head hinders communication. Interviewees who are embarrassed at their lack of understanding may either not answer or guess at the meaning, which can lead to incorrect answers. Or interviewees may get the impression that the auditor really does not care about the answer and lose interest in the interview.

(C) Speaking Down to an Interviewee Speaking down to an interviewee is just as bad as speaking over the interviewees head. Oversimplifying the language in the data collection instrument can make interviewees feel that the auditor regards them as ignorant. This approach is demeaning. The auditor has contacted these individuals because they have important information to impart. To treat a person condescendingly—or to let it appear that one does—negates that importance. Likewise, care should be taken in using slang, folksy expressions, and certain jargon. While such language may help the auditor develop rapport with the interviewee, the exactness of the communication may be lessened. To avoid error in either direction, it is useful to **pretest** both the final wording of the data collection instrument and the interview questions.

(D) Use of Qualifying Language After composing an interview question, the auditor may find it requires an adjective or qualifying phrase or a time specified to make the item complete or to give the interviewee sufficient or complete information. For example, "How many employees do you have?" might become "How many full-time-equivalent employees do you have?" If the auditor did not include the necessary qualifiers in the data collection instrument, another auditor may qualify it in a different way. This could make the resulting data difficult to summarize and analyze. Also interviewees, not realizing that qualifying language is absent, may answer the question as they interpret it. Thus, different interviewees would be responding to different questions, based on their own interpretations.

(E) Clarity of Language The style in which a question is couched can affect the clarity of communication. A question that contains too many ideas or concepts may be too complex for the interviewee to understand, especially if it is presented orally, which makes it difficult for interviewees to review parts of the question. The auditor should limit one thought to one sentence and give the interviewee the proper framework.

Likewise, a sentence may contain clutter—words that do not clarify the message. Questions should be worded concisely. Here are a few suggestions to reduce sentence clutter.

- Delete "that" wherever possible—for example, "Others suggest [that] training can be improved."
- Use plain language. For example, for "aforementioned," use "previous" or "previously mentioned."
- Avoid the passive voice. Substitute pronouns ("I," "we," or "they") and active verbs; instead of "It is necessary to obtain," use "We need."

A double-barreled question is a classic example of an unclear question. In this case, it is good to state the question separately if it contains too many parts. In phrasing a question, it is best to avoid the double negative, which is difficult to answer. For example, "Indicate which of the organizational goals listed below are not considered unattainable within the two-year period" should be reworded to read "Indicate which of the organizational goals listed below are considered attainable within the two-year period."

Words such as "all," "none," "everything," "never," and others that represent extreme values should be avoided. There are cases when the use of "all" or "none" is appropriate, but they are few. Where "yes" or "no" answers are expected, the results can be misleading. For example, if one employee is not covered in a question such as "Are all of your employees covered by medical insurance," a "yes" answer is impossible. This is because some employees may not have been covered. A better question would be "About what percentage of your employees are covered by medical insurance?" Where possible, key words and comments used in questions should be defined. For example, when speaking of "employees," the term should be defined and clarified. Are we talking about part-time, full-time, permanent, temporary, volunteer, white-collar, blue-collar employees?

(iv) Biased Questions in Interviews

A question is biased when it causes interviewees to answer in a way that does not reflect their true positions on an issue. An interviewee may or may not be aware of the bias. Problems result when the interviewees are:

- Unaware of the bias and influenced to respond in the way that is directed by the wording.

- Aware of the bias and either deliberately answer in a way that does not reflect their opinions.

- Refuse to answer because the question is biased.

Bias can appear in the stem (or statement) portion of the question or in the response-alternative portion. Bias may also result when a question carries an implied answer, choices of answer are unequal, "loaded" words are used, or a scaled question is unbalanced.

(v) Conducting Interviews

Each participant in the interview—interviewer (auditor) and interviewee (auditee)—has a role to perform and a set of behaviors that assist in the performance. Because the role and behaviors of each one influence the conduct of the interview, they affect the other participant. To oversimplify, the role of the auditor is to ask the questions; that of the auditee is to respond with answers. Actually, the auditor must perform these major tasks:

- Develop rapport with the auditee and show interest.
- Give the auditee a reason to participate.
- Elicit responsiveness from the auditee.
- Ask questions in a prescribed order and manner.
- Ensure understanding.
- Ensure nonbias.
- Obtain sufficient answers.
- Show sensitivity to the auditee's burden.

(A) Developing Rapport and Showing Interest Auditors should seek to establish a balance relationship between the auditee and themselves as empathetic, friendly individuals who are not too different from the auditee but who are also independent, unbiased, and honest collectors of data. The auditors' appearance, verbal mannerisms, body language, and voice will determine the rapport, starting with the contact that sets up the interview.

Auditors should make their verbal and voice cues calm and unflustered. They should speak so the auditee need not strain to hear and understand. Changes in voice inflection, sighs, or other noises give clues to the auditors' feelings or moods, as do facial expressions and body language. These nonverbal communications can be imprecise. Auditors should control these so that the auditee does not pick up impatience, disapproval, or other negative feelings. Ideally, auditors should not experience such feelings during the interview, since they are supposed to be impartial, unbiased, and tolerant observers. Likewise, auditors should control expressions of positive feelings or agreement with what the auditee is saying.

It is important that auditors be aware of characteristic nonlinguistic cues, such as change in voice, facial expressions, or gestures, since as much as half of the communication that takes place during the interview is conveyed by these modes of expression. Failure to understand those cues may result in miscommunication.

Auditors' appearance is still another variable that influence rapport and, therefore, the tone of the interview. Auditors should dress to fit both the interview and the interviewee. This means wearing warehouse-type clothing (e.g., casual) to meet the auditee during physical inventory taken in a warehouse or manufacturing plant and wearing office-type clothing (e.g., suit and tie) to meet an auditee manager in the office. Auditors' appearance indicates to the auditee that the auditors (1) understand the nature of the auditee's circumstances and (2) are not totally different from the auditee.

(B) Giving the Auditee a Reason to Participate   Some auditees understand the nature of audits in general and the role of the auditor in the organization, while the others do not. Auditees who are not aware of the importance of the audit work and how they can help may not give sincere and well-thought-out answers. Therefore, an auditor's explanations to the auditee are important to the validity of the resulting data.

(C) Helping the Auditee to Be Responsive   Some auditees may have never before been interviewed during an audit. The auditor needs to make the auditee comfortable and capable as a respondent. This can be done by reinforcing the auditee with such verbal cues as "I see," "Let me get that down," "I want to make sure that I have that right," "I see, that is helpful to know," "It is useful to get your ideas on this."

(D) Asking Questions in a Prescribed Order and Manner   Questions should be ordered so as to lead the auditee through various topics, correctly position sensitive questions, and hold the auditee's interest. The next suggestions may help.

- Ask the questions exactly as they are worded in the questionnaire.
- Ask the questions in the order in which they are presented in the questionnaire.
- Ask every question specified in the questionnaire.
- Read each question slowly (i.e., two words per second).
- Repeat questions that are misunderstood or misinterpreted.
- Do not let the auditee stray from the questions in the interview.
- Keep nonverbal cues as neutral as possible.

Remember that for telephone interviews, the lack of visual contact decreases the auditor's ability to make the auditee understand.

(E) Ensuring Understanding At times, an auditee will not understand a question, as indicated by telling the auditor so, by not answering, or by providing an answer that seems inconsistent or wrong. When this happens, the auditor should use an appropriate probing technique, such as:

- Repeating the question.
- Giving an expectant pause.
- Repeating the respondent's reply.
- Making neutral questions or comments, such as "Anything else?" "How do you mean?" "What do you mean?"

The auditor should use these probing questions with care so as not bias the auditee. At this time, rephrasing the question or adding new questions should be avoided as much as possible to minimize confusion.

(F) Ensuring Nonbias A bias can be introduced in many ways, such as in the way a question is written, in the selection of auditees, in the way the auditor poses the contents of the query, in the introduction of an auditor's own ideas into a probe, or in the auditor adding certain verbal emphasis or using certain body language. All these can destroy the neutrality that should characterize the auditor's presentation.

(G) Obtaining Sufficient Answers Auditors must learn to judge when an answer is sufficient before going to the next question. If the answer is incomplete or vague, auditors should ensure that the question is understood or draw more out of the auditee to complete the answer. Auditors can check the accuracy of the answers given by asking for supporting documentation from the auditee.

(H) Showing Sensitivity to Auditee's Burden Before conducting an interview, the auditor should make a general statement regarding how long it is expected to take. Then the auditor is under obligation to adhere to this time limitation. Besides the length of time taken, the interview can be burdensome because of the amount of work the auditee needs to go through to produce the information requested.

(b) Questionnaires

(i) Purpose of Questionnaires

Three phases occur in questionnaires: (1) data design, (2) data collection, and (3) data analysis. A questionnaire is a data collection instrument, and auditors employ it to:

- Ask auditees for figures, statistics, amounts, and other facts.
- Describe conditions and procedures that affect the work, organizations, and systems with which they are involved.
- Obtain from auditees' their judgments and views about processes, performance, adequacy, efficiency, and effectiveness.
- Report past events and make forecasts.
- Describe auditees' attitudes and opinions.
- Describe auditees' behavior and the behavior of others.[2]

---

[2] Ibid.

Questionnaires are popular because they can be a relatively inexpensive way of getting auditees to provide information. However, because questionnaires rely on people to provide answers, a benefit–risk consideration is associated with their use. People with the ability to observe, select, acquire, process, evaluate, interpret, sort, retrieve, and report can be a valuable and versatile source of information under the right circumstances. However, the human mind is a very complex and vulnerable observation instrument. *If we do not ask the right people the right questions in the right way, we will not get high-quality answers. .*

WHAT KINDS OF QUESTIONS SHOULD BE ASKED?

Three kinds of audit questions should be asked: descriptive, normative, and causal (impact). As the name implies, the answers to **descriptive questions** provide descriptive information about specific conditions or events, and focus on "what is." An example is the number of people who received certain types of medical benefits in a given year.

The answers to **normative questions** compare an observed outcome to an expected level of performance and focus on "what should be." An example is the comparison between airline safety violations and the standard that has been set for safety.

The answers to **impact (cause-and-effect) questions** help reveal whether observed conditions or events can be attributed to business operations. An example is determining the effect of changing a policy or a procedure.

Auditors should use these three kinds of questions in questionnaires since they are all relevant to most common audit situations. The best way to achieve the right balance is to see if each question can be labeled as one of the three kinds of questions. If a question does not belong to any of these types of questions, auditors need to decide whether to drop the question or use it as a general background, information-gathering information.

Questions must be clear, interesting, and easy to understand and answer. The answers to the questionnaires become input to audit report writing

(ii) When to Use Questionnaires

The decision to use a questionnaire should be made only after carefully considering the comparative advantages and disadvantages of the various ways of administering a questionnaire over other data collection techniques.

Data can be collected in a variety of ways, such as field observations, reviews of records or published reports, interviews, mail questionnaires, and face-to-face or telephone questionnaires. The selection of one technique over another involves trade-offs between staff requirements, costs, time constraints, and, most important, the depth and type of information needed.

Questionnaires are frequently used with sample survey strategies to answer descriptive and normative audit questions. They are often less central in studies answering cause-and-effect questions since good answers require an in-depth qualitative and quantitative analysis. Questionnaires can be used in all types of audits—operational, financial, and compliance—to confirm or expand the audit scope.

Questionnaires can be useful when the auditor needs a cost-effective way to collect a large amount of standardized information, when the information to be collected varies in complexity, when a large number of auditees are needed, when different populations are involved, and when auditees in those populations are in widely separated locations.

CONSTRAINTS IN USING QUESTIONNAIRES

■ In using and administering questionnaires, time, cost, and staff expertise are examples of primary constraints while location and facilities are a secondary constraint. For example, if location and facilities are a constraint, use of a mail questionnaire or telephone interviews are advised compared to face-to-face interviews.

■ If money is tight and the subject matter can be phrased intelligibly for the respondent population, the mail should be used. Online interviews are becoming popular.

■ If time is tight and staff time is not, the face-to-face or telephone interview methods should be used.

Furthermore, questionnaires are usually more versatile than other methods. They can be used to collect more types of information from a wider variety of sources than other methods because they use people, who can report facts, figures, amounts, statistics, dates, attitudes, opinions, experiences, events, assessments, and judgments during a single contact.

Questionnaires are difficult to use if the respondent population cannot be readily identified or if the information being sought is not widely distributed among the population of those who hold the knowledge. Furthermore, questionnaires should not be used if the respondents are likely to be unable or unwilling to answer or to provide accurate and unbiased answers or if the questions are inappropriate or compromising.

In general, questionnaires should not be used to gather information that taxes the limitations of respondents. Sometimes people are not knowledgeable as accurate reporters of certain kinds of information. They remember recent events much better than long-past events. They remember salient and routine events and meaningful facts but do not remember details, dates, and incidental events very well.

Structured questionnaires are also not particularly well suited for broad, global, or exploratory questions. Because respondents have many different forms of reference, levels of knowledge, and question interpretations, the structured methodology limits the auditor's ability to vary the focus, scope, depth, and direction of the line of inquiry. Such flexibility is necessary to accommodate variances in the respondents' perceptions and understanding that result from such questions.

Mail questionnaires are usually more cost-effective but require longer time periods than personal or telephone interviews. While mail questionnaires usually have higher development costs than telephone or face-to-face interviews, this is generally offset by the relatively inexpensive data collection costs. Extra care must be taken with the mail questionnaires because, unlike the other choices, there is no interviewer (auditor) to help the respondent (auditee). Also, mail is a slow means of transmission, and mail questionnaires take two or three follow-ups. Online interviews are becoming popular.

If the contacted people are likely to conceal the identity of the intended respondent, and this is likely to make a difference, or if the auditor is not sure that the intended respondent will get the questionnaire, then personal contact is better than telephone and telephone is better than mail.

KEY CONCEPTS TO REMEMBER: Questionnaires versus Interviews

- Auditors should review the conditions and requirements of the data collection methods before deciding to use questionnaires and again before deciding the methods for administering the questionnaire.

- Mail questionnaires are a versatile, low-cost method of collecting detailed data. They are particularly adaptable to survey methods when the population is big, difficult to contact, likely to be inconvenienced, concerned about privacy, and widely dispersed. But mail questionnaires usually have a long turnaround time. Auditors must be willing to invest the time required to carefully design and test questions used in mail questionnaires. And respondents must be willing and able to provide unbiased answers.

- Interview methods, while much more expensive and more prone to bias than, help ensure against respondent error, have less turnaround time if sufficient staff is provided, and can be used to provide some auditor verifications during the interviews.

(iii) Formatting the Question

Before preparing the questionnaire, auditors need to choose the format for each question, which is a design issue. Basically, two types of formats exist: open-ended and closed-ended questions (see Exhibit 3.3).

(iv) Open-Ended Questions

Open-ended questions are easy to write and require very little knowledge of the subject or operation. These types of questions provide very unstandardized, often incomplete, and ambiguous answers, and it is very difficult to use such answers in a quantitative analysis. Respondents will write some salient factors that they happen to think of but will leave out some important factors because they did not think of them at that moment.

CARE IN DEVELOPING QUESTIONNAIRES

Good questionnaires can be seriously compromised if they are not presented in a format that is easy to read and understand by respondents.

Open-ended questions do not help respondents consider a range of factors; rather, they depend on the respondents' unaided recall. There is no way of knowing what is important but not recalled, and because not all respondents consider the same set of factors, it may be extremely difficult or impossible to aggregate the responses. *Open-ended questions are easy for auditors and difficult for auditees.*

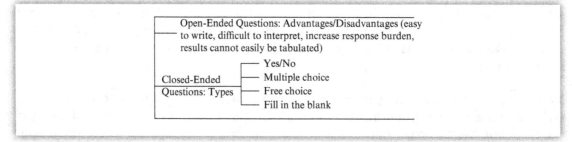

EXHIBIT 3.3 Questions

Also, auditors may not know how to interpret the answers due to their descriptive nature. Another problem is that open-ended questions cannot easily be tabulated. Rather, a complicated process called content analysis must be used, in which someone reads and rereads a substantial number of the written responses, identifies the major categories of themes, and develops rules for assigning responses to these categories.

Still another problem is that open-ended questions substantially increase response burden. They usually take several minutes to answer rather than a few seconds. Because respondents must compose and organize their thoughts and then try to express them in concise language, they are much less likely to answer such questions.

However, open-ended questions sometimes do have advantages. Their use may be unavoidable when, for example, auditors are uncertain about criteria or are engaged in exploratory work. If auditors ask enough people an open-ended question, a list of alternatives for closed-ended questions can be developed, but not the other way around. Auditors can also use open-ended questions to make sure the list of structured alternatives does not omit an important item or qualification. Auditors can also ask open-ended questions to obtain responses that might further clarify the meaning of answers to closed-ended questions or to gather respondent examples that can be used to illustrate points. In other words, *answers to open-ended questions can become an input to the closed-ended questions.*

(v) Closed-Ended Questions

Yes/no questions are very popular. Although they have some advantages, they have many problems and few uses. Yes/no questions are ideal for dichotomous variables, such as black and white, because they measure whether the condition or trait is present or absent. They are therefore very good for filters in the line of questioning and can be used to move respondents to the questions that apply to them.

Yes/No Filter Question

Did you get training? (Check one)

☐ Yes (continue)

☐ No (go to question 5)

Consider the question: "Were the terms of the contracts clear?" Most auditees would have trouble with this question because it involves several different considerations: (1) Some contracts may have been clear and others may not have been; (2) some contracts may have been neither clear nor unclear or of marginal clarity; (3) parts of some contracts may have been clear and others not clear.

WHEN TO USE YES/NO QUESTIONS

Yes/no questions are good in dealing with measures that are absolute. They are not good for measures that span a range of values and conditions.

Because so little information is obtained from each yes/no question, several rounds of questions individually have to be administered to get the information needed. "Did you have a plan?" "Was the plan in writing?" "Was it a formal plan?" "Was it approved?" This method of inquiry is usually so boring as to discourage respondents.

Sometimes question writers try to compress their line of inquiry and cause serious item-construction flaws. They ask for two things at once—a double-barreled question. For instance, a yes/no answer to "Did you get mission and site support training?" is imprecise. How do respondents answer if they got mission but not site support training? A related question-writing mistake is mixing yes/no and multiple choice.

Yes/no questions are prone to bias and misinterpretation for two reasons:

1. Many people like to say "yes." Some have the opposite bias and like to say "no."

2. Questions such as "Do you submit reports?" have what is called an "inferred bias" toward the "yes" response. The most common way to counter this bias is to add the negative alternative—for example, "Do you submit reports or not?" However, if this is done, the use of yes/no choices in the answer must be qualified or avoided. Without this precaution, a simple "yes" answer may be read as applying to both parts of the question: "Yes, I submit" and "Yes, I do not submit." A simple "no" might also be read as "No, I do not submit"—a double negative. To prevent confusion, answer choices should be qualified to avoid yes/no answers.

Balanced and Unambiguous Yes/No Question

Do you submit reports? (Check one)

☐ Yes, I submit reports

☐ No, I do not submit reports

(A) "Implied-No" Choices   The implied-no choice format, a variation of yes/no format, is used because it is easy to read and quick to answer. A failure to check an item implies "no." When auditors want to emphasize the "no" alternative, they can expand the implied-no format to include one column for "yes" answer and one for "no." If "no" is not included as an alternative, noes will be overreported, because the auditors will not be able to differentiate real noes from omissions and nonresponses.

(B) Single-Item Choices   In single-item choices, which is another variation of the yes/no format, respondents choose not "yes" or "no" but one of two or more alternatives. This is because "yes" and "no" are not one of the choices given. Since yes/no and single-item choices are similar, they have the same types of problems, but the difficulties are less pronounced in some respects and accentuated in others.

If used carefully, the single-item choice can be efficient. It often serves to filter out people or to skip them through parts of the questionnaire. It is not likely to be overused and cause excessive cycles of repetition. Furthermore, the question writer is not likely to compress the question into a double-barreled item. The single-item-choice format is also not subject to bias from yea-sayers or naysayers, and eliminating the negative alternative reduces misinterpretation.

But there are problems. In the single-item choice format, the writer is more apt to bias one of the choices by understating or overstating it. Some writers may not properly emphasize the second alternative; others, aware of this tendency, overcompensate.

(C) Expanded Yes/No Questions   One way around the yes/no constraints is to use an expanded yes/no format. The expanded yes/no format gives: a measure of intensity; avoids some of the biases common to yes/no, implied-no, and single-item-choice questions; and resolves the problem of quibbling.

> *Expanded Yes/No Format*
> ☐ Yes
> ☐ Probably yes
> ☐ Probably no
> ☐ No

The expanded alternatives can have qualifiers other than "probably yes" and "probably no." Qualifiers can be changed to meet the situation—"generally yes" and "generally no" or "for the most part yes" and "for the most part no."

(D) Multiple-Choice Questions The most efficient format—and the most difficult to design—is the multiple-choice question. The respondent is exposed to a range of choices and must pick one or more. Usually four or five choices are included, the "other—specify" being the final choice.

Multiple-choice questions are difficult to write because the writer must provide a comprehensive range of nonoverlapping choices. They must be a logical and reasonable grouping of the types of experience the respondents are likely to have encountered.

(E) Free-Choice Questions Yes/no, implied-no, single-item, and expanded formats are forced choices in that respondents must answer one way or the other. Forced-choice items generally simplify measurement and analysis because they divide the population clearly into those who do and those who do not or those who have and those who have not. Unfortunately, putting the population into just two categories may also oversimplify the picture and yield error, bias, and unreliable answers. To avoid this problem and to reduce the respondent's burden, a middle category can be added.

> *Expanded Yes/No Format with Middle Category*
> ☐ Yes
> ☐ Probably yes
> ☐ Uncertain
> ☐ Probably no
> ☐ No

Even though the proportion of yesses to noes will not change, the auditor will have a better measure of the yes/no polarization, because the middle category absorbs those who are uncertain. *A good rule of thumb is that if we are not certain that nearly everyone can make a clear choice, we include a middle category.*

Usually the question writer will also put in an escape choice to filter out those for whom the question is not relevant. Examples are "not applicable," "no basis to judge," "have not considered the issue," and "can't recall."

Expanded Yes/No Format with Escape Choice

☐ Yes

☐ Probably yes

☐ Uncertain

☐ Probably no

☐ No

☐ Have not considered the issue

(F) Fill-in-the-Blank Questions Each questionnaire usually has some fill-in-the-blank questions. They are not open-ended because the blanks are accompanied by parenthetical directions that specify the units in which the respondent is to answer.

Fill-in-the-Blank Questions

What size is your manufacturing plant? _____ (in square feet)

What is your department budget? _____ (in dollars)

Fill-in-the-blank questions should be reserved for very specific requests. The instructions should be explicit and should specify the answer units. Sometimes several fill-in-the blank questions are asked at once in a row, column, or matrix format.

(vi) Quality of Questionnaires

The quality of questionnaires can be checked by several methods, some of which are carried out during the design phase and others during the data collection or analysis phase. During the design phase, the questionnaire should be pretested (or pilot tested) on selected persons or departments that represent the range of conditions likely to influence the auditor's results. The questionnaires should also be sent out for review by experts who are familiar with both the issue area and the respondent group. In addition to expert reviews, peer reviews can be done by an auditor who worked on the auditable area before or a new auditor who never worked before in that area.

QUALITY ASSURANCE OF QUESTIONNAIRES

The quality of questionnaires can be checked by four methods:

1. Pretesting
2. Expert review
3. Peer review
4. Validation and verification techniques

The first three methods belong to the data design phase, while the fourth method is used in the data collection and data analysis phases.

Pretesting and expert review are some of the best ways to ensure that the instrument actually communicates what it was intended to communicate, that it is standardized and will be uniformly interpreted by the target population, and that it will be free of design flaws that could lead to inaccurate answers.

Important parts of quality assurance effort are validating, verifying, or corroborating responses; conducting reliability studies; and analyzing nonresponses. These tasks are conducted during the data collection and analysis phases.

(vii) Pretesting

By testing the questionnaire before it is distributed, auditors can assess whether they are asking the right group of auditees the right questions in the right way and whether the respondents are willing and able to supply the information the auditors need. Pretests are conducted with a small set of respondents from the population that eventually will be considered for the full-scale study. Troublesome questions discovered in the pretest can be dropped.

Mail questionnaires are pretested by means of personal interviews. During the interviews, a wealth of information can be obtained by observing respondents as they complete the form and by debriefing them about the question-answering experience. The purpose of debriefing is not only to identify items that are difficult or misunderstood but also to get at the cause of these problems.

(viii) Expert Review

Expert review seeks outside comments on the questionnaire approach. The purpose of this expert review is twofold: (1) to determine whether the questions and the manner in which they are asked are adequate for addressing the larger questions posed by the audit; and (2) to find out whether the target population for the survey has the knowledge to answer the questions. People who provide expert reviews do not act as pretest interviewees; they do not answer the questions but provide a critique. Some sources of expert reviews include audit managers from the same or other business units or divisions, auditee managers, and business school professors.

(ix) Data Validation, Verification, Corroboration, and Reliability of Questionnaires

Validation is an effort to ensure that the questionnaire is actually measuring the variables it was designed to measure. The concept of construct validation requires the demonstration of the relationship between the measurement and the construct being measured in a setting as controlled as possible. Construct validity is tested with a number of people under controlled conditions. A very practical method of assessing validity is to use content validity. In this approach, auditors might ask experts to make sure that the measure includes the content they want to measure. Validity can be tested by looking at the relationships between factors that should be positively correlated or negatively correlated. For example, measures of the quality of training ought to correlate positively with productivity. If they do, we have some confidence in the validity of the measures. The measure of a participative management style ought to correlate inversely with a measure of an authoritative management style. If it does, confidence in the validity of the measure is strengthened.

CRITERIA FOR QUESTIONNAIRES

- The term "validation" refers to the purpose of measure (shows that the observation measures what it is supposed to measure).
- The term "verification" refers to the accuracy of data.
- The term "corroboration" refers to validation in some cases.
- The term "reliability" refers to the consistency of measures.

Validation is important because if the questions are not valid measures of the constructs being studied, even answers verified as accurate will not provide the quality data needed for findings, conclusions, and recommendations.

Verification is a way of checking or testing questionnaire answers with records or direct observation to reduce the risk of using data that are inaccurate. The accuracy of data is tested by comparing the data against an accurate source, by putting in controls that reduce observation errors, or by repeating the measurement process. The extent of verification should be based on the type of data, their use as evidence to address the assignment's objectives, the relative risk of the data being erroneous, and an alternative available to verify data, including time and resource constraints.

The most convincing method of verification is to compare on a test basis the respondent's answers with evidence developed from an on-site inspection that involves direct observation or a review of documents and records. Ideally, such verifications are conducted on a statistical sample of the respondent population. Practically, a judgment sample considered typical of the population is often used.

VERIFICATIONS VERSUS VALIDATION

- Verification is different from validation.
- Ideally verification is conducted by testing a sample, which is time consuming and expensive.
- Validation does not require sampling approaches.

Corroboration (referred to as validation in some circumstances) of questionnaire results against similar information from another, independent source can also provide supporting evidence to increase confidence in the relative accuracy of questionnaire data.

The **reliability** of questionnaire results tests whether a question always gets the same results when repeated under similar conditions. *Answers can be highly reliable without being either verified or valid.* A reliable measure is one that, used repeatedly in order to make observations, produces consistent results. Testing reliability is difficult and expensive, because auditors have to either replicate the data collection or return to those who were questioned before. People do not like to be retested.

VERIFICATION VERSUS RELIABILITY

- The procedures for testing the reliability of answers are different from those for verifying answers.
- When information is verified, auditors usually go to a different source for the same information or use a different technique on the same source, such as observations or in-depth interviews.
- To test reliability, auditors have to administer the same test to the same source.

Why do auditors have to validate, verify, corroborate, and make reliability checks during data collection or analysis phases? Nonstandardized questionnaires require this kind of checking. Auditors are either measuring things that have not been measured before or measuring previously measured things under different circumstances. Standardized questionnaires have already been tested during their design and development phase.

(x) Analysis of Questionnaire Nonresponses

Nonresponses to questionnaires, whether an individual item or a section that is not completed, must be analyzed because high or disproportionate nonresponse rates can threaten the credibility and generalizability of the findings. The real problem is not so much the decreased sample size but whether those who chose not to answer had disproportionately different views from those who did. This would threaten the representativeness of the sample and the ability to generalize from the sample to the population. Inductive generalizations cannot be made under these circumstances. Therefore, reasons for nonresponses should be investigated.

(xi) Quality Instructions for Questionnaires

A questionnaire should be easy to read, attractive, and interesting. Good graphics and layout can catch the respondent's attention, counteract negative impressions, cut the answer time in half, and reduce completion errors.

The first part of the questionnaire should present the introduction and instructions. The instructions should:

- State the purpose of the survey.
- Explain who the data collector is, the basis of its authority, and why it is conducting the survey.
- Tell how and why the respondents were selected.
- Explain why their answers are important.
- Tell how to complete the form.
- Provide mail-back instructions.
- List the person to call if help is needed to complete the form.
- Provide assurances of confidentiality and anonymity when appropriate.
- Tell how long it will typically take to complete the form.
- Explain how the data will be used.
- Explain who will have access to the information.
- Disclose data uses that may affect the respondents.
- Present the response efforts as a favor and thank the respondents for their cooperation.

The instructions should be concise, courteous, and businesslike.

(xii) Use of Rating Scales for Questionnaires

Questions are subject to ranking and rating. Ranking questions are used to make very difficult distinctions between things that are of nearly equal value. The question forces the respondent to value one alternative over another no matter how close they are. The value that is assigned is a relative value. Rating questions are used when the alternatives are likely to vary somewhat in value and when auditors want to know how valuable the alternative is rather than if it is a little more or less valuable than the next alternative. The next list discusses ranking and rating.

- **Ranking.** In ranking, the respondents are asked to tell which alternative has the highest value, which has the second highest, and so on. They rank the choices with respect to one another, but their answers tell little about the intrinsic value of their choices. Ranking starts to get hard for people when there are more than seven categories. Respondents begin to lose track of where they are with respect to the first, last, and middle positions. When this happens, they make mistakes. Ranking questions have to be written very carefully. The slightest lapse in clarity in the question or the instruction given will cause some people to rank in the reverse order or to assign two alternatives the same rank or to forget to rank every alternative. Nonetheless, sometimes ranking must be used, as when an order of issues or items is important.

- **Rating.** Rating questions are perhaps the most useful format because we usually want to know the actual or absolute value of the trait we are measuring. Ratings are assigned solely on the basis of the score's absolute position within a range of possible values. For example, a rating scale might be assigned these categories: of little importance, somewhat important, moderately important, and so on. In writing rating questions, it is useful to categorize the scales in equal intervals and anchor the scale positions whenever possible. Aside from the scaling, rating questions are easier to write properly and cause less error than ranking questions. Ratings usually provide an adequate level of quantification for most purposes, and rating formats are simpler than ranking formats.

> *Examples of a Rating Question*
>
> Based on what we discussed, how would you classify the risk involved in your accounts receivable operations? (Check one)
>
> ☐ Maximum risk
>
> ☐ Moderate risk
>
> ☐ Minimum risk
>
> ☐ No risk

Other question formats include the Gutman format and intensity scale format, where the latter includes the Likert scale and amount and frequency intensity scales. In questions written in the **Gutman format**, the alternatives increase in comprehensiveness; that is, the higher-valued alternatives include the lower-valued alternatives. The intensity scale format is usually used to measure the strength of an attitude or an opinion.

Another frequently used intensity scale format is the **Likert or agree-or-disagree scale**. The Likert scale is easy to construct. However, if the writer is not careful, the simplicity and adaptability of the Likert scale format are often paid for by greater error and threats to validity.

Consider an example of the Likert scale: "My supervisor never lets me participate in decisions (agree or disagree)." First, there is bias. The Likert scale presents only one side of an argument, and some people have a natural tendency to agree with the status quo or the argument presented. This bias can be countered by presenting the converse statement also: "My supervisor lets me participate in decisions (agree or disagree)."

Another problem is that the extent of the respondent's agreement or disagreement with a statement may not correspond directly to the strength of the respondent's attitude about the Likert statement posed in the question. The respondent may consider the statement either true or false and respond as if the question were in an either/or format rather than a graduated scale measuring the intensity of a belief.

The Likert question uses the statement as a reference point or anchor. Hence, what is measured may be not the strength of the respondent's attitude over the complete range of intensities but rather the range of intensities bounded or referenced by the position of the anchoring statement at one end of the range and unbounded at the other end of the range. The indirect approach in the Likert scale may produce misleading results for a variety of reasons. It is usually better to use a direct approach that measures the strength of the respondent's actual attitude over a complete range of intensities. For example, it is better to reformulate the item from "My supervisor never lets me participate in decisions" to "To what extent, if at all, do you participate in decisions?"

However, one situation in which the Likert scale is very useful is when the extent of an agreement or disagreement is closely and indirectly related to the statement. For instance, the respondent may be asked about the extent to which he or she agrees or disagrees with a policy.

Example of a Likert Scale Question

How do you feel about policy A? (Check one)

☐ Strongly agree

☐ Agree more than disagree

☐ Undecided

☐ Disagree more than agree

☐ Strongly disagree

Many audit questions ask the respondent to "quantify" either amounts or frequencies. These questions are relatively simple. They use certain derivative words to characterize the amount, frequency, or number of items being measured. For example, traits like "help," "hindrance," "effect," "increase," or "decrease," can be quantified by adding "little," "some," "moderate," "great," or "very great." Certain adjectives, such as "some" and "great," have a stable and relatively precise level of quantification. Quantities can also be implied by the sequence of numbered alternatives ordered with respect to increasing or decreasing intensity.

Examples of Amount Intensity Scale

☐ Little or no hindrance

☐ Some hindrance

☐ Moderate hindrance

☐ Great hindrance

☐ Very great hindrance

Frequencies or occurrences of events are treated the same way. Question writers know that words like "sometimes," "great many," or "very often" mean about one-fourth of the amount or 25% of the time and three-fourths or 75% of the time, respectively, to most people. Similarly, "about half" and "moderate" anchor the midpoints. As with amount intensity scales, it is important to use both numbered, ordered scalar presentations and words to quantify the scale intervals.

Examples of Frequency Intensity Scale

☐ Seldom if ever

☐ Sometimes

☐ Often

☐ Very often

☐ Always or almost always

In many amount and frequency measures, where ambiguities are likely to occur, it is also important to use proportional anchors, such as fractions and percents, or verbal descriptive anchors, such as once a day or once a month, in addition to the adjective and scale number anchors.

Examples of Frequency Intensity Scale with Proportional Anchors

- ☐ Seldom if ever (0 to 10% of the time)
- ☐ Sometimes (about one quarter of the time)
- ☐ Often (about one half of the time)
- ☐ Very often (about three quarters of the time)
- ☐ Always or almost always (90 to 100% of the time)

(xiii) Application of Rating Scales

Rating scales can be applied in many instances. For example, rating scales can be used as a method of employee performance evaluation. In the graphic rating scale method, a set of performance factors, such as quantity and quality of work, depth of knowledge, cooperation, and initiative, can be used to rate each factor on an incremental scale of 1 (poor) to 5 (excellent). Advantages of rating scales are that they are less time consuming to develop and administer and allow for quantitative analysis and comparisons. The disadvantage is a lack of depth of information on the performance factors when compared to anecdotal records (discussed below).

Behavioral anchored rating scales combine major elements from the anecdotal records and graphic rating scale approaches. Examples of behavioral descriptions that are used to rate include "plans," "anticipates," "executes," and "solves problems." The appraiser rates the employee based on actual behavior on the job rather than general descriptions or traits.

(xiv) Methods for Gathering Feedback

Auditors face some degree of nonrespondent problem whether they are conducting personal interviews or mailing questionnaires. The reason is that auditees may not be available, may be unable to locate, or do not answer the questions completely or sufficiently. In some cases, auditors may want to obtain feedback on the quality and relevancy of interview or the questionnaire. The higher the nonrespondent problem, the lower the feedback.

The best approach to gather feedback would be to conduct a short phone survey of auditees, using some of the critical questions on the data collection instrument, or second-mail the questionnaire.

Some other common methods for gathering feedback include sending standardized letters for comments, requesting customized written responses, receiving voice mail answers, and receiving electronic mail answers. A stratified sample can be selected to determine the number of auditees to request for feedback.

(c) Checklists

Auditors are familiar with using checklists for various purposes. They are memory aids to ensure that all required steps or actions are completed. Checklists can be used in any phase of the audit: planning, survey, fieldwork, report writing. Checklists are especially useful during

KEY CONCEPTS TO REMEMBER: Questionnaires

- The primary purpose of an internal control questionnaire (ICQ) is to make preliminary appraisals of controls to be tested.

- The primary advantage of using an ICQ is that it reduces the risk of overlooking important aspects of the system.

- The major disadvantage of using an ICQ is that questionnaires may be completed routinely by users without auditors really understanding overall operations of internal control systems.

- ICQ provides indirect audit evidence that might need corroboration. The verification technique is most appropriate for testing the quality of the preaudit of payment vouchers described in an ICQ.

- The most appropriate use of questionnaires is to help review internal control.

- The ICQ does not highlight the interaction of departments; it is a static data collection instrument.

working paper review to ensure that all components of the quality assurance program are addressed properly.

Supervisors can use checklists to document their review comments when they look at the auditor's working papers. Supervisors can later use the review comment sheet (also called point sheet) for follow-up to ensure that all points that were raised are cleared by the auditor who worked on the audit. There is no limit to the number of applications of the checklists, and it really depends on the creativity of the auditor. Audit quality can be enhanced with the use of checklists since they provide a discipline and framework to work with by all parties involved in an audit. For example, checklists can be used during a peer review of working papers to mark compliance with the requirements.

(d) Focus Groups

(i) Purpose of Focus Groups

The primary purpose of focus groups is to collect qualitative data, with quantitative data being the secondary purpose. Focus groups do represent an important tool for discovery and exploration of ideas and opinions. They are a choice between individual interviews or focus group interviews. Focus groups, which consist of 6 to 12 people, produce a rich body of data expressed in the respondents' own words and context.

Surveys ask for responses expressed on point rating scale or other constrained response categories. Surveys produce more artificial responses than focus groups due to absence of interaction among respondents. The data provided by focus groups are idiosyncratic and difficult to summarize. In surveys, the response categories may or may not be those with which the respondents are comfortable, although they may still be selecting answers.

SURVEY VERSUS FOCUS GROUP

- Surveys produce artificial responses due to lack of interaction among respondents.

- Due to interaction among respondents, focus groups do not produce artificial responses.

(ii) The Process

The process begins with a statement of the problem. The group has focus and a clearly identifiable agenda. Then a sampling frame is identified. A moderator needs to be located to design the questions used in the group interview. The moderator leads the group through the questions and seeks to facilitate discussion among all the group members. The moderator should be perceived as nonevaluative and nonthreatening. Analysis and interpretation of data and report writing concludes the process.

(iii) Uses and Misuses

Focus group interviews should be considered when these circumstances are present:

- Insights are needed in exploratory or preliminary studies, with limited scope or limited resources. The goal might be to gain reactions to areas needing improvement.

- There is a communication or understanding gap between groups or categories of people. Focus groups bring people together.

- The moderator desires ideas to emerge from the group. Focus groups possess the capacity to become more than the sum of their participants, to exhibit a synergy that individuals alone cannot achieve.

Focus group interviews should **not** be considered when these circumstances are present:

- The environment is emotionally charged, issues are polarized, trust had deteriorated, and the participants are in a confrontational mode.

- The moderator has lost control over critical aspects of the study. The moderator should maintain control over the selection of participants, question development, and analysis protocol.

- Statistical projections or estimations are needed. Focus groups do not involve sufficient number of participants, nor does the sampling strategy lend itself to statistical projections. The types of generalizations that arise from focus group results tend to be more general than specific, more tentative, and more descriptive.

(iv) Advantages and Disadvantages of Focus Groups

Some major advantages resulting from focus groups include:

- Focus groups provide data from a group of individuals much more quickly and at less cost than would be the case if each individual were interviewed separately. They also can be assembled on much shorter notice than would be required for a more systematic and larger survey.

- The focus group interview process is objective and rigorous as it rests on an extensive body of empirical theory and research as well practice.

- Focus groups allow the moderator to interact directly with respondents. This provides opportunities for the clarification of responses, for follow-up questions, and for the probing of responses. Respondents can qualify responses or give contingent answers to questions. In addition, it is possible for the moderator to observe nonverbal responses, such as gestures, smiles, frowns, and so forth.

- The open response format provides an opportunity to obtain large and rich amounts of data in the respondents' own words. It allows respondents to react to and build on the responses of other group members.

Some major **disadvantages** resulting from the focus groups include:

- The results obtained in a focus group may be biased by a very dominant or highly opinionated member of the group. More reserved group members may be hesitant to talk.

- The open-ended nature of responses obtained in focus groups often makes summarization and interpretation of results difficult.

- The moderator may bias results by knowingly or unknowingly providing cues about what types of responses and answers are desirable.

- Each focus group really represents a single observation, although it is a group of people. Group consensus is given here. Therefore, more than one focus group should be conducted on a specific topic.

(v) Audit Application of Focus Groups

Focus groups can be used in the survey phase of an audit when little is known about the area to be audited. For example, they can be used to obtain general background information about an area; to diagnose the potential for problems with a new policy, program, product, or service; to generate impressions of policies, products, programs, or services; and to interpret previously obtained quantitative data through mail surveys.

(e) Observations

Observation is a direct notice of things, events, and people's actions. It is the ability to see what is happening in an individual and/or within a group and to respond appropriately. Watching body language in addition to words and actions is an additional benefit of observation. In other words, body language says more than the words and actions of people.

Observation is considered a reliable audit procedure but one that is limited in usefulness. It is not sufficient to satisfy any audit assertion other than existence. Observation provides information on how transactions are handled at one particular point in time, not how they are processed throughout the period under study. It provides a snapshot of operations. The reason why observation is limited is that individuals can react differently when being observed.

(f) Unobtrusive Measures

An unobtrusive measure is the one that is not readily noticeable to others. An auditor can use an unobtrusive measure, for example, to check to see if all hourly employees in a manufacturing plant are clocking in when they report to their workstation, as opposed to someone else clocking in for them. An auditor would stay unobtrusively in an area where employees clock in to determine their natural motions and actions. Compliance with procedure is the auditor's major objective here.

Another application is to determine whether security guards at a retail store are checking all bags and personal belongings of all employees when they leave the store building. An auditor would observe this in an unobtrusive manner so that the security guard would not notice him or her. It is a test of control compliance with the store policy that all employee bags are checked every day at quitting time.

(g) Anecdotal Records

Anecdotal records constitute a description or narrative of a specific situation or condition. For example, during the employee performance evaluation process, the appraiser writes down anecdotes that describe what the employee did that was especially effective or ineffective. The appraiser can be the immediate supervisor, peers, self-evaluation by the employee, or immediate subordinate(s).

Another example of use of anecdotal records is allowing a fraud suspect to make a narrative response concerning the incident after the interviewer has established rapport and sold the suspect on the need to cooperate in the interview.

(h) Nonstatistical Sampling Method

This section discusses sampling theory, sampling plan and operations, and the similarities and differences between statistical sampling and nonstatistical (judgmental) sampling.

(i) Sampling Theory

The primary reason for an auditor to use statistical sampling is to allow him or her to quantify, and therefore control, the risk of making an incorrect decision based on sample evidence. Statistical sampling does not prevent auditors from using professional judgment in conducting reviews. Statistical sampling is merely a tool to help them make wise decisions. Auditors still decide what type of review to make, how and when to use sampling, and how to interpret the results. In applying statistical sampling techniques to audit testing, auditors must make six decisions that involve professional judgment.

1. **Auditors must define the problem.** They must decide what to measure, what type of information will provide sufficient facts for the formation of an opinion, and what testing procedures to use.

2. **They must specify the level of confidence.** This is precision, or the probability that an estimate made from the sample will fall within a stated interval of the true value for the population as a whole. Auditors may think of it as the percentage of times that a correct decision (within the specified precision limits) will result from using an estimate based on a sample.

3. **Auditors must define the population for size and other characteristics.** They decide what type of items will be included and excluded, and specify the time period to be covered.

4. **They must determine the areas applicable to sampling.** The auditors' assessment of the internal control system for an area may determine whether statistical sampling is appropriate. A strong internal control system may reduce testing to the minimum necessary for verification and may therefore call for a different sampling plan or no statistical sampling at all. Prior experience, as well as information from prior audits, plays a role here. Prior audits may suggest that certain kinds of records are more prone to error and need higher verification rates than other kinds of records. Thus, auditors may have to stratify the population between records likely to have a high error rate and those likely to have a low error rate.

5. **Auditors must decide the maximum error rate that they will consider acceptable, and they must define an error.** Or, if auditors are attempting to estimate the value of some balance sheet amount, they must determine the required precision of the estimate in terms of the materiality of the amount being examined and the overall objective.

6. **They must draw conclusions about the population from the sampling results.** In arriving at these conclusions, auditors must judge the significance of the errors they have discovered.

Because statistical sampling provides more and better information than guesswork, it permits greater use of professional judgment and enables auditors to analyze the results of tests more effectively. And by reducing the workload, statistical sampling allows auditors more time to use professional judgment.

Basically there are two approaches to audit sampling: (1) statistical and (2) nonstatistical. The choice is based on costs and benefits. Sampling risk—the risk that the sample is not a representative of the population—is present in both approaches.

KEY CONCEPTS TO REMEMBER: What Makes a Good Sample?

- A good sample should have four characteristics: representative, corrective, protective, and preventive.

- "Representative" means that the sample estimates the true population characteristic as accurately as possible.

- "Corrective" means that the sample will locate as many error items as possible, so that they can be corrected.

- "Protective" means that the person who does the sampling attempts to include the maximum number of high-value items in the sample. This approach is common when auditors isolate the high-value items from the rest of the population, gather data on all these items, and gather data from a sample of the remaining items.

- "Preventive" means that the sampling method gives auditees no idea which items will be selected during the audit.

(ii) Sampling Plan and Operations

Topics covered include in sampling, sampling operations, sample size, precision, and confidence, and types of risks.

(A) Sampling Plan When designing a sampling plan, auditors should keep in mind the desirability of obtaining a sample that is as representative, corrective, protective, and preventive as possible. To do so, they should stratify the population on the basis of dollar value and the likelihood that the items contain errors, use some random method to select the sample from each stratum, and weight the results from each stratum to compute overall estimates for the population. It is not possible, however, to optimize all four characteristics in a single sample. Instead, a balance must be struck, depending on which characteristic is most important in view of the audit objective. Also, in certain types of audits, one or more of the characteristics may not require consideration at all.

One of the auditor's objectives is to answer questions about a universe of people or things. This universe is called the population. This objective can be achieved by looking at a sample of things, if the sample is representative of the population. A representative sample has approximately the same distribution of characteristics as the population from which it was drawn.

(B) Sampling Operations There are three components in the sampling operations: (1) sample design, (2) sample selection procedures, and (3) estimation procedures. The term "sample design" refers to the plans made for the overall way in which a sample will be related to a population. Selection procedures are the methods used to select units of samples from a population. Estimation procedures are the ways of estimating the characteristics of a population from information acquired about a sample.

Interrelationships exist among these three components:

1. The sample design will affect the estimation procedures to be used, and it may also affect the selection procedures. Conversely, the sample design is often affected by the estimation procedures to be used.

2. Selection procedures can have a major effect on how precision is estimated.

3. The types of estimates to be developed can have a bearing on the selection procedures to be used.

Auditors usually form conclusions through testing, or "sampling," a portion of a collection of items from a population. The method by which they choose a sample and the degree to which the sample is representative of every item in the population determine whether auditors can form valid conclusions based on testing results.

(C) Sample Size   The determination of an appropriate sample size is part of sample design. Before selecting the sample size, the auditor should decide on the sampling method to be used, the estimation procedure, the sample precision required, and the confidence level desired.

If all other factors in a sampling plan are held constant: (1) changing the measure of tolerable error to a smaller value would cause the sample size to be larger, or (2) changing the audit risk from 5% to 3% would cause the sample size to be larger.

KEY CONCEPTS TO REMEMBER: Sample Size

- A decision to decrease the precision interval (i.e., high precision) would result in an increase in the required sample size.

- A decision to increase the precision interval from 4% to 5% (i.e., less precision) would result in a decrease in the required sample size.

- Sample size varies directly with changes in confidence level, inversely with changes in precision.

- Sample size increases with the use of higher confidence levels.

- Sample size decreases when the auditor increases the amount of tolerable error.

- A stop-and-go sampling plan will minimize the sample size whenever a low rate of noncompliance is expected.

- When relatively few items of high-dollar value constitute a large proportion of an account balance, stratified sampling technique and complete testing of the high-dollar-value items will generally result in a reduction in sample size.

- In an attribute sampling application, holding other factors constant, sample size will increase as the planned precision becomes smaller.

- In a variables sampling application, sample size will increase when the confidence level is changed from 90% to 95%.

(D) Precision Specifying the precision needed for sample estimates is an important part of sample design. The desired precision is the amount of sampling error that can be tolerated but that still permits the results to be useful. It is sometimes called tolerable error or the bound on error. In terms of a stated confidence level, precision is the range into which an estimate of a population characteristic is expected to fall. Factors in the choice of a desired precision include the tolerable level of sampling error, the size of an account balance error considered material, and the objectives of the audit test being conducted. Audit resources available for execution of the sampling plan are not a factor.

Consider this application of precision: Based on a random sample, it is estimated that 4%, plus or minus 2%, of a firm's invoices contain errors. The plus or minus 2% is known as the estimate's precision.

PRECISION VERSUS SAMPLING RISK

- Precision is under the auditor's full control because he or she specifies it.

- Sampling risk is not under the auditor's full control.

- Precision applies to both attributes sampling and variables sampling.

- Sampling risk is present in both attribute sampling and variables sampling work.

KEY CONCEPTS TO REMEMBER: Precision

- The application of the finite correction factor to the precision interval will cause the precision interval to become smaller.

- When a confidence level is changed from 95.5% to 99.7%, and no change in sample standard deviation takes place, the sample size would be larger but achieved precision would not change.

- When planning an attribute sampling application, the difference between the expected error rate and the maximum tolerable error rate is the planned precision.

- In an attribute sampling application, holding other factors constant, sample size will increase as the planned precision becomes smaller.

(E) Precision and Confidence Because precision is a way of expressing the amount of error that can be tolerated, it is related to the accounting concept of materiality. Materiality, or importance, is a relative concept rather than an absolute one. For example, a $100,000 overstatement of the assets for a company whose total assets are only $200,000 would be material while it would be immaterial for a company with total assets of multibillions of dollars.

In addition to specifying the precision of the estimate, auditors must specify the degree of confidence that they want placed in the estimate. This is referred to as confidence level, expressed as a percentage. Confidence level is the complement of the chance that our estimate and its precision will not contain the true but unknown population value. The confidence level should be determined by the importance of the sample results to the overall objectives of the audit.

Two examples will illustrate the relationship between confidence level and risk.

1. A confidence level of 90% means that there are 90 chances out of 100 that the sample results will not vary from the true characteristics of the population by more than specified amount.

2. The complement of the risk that an internal auditor will erroneously conclude adequate compliance with a specific management policy is the confidence level.

PRECISION VERSUS ACCURACY

- "Precision" refers to the maximum amount, stated at a certain confidence level, that we can expect the estimate from a single sample to deviate from the results obtained by applying the same measuring procedures to all the items in the population.

- "Accuracy" refers to the difference between the value of the population from which the sample is selected and the true characteristic that we intend to measure.

(F) Types of Risks Basically, there are two types of risks: (1) sampling and (2) nonsampling risks. **Sampling risk** is the risk that the conclusions reached based on a sample will differ from those conclusions that would be reached by examining the entire population. Usually, the smaller the sample size, the greater will be the sampling risk.

Nonsampling risk arises even if the entire population is tested and is due to errors in auditor judgment, such as use of inappropriate audit procedures and not recognizing errors during sampling. This risk can be controlled with better audit planning and supervision.

The American Institute of Certified Public Accountants in its Statement on Auditing Standards (SAS) 39 describes the two aspects of sampling risk in performing substantive testing.

1. The **risk of incorrect rejection** is the risk that the sample supports the conclusion that the recorded account balance is materially misstated when it is not materially misstated. *This is known as alpha risk, Type I error.*

2. The **risk of incorrect acceptance** is the risk that the sample supports the conclusion that the recorded account balance is not materially misstated when it is materially misstated. *This is known as beta risk, Type II error.*

According to SAS 39, the auditor is also concerned with two aspects of sampling risk in performing compliance tests of internal accounting control.

1. The **risk of overreliance** on internal accounting control is the risk that the sample supports the auditor's planned degree of reliance on the control when the true compliance rate does not justify such reliance.

2. The **risk of underreliance** on internal accounting control is the risk that the sample does not support the auditor's planned degree of reliance on the control when the true compliance rate supports such reliance.

The risk of incorrect rejection and the risk of underreliance on internal accounting control relate to the efficiency of the audit. For example, if the auditor's evaluation of an audit sample leads him or her to the initial erroneous conclusion that a balance is materially misstated when it is not, the application of additional audit procedures and consideration of other audit evidence would ordinarily lead the auditor to the correct conclusion.

Similarly, if the auditor's evaluation of a sample leads him or her to unnecessarily reduce the planned degree of reliance on internal accounting control, the auditor would ordinarily increase the scope of substantive tests to compensate for the perceived inability to rely on internal accounting control to the extent originally planned. Although the audit may be less efficient in these circumstances, the audit is nevertheless effective.

The risk of incorrect acceptance and the risk of overreliance on internal accounting control relate to the effectiveness of an audit in detecting an existing material misstatement.

KEY CONCEPTS TO REMEMBER: Sampling Risk

- Sampling risk is choosing a sample that has proportionately more errors than the population.
- The term "sampling risk" refers to the possibility that even though a sample is properly chosen, it may not be representative of the population.
- Each time an auditor draws a conclusion based on evidence drawn from a sample, a sampling risk is introduced that draws an erroneous conclusion from sample data.

(iii) Statistical Sampling and Nonstatistical (Judgmental) Sampling

The use of any statistical sample requires a high degree of professional judgment to determine the confidence level and the reliability desired and thus what sample criteria to use. It takes judgment to evaluate the effectiveness of internal control procedures in order to test the accuracy and reliability of records as well as to recognize any errors in the items examined.

In using a statistical sample, the auditor must investigate by appropriate means any exceptions or irregularities noted in performing any auditing procedure. This may include a subsequent increase in the sample size. If there are no exceptions, the sample size should not be arbitrarily increased. Statistical sampling helps ensure that audit tests are adequate but not excessive and demonstrates objectivity.

When the choice is made to use statistical sampling, the first step is to devise a sampling plan. A statistical sampling plan includes five major steps.

KEY CONCEPTS TO REMEMBER: Steps Involved in a Statistical Sampling Plan

1. Define the audit objectives.
2. Define the population as clearly as possible, noting any distributional or systematic patterns. This step will establish the population size.
3. Determine the appropriate sampling method and sample selection technique that best fits the characteristics of the population.
4. Determine the precision and reliability desired.
5. Calculate the sample size.

One common error is the assumption that statistical sampling techniques are limited to customer confirmation programs. Auditors should look at all records and transactions that should be reviewed but, due to volume, must be sampled. Statistical sampling may apply to documentation tests, signature verifications, expenses, and so forth.

The auditor must be careful with statistical sampling. There are many different sampling techniques, and not all of them are appropriate in a given circumstance. Correct application of the wrong method is an error that is fairly common and should be avoided.

The auditor must not let the mere application of a statistical method lead to a false sense of security. Statistical samples are subject to some degree of error. Absolutely no inferences can be made from a statistical sample except that of the likelihood of the sample being representative of the population from which it is drawn. Statistical sampling is no substitute for judgment. The auditor must decide the sampling method most appropriate, the confidence level and precision that are appropriate, and even the correct definition of "population." An error in any of these judgments can lead to incorrect conclusions in spite of the elegance of the mathematics.

Although using statistical methods to select samples is almost always preferable to selecting samples judgmentally, judgmental sample selection may be appropriate in some circumstances. However, auditors should always justify their use of judgmental sample selection in the working papers.

Sampling, whether statistical or nonstatistical (judgmental), is **not** appropriate when examination of 100% of an account balance is required, inquiry and observation techniques are used to collect audit evidence, and analytical procedures are used to evaluate the appropriateness of values reported by the auditee. Analytical procedures examine the entire population instead of examining only part, as in sampling. Accounts with low risk of material errors are included in the sample, and examination of few items is done without evaluating the characteristics of the population.

Auditors should document the conclusions drawn from the samples, whether the samples are statistically or judgmentally selected. When the population size and audit objectives are sufficient to warrant statistical samples, the samples will provide certain mathematical confidence levels to support the conclusions.

Exceptions must be classified as either critical or noncritical. Critical errors are those that cannot be tolerated (e.g., errors caused by deliberate falsification of transactions or account balances). Any critical errors must be analyzed and the underlying causes determined. The scope of the work also must be increased.

Noncritical errors are those exceptions that have a lesser impact (e.g., clerical or typing errors). If numerous clerical errors exist, the department should be required to resolve the problems, and sufficient follow-up audit procedures should be pursued.

Exhibit 3.4 summarizes similarities and differences between statistical and nonstatistical sampling approaches.

3.2 Data Analysis and Interpretation

Topics such as computerized audit tools and techniques and analytical review techniques are covered in this section.

Statistical sampling approaches	Nonstatistical sampling approaches
• Require auditor's judgment	• Require auditor's judgment
• Basic audit procedures are the same	• Basic audit procedures are the same
• Permitted as a professional standard	• Permitted as a professional standard
• Use the laws of probabilities to measure sampling risk associated with the sampling procedures	• Cannot measure the sampling risk
	• Sample selection methods may use statistics, but evaluation of the sample results could be nonstatistical
• Sample selection methods use statistics	
• Involve additional costs due to technical training required	• Fewer costs due to minimal training requirements
• Can explicitly measure and control sampling risk	• Sampling risk cannot be explicitly measured or controlled
• Require computer software and hardware for efficient use	• Do not require computer facilities
	• Provide subjective conclusions that are subjected to challenge
• Provide objective conclusions based on sample results	• Compatible with a wider variety of sample selection methods
• Compatible with limited number of sample selection methods	• Sample is smaller and is based on judgment
• Sample is larger and is based on mathematics	

EXHIBIT 3.4 Statistical and Nonstatistical Sampling Approaches

(a) Computerized Audit Tools and Techniques

(i) Auditing around the Computer versus Auditing with the Computer

There are two approaches to testing computer-based data. They are characterized as auditing around the computer and auditing with the computer. The appropriate approach or combination of approaches is dependent on the nature of the related system (see Exhibit 3.5).

	Auditing around the computer	Auditing with the computer
Time involved to do the audit	High	Low
Cost involved to do the audit	Low/Medium	Medium/High
Audit effectiveness	Low/Medium	High
Technical knowledge required of auditor	Low	High

EXHIBIT 3.5 Auditing Around the Computer and Auditing with the Computer

(A) Auditing Around the Computer   Auditing around the computer assumes that techniques and procedures the computer uses to process data need not be considered as long as there is a visible audit trail and/or the result can be manually verified. This approach bypasses the computer in either of two ways.

In the first way, computer output is compared to or confirmed by an independent source. This approach confirms computer-processed data with third parties or compares data with physical counts, inspections, records, files, and reports from other sources. Physical counts and inspections can verify quantity, type, and condition of tangible assets.

Auditors can also conduct commonsense examinations of printed data output to reveal potential reliability problems. These inspections can establish data reliability when a low to very low level of data testing is required. When a moderate to high level of testing is required, these tests should be supplemented by more extensive procedures. These questions are examples of commonsense data tests: Are amounts too small? Are amounts too large? Are data fields complete? Are calculations correct?

Although confirmations and comparisons directly test the accuracy of computer output and effectively disclose fictitious data, they may not detect incomplete data input. When data completeness is in doubt, confirmations or comparisons should be supplemented by tracing a sample of source records to computer output.

The second way to bypass the computer in confirming data reliability is to select source transactions, manually duplicate the computer processes, and compare the results with the computer output. Examples include salary payments, specific benefit payments, and loan balances and delinquent amounts.

Although this approach can test the completeness of computer output as well as the accuracy of computer processing, it does not disclose fictitious data (i.e., data that have been entered into the computer but are not supported by source records). If fictitious data are an issue, tracing data from the computer to source records should be considered.

The usefulness of auditing around the computer diminishes as the number and complexity of computer decisions increases. The process may be impractical when sophisticated data processing activities are involved. *A principal disadvantage of auditing around the computer is that the integrity of the audit trail through the computer is not tested.*

(B) Auditing with the Computer Auditing with the computer means that computer-programmed tests are used, in part, to measure data reliability.

After determining the completeness and accuracy of computer input by manually tracing data to and/or from a sample of source records, this approach uses auditor-developed computer-programmed tests to examine data reasonableness and identify defects that would make data unreliable.

An advantage of auditing with the computer is that it can be used regardless of the computer system's complexity or the number of decisions the computer makes. Auditing with the computer is also fast and accurate, permitting a much larger scope of testing than would be practical with other methods.

The first step in developing computer-programmed tests is to identify what computer information is to be used as evidence and what data elements were used to produce it. Auditors should test all data elements that affect the assignment objective(s).

When an audit-significant data element is derived (i.e., calculated by the computer based on two or more data elements), auditors should also test the source data elements. For example, the element "net pay" might be planned for use as evidence to meet an assignment's objective(s). Review of the system's data dictionary shows that a computer program uses three other data elements to calculate net pay: "hourly rate," "hours worked," and "deductions." Errors in any of these data elements would make "net pay" incorrect. Therefore, auditors should determine the accuracy of each data element.

After identifying the relevant data elements, the data dictionary can be examined to define the attributes of each data element and identify rules that each should meet. If a data element fails these requirements, the computer may exclude it or process it in a way that does not ensure an accurate result. Computer programs frequently have default logic that may cause a missing or defective data element to be erroneously processed due to incorrect assumptions.

Understanding a data element also makes it possible for audit staff to develop reasonableness assumptions that can be programmed as commonsense tests. Data attributes should also consider expected relationships among data elements. Although developed independently, a data element may have a reasonable relationship to another data element. For example, some kinds of medical procedures are related to age or gender. Determining and testing relationships can reveal errors by disclosing irrational or unlikely relationships, such as a hysterectomy on a male patient.

When auditors have learned about each of the data elements that affects the information relied on, tests are developed to detect errors. Tests are of two types: (1) those that disclose failures of data elements to meet established requirements (called unconditional data tests) and (2) those that disclose illogical relationships (called conditional data tests).

After data tests are developed, the computer is programmed to apply them. The programmed data tests must be validated and tested to ensure that errors revealed during the data testing are the result of incorrect data and not the result of invalid test programs. *Data tests can be developed without knowledge of the technical design of the database or its structure, and layout. This knowledge, however, is needed to program the tests.*

Whether a personal computer or a mainframe computer should be used to process data test depends on factors such as the size of the database, the number and complexity of data tests, required processing speed, computer accessibility, and team expertise. The key point is to ensure that test requirements are properly matched to the application and to the operating environment (personal versus mainframe computer).

(ii) Embedded Audit Modules

Embedded audit data collection modules use one or more specially designed data collection modules embedded in the computer application system to select and record data for subsequent analysis and evaluation. The data collection modules are inserted in the application system or program at points that the auditor determines to be appropriate. The auditor also determines the criteria for selection and recording. Other automated or manual methods may be used to analyze the collected data. This technique is intended to highlight unusual transactions and subject them to audit review and testing. Another name given to this technique is system control audit review file (SCARF).

Unlike other audit methods, this technique uses in-line code; that is, the computer application program performs the audit data collection function at the same time it processes the data for normal production purposes. This has two important consequences for the auditor: (1) in-line code ensures the availability of a comprehensive or very specialized sample of data as desired by the auditor, since strategically placed modules have access to every data element being processed; and (2) retrofitting this technique to an existing system is more costly than implementing the audit module during system development. Therefore, it is preferable for auditors to specify requirements in this regard while the application system is being designed. Ideally, data collection control points should be inserted in the application program processing logic where errors, irregularities, or security breaches are most likely to occur.

(iii) Data Extraction Techniques

Many data extraction tools and techniques are available, such as fourth-generation programming languages, audit hooks, and extended records, and others.

(A) Fourth-Generation Programming Languages Relatively speaking, the fourth-generation programming languages (4GLs) are easy to learn and easy to use than the third-generation languages. 4GLs have online real-time, interactive, query characteristics with a quick turnaround time. 4GLs are command driven and user-friendly software and use nonprocedural statements, unlike the third-generation programming languages (e.g., COBOL) and the traditional audit software packages. Some 4GLs contain both procedural and nonprocedural statements.

With the use of 4GLs, the auditor can make inquiries against online data files. 4GLs can merge different data records and data files. Many 4GLs perform most of the functions that a traditional audit software package does, but 4GLs do not come with some functions, such as accounts receivable aging and confirmations and statistical sampling, that are common to traditional audit software packages. If these functions are needed, the auditor has to insert them in the 4GLs by developing them as special subroutines written in COBOL, FORTRAN, or PL/1 programming languages.

An advantage of 4GLs is their free-format report requests. The use of a 4GL package may enhance auditors' productivity. Any viable 4GL package can be used as a supplement to traditional audit software packages but not as substitute for them.

(B) Audit Hooks Audit hooks are similar to red flags to auditors. They are computer programs used in high-risk systems and are triggered by a condition or event designed by the auditor in conjunction with the information systems (IS) staff and the user. The objective is to act before an error, abnormality, or irregularity gets out of hand. Audit hooks are inserted in application programs to function as red flags. For example, bank internal auditors can use the audit hook in a program that processes dormant customer accounts to observe the activity in the account and, if need be, initiate timely action to correct or eliminate any irregularities that are identified. The difference between the audit hooks technique and the SCARF technique is that an audit hook is used more discreetly for sensitive applications.

(C) Extended Records The extended record technique collects, by means of a special program(s), all the significant data that have affected the processing of an individual transaction. This includes the accumulation of the results of processing into a single record covering the time period that the transaction required to complete processing. The extended record includes data from all the computer application systems that contributed to the processing of a transaction. Such extended records are compiled into files that provide a conveniently accessible source of transaction data. Auditors can extract the transactions that have such extended records using generalized audit software or utility programs and prepare reports for audit review and analysis.

With this technique, the auditor no longer needs to review several computer data files to determine how a specific transaction was processed. With extended records, data are consolidated from different accounting periods and from systems interfacing with the application system being reviewed so that a complete transaction audit trail is physically included in one computer record. This facilitates tests of compliance to organization policies and procedures.

(iv) Generalized Audit Software

Generalized audit software (e.g., ACL and IDEA) should be used to achieve cost-effective audits of computer-based systems where similar audit tasks are required to meet a variety of objectives. Generalized audit software can:

- Provide totals of unusual items.
- Check for duplications, missing information, or range of values.
- Verify calculation totals and analyses produced.
- Examine the existence and consistency of data maintained in files.
- Perform concurrent auditing of data files.
- Select and generate audit confirmations.

The audit software is most effective in verifying the clerical accuracy of an account balance. It is least effective in evaluating the logic of a specific computer program, evaluating the adequacy of internal controls embedded in a computer program, or confirming the existence of internal controls in manual operational procedures.

A limitation to using the audit software is that it can be used only on hardware with compatible operating systems. The audit software does not require significant programming knowledge to be used effectively. It does not require lengthy detailed instructions in order to accomplish specific tasks. It does not require significant modification of the program to be of use. The audit software cannot specify which data elements will be tested and the criteria to be used. The auditor specifies the criteria.

Generalized audit software is the most widely used technique for auditing computer application systems. This technique permits the auditor to analyze a computer-application system data file independently.

Most generalized audit software packages, because of their widespread use and long history, are reliable, highly flexible, and extensively and accurately documented. They are used to test the functions of data editing and validation routines in computer programs.

Generalized audit software packages can foot, cross-foot, balance, stratify, select a statistical sample, select transactions, total, compare, and perform calculations on diverse data elements contained within various data files.

These extensive capabilities are available to the auditor to substantively test computer application programs. Generally, this audit method is used to test the integrity of computer records in a data file or files and not to test the application program logic. However, some insights into the logic may surface through the use of generalized audit software.

Generalized audit software packages are available for batch and online systems. However, in a database environment, generalized audit software may not be usable directly because of complex data storage and access structures. In this case, there are two approaches to this problem.

1. Copy the required portion of the database onto a sequential file that can be accessed with the generalized audit software.
2. Develop a computer interface program that uses the database management system software to access the database.

Many audit software packages that are currently available examine data in personal computer files independently and interactively. Required data files can be downloaded from the host to a personal computer based on some selection criteria. Downloading is a process for selecting and retrieving data from another computer system in a way that makes it usable on a personal computer. It requires the establishment of a compatible communication link between the personal computer and the mainframe computer. This method is used when data already exist in automated form. The data may be available on the computer system or on another electronic medium, such as magnetic tape.

Downloading is frequently used when selecting data from very large data files stored on a mainframe or on tape used on the mainframe. To establish the link between the micro- and mainframe computer, the auditor must determine the appropriate communication protocol and have access rights on the mainframe computer. Standard software for downloading data can be used to select the desired data elements for use. Once the data have been downloaded to the personal computer, they may have to be reformatted for use with available personal computer software.

Another method of entering data into a particular personal computer is to communicate it from another personal computer. Two compatible personal computers can exchange data by using disks, flash drives, thumb drives, pen drives, USB drives or by using existing phone lines and a communications program. Communication links among personal computers permit data entered into a personal computers in the field to be transferred to a headquarters system. A local area network permits data to be transferred to designated recipients on the network or to be stored in common storage files with relative ease.

In some cases, the audit software can be developed on the personal computer and then uploaded to the host computer for program execution. After the program is executed, the results can either stay on the host or be downloaded to a personal computer.

Some personal computer-based packages include interactive procedures for performing a full range of audit tests, such as analyzing data fields, sampling transactions and records, validating data, testing and converting dates, and producing statistical summaries. Reports required by the auditor can be produced in the graph, tables, charts, or hard-copy format.

Two examples of the application of personal computer audit software in a payroll audit follow.

1. Compare current period amounts with previous period amounts for employee gross and net payroll wages. Identify employees with unusual pay amounts after performing reasonableness tests.

2. Select all transactions in specified activity codes and in excess of predetermined amounts. Trace them to proper authorization in personnel files in order to determine if payroll changes are authorized.

Advantages of generalized audit software are:

- It is most widely used to analyze and extract data from computer files.
- It allows the auditor to examine more data on computer records in more detail than when using manual records.
- It can be used to automate working paper preparation.
- It enables auditors to control their own programming and testing work.
- It minimizes the audit staff time allocated to audit testing.

- It minimizes the cost of adapting audit program routines to frequent changes in the application program being used due to a parameter-driven approach used in the audit software.

Disadvantages of generalized audit software are:

- It is least likely to be used for inquiry of online data files.
- It cannot flowchart an application program logic.
- It cannot perform a physical count of inventory or cash.
- It cannot perform continuous monitoring and analysis of transactions.
- It can require IS technical knowledge.

(A) Terminal Audit Software   Terminal audit software accesses, extracts, manipulates, and displays data from online databases using remote terminal inquiry commands. This technique provides the same basic functional capability as the more widely used batch-oriented generalized audit software. It has the advantages of a quicker turnaround and interactive investigation. It provides direct access to data files for periodic audit examination without extensive setup procedures or separate processing. It is, however, useful only in situations where online databases have been established and are already in use.

(B) Special-Purpose or Customized Audit Software   Special-purpose or customized audit software consist of specially developed computer programs to extract and report data from a specific application system's data files. A focused approach in meeting audit needs is the major advantage.

Disadvantages associated with the use of these audit programs are their limited applicability, inflexibility, development cost and time, and high level of computer programming expertise required.

Another problem encountered in using these programs is the maintenance needed to keep pace with changing audit requirements and changing application system functions. On occasion, utility programs can be used for audit purposes.

(v) Spreadsheet Analysis

Auditors perform spreadsheet analysis very extensively with the use of personal computer-based software packages, such as Spreadsheet Auditor and Spreadsheet Analyst. These software packages are designed to serve as an aid in creating error-free spreadsheets. The software prints out: a description of ranges; a map indicating which cells contain formulas, labels, numbers, or macros; and a formula report. A critical point is the accuracy of formulas used in spreadsheet cells and their applicability to business rules.

A list of suggested controls for spreadsheet work follows.

- Spreadsheets should be mapped out clearly to show how the spreadsheet should look. A record of changes should be maintained for important data.
- Proper analysis should be conducted to ensure that the data required for analysis are included and entered in a format amenable to the analytic techniques planned.
- A specific area within the spreadsheet should be designated for data entry to minimize data entry errors. All data should be entered in that area and verified before the data are used.
- A specific area should be denoted in the spreadsheet for parameters of the data entry.

- Sampling and validation criteria should be established for each individual spreadsheet based on principles and judgment.

- Critical data should undergo more vigorous verification methods.

- Adequate quality assurance measures should be implemented during the data entry and analysis stage. This will help eliminate errors and facilitate supervisory review and referencing. Some guidelines include:

  - Minimize data entry errors by using the pointer method to specify a cell or range rather than typing in cell addresses and copying formulas and then editing. Take the time to verify the formula before copying it.

  - Use range names, as they are a good way to identify cells. To facilitate the supervisor's and referencer's review, prepare a list of all named ranges and their locations in the spreadsheet.

  - Protect formulas and key data by using the range protect command.

  - Test the spreadsheet's features, including its formulas and macros, with a small part of the database to ensure that the spreadsheet works as planned. Using a partial database rather than a complete spreadsheet saves time and makes it easier to identify errors in logic.

  - Correct mistakes as soon as they are identified.

  - Format cells using two decimals.

  - Write out macros by spelling what each macro command means.

- To ensure the accuracy of data entry, these precautions should be taken prior to printing the spreadsheet:

  - Use foots and cross foots. By adding an extra row and column of formulas that bracket the totals, the accuracy of the preliminary results can be checked.

  - Use hash totals. To verify that all records are included in the spreadsheet, various hash totals can be used. These totals can be arrived at by adding up the data elements to be used in the subsequent analysis.

  - Use automatic recalculations feature. Each spreadsheet should be set on automatic recalculation for a final recalculation before the information is used in the report and the spreadsheet is given to a referencer or supervisor to be used as support for a statement of fact.

  - Protect the spreadsheet. After verification, when no further changes are anticipated to the spreadsheet, the entire spreadsheet should be protected using the global protect feature.

  - Print out spreadsheet formulas. Printing the formulas facilitates spreadsheet review for accuracy.

  - Include reasonableness checks into formula or particular cells; for example, tax rate should not exceed a certain percentage.

- Some spreadsheets may require more extensive documentation than is practical to place within the spreadsheet itself. In such instances, external documentation should be used for detailed explanation of the spreadsheet. The external documentation should be placed in word processing software or other means. The internal documentation would still contain the next elements, with keys to the external documentation.

  - Job title and code, title of the spreadsheet, work paper index.

- ☐ Purpose of the spreadsheet, reviewer and date, description of the spreadsheet, source of data entered.

- ☐ Documenting the cell addresses for each component of the spreadsheet showing data entry, formula explanations, macro explanations and purpose, range names and their cell addresses.

■ Maintain backup copies of spreadsheet data whenever changes are made. Backup copies should be kept in a location that is secure and different from the location where originals are kept.

■ Spreadsheet applications should be reviewed and tested, both manually and by using audit software. Typical functions that can be provided by spreadsheet audit software include:

- ☐ Documenting the contents of macros used within the spreadsheet as a basis for verifying the logic.

- ☐ Providing a global view of the contents of the spreadsheet application to scan reports for particular patterns or configurations.

- ☐ Verifying for circular references.

- ☐ Displaying the contents of a cell.

Adequate training should be provided to potential users of the spreadsheet software.

(vi) Automated Work Papers

Automated work paper software helps auditors to increase efficiency and productivity because it relieves the boredom of writing out by hand. The software automatically refers to audit work program sections and related audit objectives. Any corrections or changes can be done with ease and without losing the continuity.

Other documentation aids can also help the internal auditor during the fieldwork. One of the ways that an auditor can make sure that the intentions of program/system changes have been achieved is through the use of automated documentation aids. If used properly, these documentation aids can provide flowcharts, tables, or graphs of the program or the system that can be compared at two different points in time (i.e., before and after the program change). Any differences indicate changes to the program logic, data file contents, and Job Control Language (JCL) procedures. The auditor then locates and analyzes the supporting documentation prepared in order to authorize and implement the changes.

Program or system flowcharts, tables, or graphs generated by the automated documentation aids provide a correct picture of what is in the computer programs and data files as opposed to relying on incorrect, obsolete, or incomplete documentation maintained on paper. Automated documentation aids include:

■ Automated flowchart software packages, which read the source code for a computer program and convert it into an easy-to-read flowchart.

■ Computer data file translation software packages, which read the data file descriptions in the computer program and convert them into a convenient and readable format (tabular and graphic).

■ JCL software packages, which depict the job control flow as a graph or table showing the sequence of jobs or steps executed and indicating their procedure names and numbers.

(vii) Source Code Comparison

The best audit tool and technique that an auditor in charge of reviewing program changes can find is a source code compare utility program. Why review and compare source code? It is where program changes, whether authorized or unauthorized, can be made. Source code explains the functions, features, and capabilities of a computerized application system. Programmers write source code in a programming language, such as COBOL. Hence it is most vulnerable to program changes. After the source code is developed, it is placed in a production source code library, which is often protected from unauthorized modifications by the use of program library management software packages.

Simply stated, a source code compare utility program takes two versions of a source code, compares each line of code, and indicates differences and whether the line of code is added, changed, or deleted. This output can be used in a structured walk-through or for management and auditor reviews. The auditor then locates and analyzes the supporting documentation (system, program, computer operations, and user) prepared to authorize and implement the program changes. Lack of supporting documentation is a weakness in controls, which is an indication of potential risk and exposure. The auditor needs to inform management to strengthen internal controls over software maintenance activities.

(viii) Object Code Comparison

As indicated in the previous section, programmers write source code in a programming language, such as COBOL. Later the source code is translated into machine-readable language—object code—for proper execution of the program. Compiler software supplied by vendors performs the translation of source code into object code. Load/executable code, which comes after the object code is link-edited, is then placed in a production library and used for the processing of live data for an application system.

By itself, a source code compare utility software package, described in the previous section, may not be sufficient to ensure that programs are changed properly and effectively. An additional approach is needed to ensure that the object code being executed in production mode is in agreement with the authorized source code.

The auditor can use object code compare utility software packages for comparison of two versions of a program's object code to report any differences. This is accomplished through four steps.

1. Identify the current version of production source code.

2. Recompile the current version of production source code to obtain the corresponding object code (say, Item 1).

3. Inspect the production JCL for correct program name and production library where the object code to be compared (say, Item 2) is placed.

4. Compare Item 1 and Item 2 of object code using an object code compare utility software package.

Any differences indicate that the object code in the production library that is used for program processing is not generated from the corresponding source code. This requires analysis and corrective action by the information technology staff and the auditor. Combined with the source code compare, an object code compare tool is an effective method of detecting, identifying, and controlling program/system changes.

(ix) File Comparison Utility Program

File compare is performed by a utility program supplied by a software vendor (e.g., IEBCOMPR by IBM). The purpose of the tool is to identify differences in data field names and values in two files of data at a static point in time. For example, in a manufacturing environment, a file compare utility program can be used to compare the "on-hand inventory balance" data field appearing in two different files to determine if the values are the same. If not, an abnormal situation exists. This may require analysis and correction if the two values are supposed to be the same.

Another example is to compare file control totals in accounts receivable or payable subsidiary ledger files to file control totals maintained in the general ledger file. Accounting logic requires that these two file control totals be the same. If they are not, an abnormal situation exists. Also, this tool can be used to compare JCL file contents at two points in time to detect any changes. The auditor needs to be imaginative to use this powerful tool in either software maintenance or development activities.

(x) Test Data Method

The test data method verifies computer-processing accuracy of application programs by executing these programs using manually prepared sets of test cases, test data, and expected results of processing. Actual processing results are compared with the expected results. If the two results are identical, the auditor may infer that the program logic is consistent with the documentation.

This method provides auditors with a procedure for review, testing, and evaluation of computer program logic. However, because of continual program changes, preparing and maintaining test data manually is very difficult and time consuming. In addition, the test data method is not an appropriate technique for verification of the accuracy and completeness of production data or master files.

Automated test data generators are available to create large volumes of test data in complex data formats with relatively little effort. They can be used as input to the application program to be tested. This technique, combined with an automated code optimizer program, provides statistics on the number of times a program statement line code was executed and highlights the program sections that were not used during computer processing. Automated code optimizer programs can be used to evaluate test data prepared either manually or by an automated test data generator program. Test data method can be used to test both batch and online programs.

(xi) Base Case System Evaluation

Base case system evaluation (BCSE) is a technique that applies a standardized body of data (input, parameters, and output) to the testing of computer application programs. User staff members, with auditor participation, establish this body of data (the base case) as the criterion for correct functioning of the computer application system. This testing process is widely used as a technique for validation of production systems.

Some organizations use the base case approach as a means to test computer programs during their development, demonstrate the successful operation of the system prior to its implementation, and verify its continuing and accurate processing during its production life. As a result, this approach requires and represents a total commitment by data processing and user department management to the principles and disciplines of BCSE.

(xii) Integrated Test Facility

Integrated test facility (ITF) is a technique to review application program logic and functions to provide the auditor with evidence on operating procedures (computer and/or manual) and error handling conditions. The auditor's test data for a fictitious entity (i.e., a branch, department, division, or subsidiary) are used to compare ITF processing results to precalculated and expected test results. Here the auditor's test data are processed with normal production data. The auditor, however, must ensure that the ITF results for the fictitious entity are removed from the regular production data files either at the end of testing process or later, in order to eliminate its impact on the organization's financial and operating transactions and records. ITF can be used in batch and online application systems.

(xiii) Parallel Simulation

Parallel simulation is the use of one or more special computer programs to process "live" data files and simulate normal computer application processing. As opposed to the test data method and the integrated test facility, which process test data through live programs, the parallel simulation method processes live data through *test* programs. Generalized audit software can be used to create a test model or simulation of relatively simple application systems or a portion of more complex application systems.

Parallel simulation programs include only the application logic, calculations, and controls that are relevant to specific audit objectives. As a result, simulation programs are usually much less complex than their application program counterparts. Often large segments of major applications that consist of several computer programs can be simulated for audit purposes with a single parallel simulation program. Parallel simulation permits the auditors to independently verify complex and critical application program controls and procedures. Parallel simulation is also used to test computer programs and complex processing logic, such as interest calculations, during system development projects.

(xiv) Snapshot

Both auditors and IT staff periodically encounter difficulty in reconstructing the computer decision-making process. The cause is a failure to keep together all the data elements involved in that process. Snapshot is a technique that, in effect, takes a picture of the parts of computer memory that contain the data elements involved in a computerized decision-making process at the time the decision is made.

Input transactions are tagged and written to an audit log file with date, time, and indication of the point in the program at which the snapshot occurred. The results of the snapshot are printed in a report for review and analysis.

The snapshot audit technique offers the ability of listing all the data that were involved in a specific decision-making process. The technique requires the necessary logic to be preprogrammed in the system. A mechanism, usually a special code in the transaction record, is added for triggering, logging, and printing of the data in question for analysis.

The snapshot audit technique may help auditors answer questions as to why computer application systems produce questionable results. It provides information to explain why the computer made a particular decision.

Used in conjunction with other audit techniques (e.g., ITF or tracing), this technique aids in the determination of what results would occur if a certain type of input were entered the application system. The snapshot technique can also be an invaluable aid to systems and programming staff in debugging the application system because it can provide "pictures" of the computer memory. Ideally, the snapshot technique should be designed as part of the original application system development process. The auditor participates in the system development process by defining requirements and reviewing system design specifications and system test results.

(xv) Tracing

A traditional audit technique in a manual environment is to follow the path of a transaction during processing. For example, an auditor picks up a customer order as it is received into an organization and follows the flow from department to department. The auditor inquires of the employee involved what actions were taken at that particular step in the processing cycle.

Since the auditor understands the policies and procedures of the organization, he or she can judge whether they are being followed adequately. By the time the auditor has walked through the processing cycle, he or she has an appreciation of how work flows through the organization.

In an IT environment, it is not possible to follow the path of a transaction through its processing cycle solely by following the paperwork flow, since the computer accomplishes many of the functions performed by employees and no hard-copy documents are produced. A new type of audit evidence (electronic) is introduced in the IT environment.

Tracing is an audit technique that provides the auditor with the ability to perform an electronic walk-through of a computer application system. The audit objective of tracing is to verify compliance with policies and procedures by substantiating, by examining the path a transaction followed through a program, how that transaction was processed. Tracing can be used to detect omissions.

Tracing shows what instructions have been executed in a computer program and in which sequence they have been executed. Since the instructions in a computer program represent the steps in processing, the processes that have been executed can be determined from the results of the tracing audit technique. Once an auditor knows what instructions in a program have been executed, he or she can perform an analysis to determine if the processing conformed to the organization's policies and procedures.

(xvi) Mapping

Mapping is a technique used to assess the extent of system testing and to identify specific program logic that has not been tested. Mapping is performed by software measurement tools that analyze a computer program during execution and indicate which program statements have been executed. The software measurement tool can also determine the amount of central processing unit time consumed by each program segment.

The original intent of the mapping concept was to help computer programmers ensure the quality of their programs. Auditors can use the same software measurement tools, however, to look for unexecuted program statements. This analysis can provide auditors with insight into the efficiency of program operation and can reveal unauthorized program segments or statements included, if any exist.

(xvii) Control Flowcharting

In a complex business environment, it is difficult to thoroughly understand the total system of control of an organization within its total business and operational context. A graphic technique, or flowchart, for simplifying the identification and interrelationships of controls can be a great help in evaluating the adequacy of those controls and in assessing the impact of system changes on the overall control profile.

Flowcharts facilitate the explanation of controls to a system analyst, auditor, or people unfamiliar with specific functions of the system. They also aid in ascertaining that controls are operating as originally intended or planned.

The control flowcharting technique provides the documentation necessary to explain the system of control. Often an organization's information about controls is fragmented. This fragmentation makes obtaining a clear picture of the controls operating within the organization difficult. The availability of an overall picture of controls, using several levels of flowcharts, facilitates understanding.

(xviii) Control Reprocessing

Control reprocessing is a technique to identify lost or incomplete records during an update cycle. An update cycle of importance is reprocessed to compare against the original update to determine whether the results are the same between the two updates, original and reprocessed. If the results are not the same, analysis is conducted to identify the sources causing the difference.

WHICH COMPUTER-ASSISTED AUDIT TECHNIQUE METHOD USES WHAT?

- The test data method uses test data with production programs.

- The parallel simulation method uses production data with test programs.

- The ITF method uses test data with production programs.

- The embedded audit data collection, generalized audit software, snapshot, audit hooks, tracing, mapping, extended records, and transaction selection methods all use production data with production programs.

(xix) Conventional and Concurrent Audit Techniques

In a conventional audit using a computer-assisted audit technique (CAAT) on an after-the-fact-basis, auditors evaluate the controls at periodic intervals. Using concurrent audit techniques, controls are evaluated on a continuing basis. Audit evidence is collected in a timely manner.

Exhibit 3.6 presents a comparison between conventional and concurrent audit techniques.

Conventional audit techniques	Concurrent audit techniques
• Examples: generalized audit software, test data method, transaction selection, extended records, tracing, mapping, utility programs.	• Examples: ITF, SCARF, simulation, snapshots, audit hooks.
• Most appropriate for computerized batch, simple, and normal application systems.	• Most appropriate for computerized online, complex, and sensitive application systems.
• Require less data processing technical knowledge on the auditor's part.	• Require more data processing technical knowledge on the auditor's part.
• Mostly use test data instead of production data.	• Mostly use production data instead of test data.
• Not part of user production application systems.	• Part of production application systems.
• Auditor has more control over test data.	• Auditor has less control over test data.
• Auditor initiates CAAT program execution to test plans and schedules.	• Application system initiates CAAT program execution according to specified event, transaction, date, time, and other criteria.

EXHIBIT 3.6 Conventional and Concurrent Audit Techniques

(b) Analytical Review Techniques

The scope of analytical review techniques includes ratio estimation, variance analysis, and reasonableness tests.

(i) Ratio Estimation

Four types of measures are used to analyze a company's financial statements and its financial position: (1) common-size analysis, (2) trend analysis, (3) comparative ratios, and (4) single (or simple) ratios (see Exhibit 3.7).

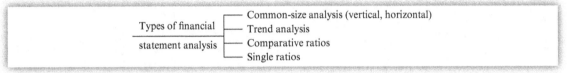

Types of financial statement analysis
- Common-size analysis (vertical, horizontal)
- Trend analysis
- Comparative ratios
- Single ratios

EXHIBIT 3.7 Types of Financial Statement Analysis

Common-size analysis expresses items in percentages, which can be compared with similar items of other firms or with those of the same firm over time. For example, common-size balance sheet line items (both assets and liabilities) are expressed as a percentage of total assets (e.g., receivables as x percent of total assets). Similarly, common-size income statement line items are expressed as a percentage of total sales (e.g., cost of goods sold as x percent of total sales).

Variations of common-size analysis include vertical analysis and horizontal analysis. **Vertical analysis** expresses all items on a financial statement as a percentage of some base figure, such as total assets or total sales. Comparing these relationships between competing organizations helps to isolate strengths and areas of concern.

In **horizontal analysis,** the financial statements for two years are shown together with additional columns showing dollar differences and percentage changes. Thus, the direction, absolute amount, and relative amount of change in account balances can be calculated. Trends that are difficult to isolate by examining the financial statements of individual years or comparisons with competitors can be identified.

Trend analysis shows trends in ratios, which gives insight whether the financial situation of a firm is improving, declining, or stable. It shows a graph of ratios over time, which can be compared with a firm's own performance as well as that of its industry.

Comparative ratios show key financial ratios, such as current ratio and net sales to inventory, by industry, such as beverages and bakery products. These ratios represent average financial ratios for all firms within an industry category. Many organizations supply ratio data, and each one designs ratios for its own purpose, such as small firms or large firms. Also, the focus of these ratios is different, such as creditor's viewpoint or investor's viewpoint. Another characteristic of the ratio data-supplying organization is that each has its own definitions of the ratios and their components. Due to these differences, examiners must be cautious when interpreting these ratios.

Another type of comparative analysis is comparing the financial statements for the current year with those of the most recent year. By comparing summaries of financial statements for the last five to ten years, trends in operations, capital structure, and the composition of assets can be identified. This comparative analysis provides insight into the normal or expected account balance or ratio, information about the direction of changes in ratios and account balances, and insight into the variability or fluctuation in an organization's assets or operations.

TREND ANALYSIS VERSUS COMPARATIVE RATIO ANALYSIS

- In trend analysis, trends are shown over time between the firm and its industry.

- In comparative ratio analysis, a single point (one-to-one) comparison is shown between the firm and its industry.

- In both analyses, the industry's ratio is an average ratio, while the firm's ratio is not.

Next, our focus will shift to **single (or simple) ratios.** Certain accounts or items in an organization's financial statements have logical relationships with each other. If the dollar amounts of these related accounts or items are expressed in fraction form, then they are called ratios. These ratios are grouped into five categories: (1) liquidity ratios, (2) asset management ratios, (3) debt management ratios, (4) profitability ratios, and (5) market value ratios. Exhibit 3.8 presents individual ratios for each ratio category.

Ratio category	Individual ratios
Liquidity (1)	Current, quick, or acid test
Asset management (2)	Inventory turnover, days sales outstanding, fixed assets turnover, total assets turnover
Debt management (3)	Debt to total assets, time-interest-earned, fixed charge coverage, cash flow coverage
Profitability (4) = (1) + (2) + (3)	Profit margin on sales, basic earning power, return on total assets, return on common equity, earnings per share, payout
Market value (5) = (1) + (2) + (3) + (4)	Price/earnings, book value per share, market/book

EXHIBIT 3.8 Ratio Categories with Examples

(ii) Variance Analysis

Budgets and standards are used to plan an operation and measure its progress. **Variance** is the difference between budget or standard and actual. For example, if actual spending is greater than the budget, a negative variance results. If actual spending is less than the budget, a positive variance results. Managers need to analyze both positive and negative variances for reasonableness because people play psychological games with budgets, such as inflating a budget for personal gain.

(iii) Reasonableness Tests

The reasonableness test procedure involves the use of selected operating data, associated financial data, and external data to predict an account balance. Reasonableness tests can be used to determine whether input data, updated data, calculated data, or output data are reasonable. Ascending or descending checks for numeric and alphabetic data can be performed. Tolerance tests measuring dollar or percentage deviation can be designed.

Reasonableness tests of expense accounts are common. Two examples are when the auditor or analyst (1) estimates a value for utilities expense based on average temperature and hours of operation, and (2) estimates payroll expense from operating data on the number of employees, the average pay rates, and the number of days of applicable operations.

The reasonableness test can be particularly effective because it links the financial data directly to relevant operating data. When variations in operations are the principal cause for variations in the related accounts (especially the expense accounts), reasonableness tests provide a relatively precise means of detecting errors and frauds affecting these accounts. That is, when a fraud is committed, it is likely that the reported financial and operating facts will not agree. The perpetrator will find it difficult to disguise both the financial data and the related operating data.

For example, a reasonableness test of payroll expense can be an effective means of detecting fraud if there are phony employees or excess time is charged, because personnel records also must be manipulated fraudulently in the same pattern to prevent detection. Because these methods effectively model the relationships between the financial data and the operating transactions that are the basis for the recorded financial data, reasonableness tests are potentially the most effective of the analytical procedures.

Examples of generic reasonableness tests include:

- Airline passenger departure flight time is not reasonable with arrival flight time for the same day.
- Customer order quantity is not reasonable with historical order.
- Prices on purchase orders are not reasonable with the prices on purchase invoices or purchase requisitions.
- Stock-status dollar values are not reasonable with general ledger amounts.
- Shipment values are not reasonable with billed amounts.

IIA STANDARD APPLICABLE TO ANALYTICAL REVIEW TECHNIQUES

2320 – Analysis and Evaluation

Internal auditors must base conclusions and engagement results on appropriate analyses and evaluations.

Practice Advisory 2320-1: Analytical Procedures

1. Internal auditors may use analytical procedures to obtain audit evidence. Analytical procedures involve studying and comparing relationships among both financial and nonfinancial information. The application of analytical procedures is based on the premise that, in the absence of known conditions to the contrary, relationships among information may reasonably be expected to exist and continue. Examples of contrary conditions include unusual or nonrecurring transactions or events; accounting, organizational, operational, environmental, and technological changes; inefficiencies; ineffectiveness; errors; fraud; or illegal acts.

2. Analytical procedures often provide the internal auditor with an efficient and effective means of obtaining evidence. The assessment results from comparing information with expectations identified or developed by the internal auditor. Analytical procedures are useful in identifying:

   ☐ Unexpected differences.

   ☐ The absence of differences when they are expected.

(continued)

- □ Potential errors.

- □ Potential fraud or illegal acts.

- □ Other unusual or nonrecurring transactions or events.

3. Analytical audit procedures include:

- □ Comparing current-period information with expectations based on similar information for prior periods as well as budgets or forecasts.

- □ Studying relationships between financial and appropriate nonfinancial information (e.g., recorded payroll expense compared to changes in average number of employees).

- □ Studying relationships among elements of information (e.g., fluctuation in recorded interest expense compared to changes in related debt balances).

- □ Comparing information with expectations based on similar information for other organizational units as well as for the industry in which the organization operates.

4. Internal auditors may perform analytical procedures using monetary amounts, physical quantities, ratios, or percentages. Specific analytical procedures include ratio, trend, and regression analysis; reasonableness tests; period-to-period comparisons; comparisons with budgets; forecasts; and external economic information. Analytical procedures assist internal auditors in identifying conditions that may require additional audit procedures. An internal auditor uses analytical procedures in planning the engagement in accordance with the guidelines contained in Standard 2200.

5. Internal auditors may use analytical procedures to generate evidence during the audit engagement. When determining the extent of analytical procedures, the internal auditor considers the:

- □ Significance of the area being audited.

- □ Assessment of risk management in the area being audited.

- □ Adequacy of the internal control system.

- □ Availability and reliability of financial and nonfinancial information.

- □ Precision with which the results of analytical audit procedures can be predicted.

- □ Availability and comparability of information regarding the industry in which the organization operates.

- □ Extent to which other procedures provide evidence.

6. When analytical audit procedures identify unexpected results or relationships, the internal auditor evaluates such results or relationships. This evaluation includes determining whether the difference from expectations could be a result of fraud, error, or a change in conditions. The auditor may ask management about the reasons for the difference and would corroborate management's explanation, for example, by modifying expectations and recalculating the difference or by applying other audit procedures. In particular, the internal auditor needs to be satisfied that the explanation considers both the direction of the change (e.g., sales decreased) and the amount of the difference (e.g., sales decreased by 10%). Unexplained results or relationships from applying analytical procedures may be indicative of a significant problem (e.g., a potential error, fraud, or illegal act). Results or relationships that are not adequately explained may indicate a situation to be communicated to senior management and the board in accordance with Standard 2060. Depending on the circumstances, the internal auditor may recommend appropriate action.

3.3 Process Mapping

Process mapping tools, including flowcharts, are discussed. In addition, interpreting charts and graphs is presented.

(a) Process Mapping

Robert Damelio identified three tools to map a process, activity, or function to understand it and to improve it.[3] These tools include relationship maps, cross-functional process maps, and flowcharts.

- **Relationship maps** show customer–supplier relationships or linkages that exist between parts of an organization. These maps show the big-picture view that portrays how the major functions of the business interact with each other. They can also be used to show any individual function.

- **Cross-functional process maps** show how an organization's major work processes cut across several functions. These maps show the sequence of steps that make up the work process as well as the inputs and outputs associated with each process step.

- **Flowcharts** are good to illustrate work processes since they help define, document, and analyze processes at the detailed level, especially about the individual performing the work or to develop the work procedures step by step. The next section presents flowcharts in a detailed manner.

Process maps can be used in a variety of ways, such as to:

- Orient new employees.
- Organize work.
- Clarify employee roles and contributions.
- Identify improvement opportunities.
- Reduce cycle time.
- Measure performance.

For example, cross-functional process maps and flowcharts can be used to reduce costs, reduce defects, conduct benchmarks, and reengineer a process. Similarly, relationship maps, cross-functional process maps, and flowcharts can be used to design performance measurement system and to measure customer satisfaction.

(b) Flowcharting

The three most widely used audit tools include flowcharts, questionnaires, and interviews. These tools will be discussed in more detail than other tools such as anecdotes (narratives), unobtrusive measures, and checklists.

Flowcharts are most valuable in providing a summary outline and overall description of the process of transactions in a system. The objective of a flowchart is to present a clear and concise picture and description of a system or operation, whether manual or automated. This description

---

[3] Robert Damelio, *The Basics of Process Mapping* (Portland, OR: Productivity, Inc., 1996).

provides a basis for an understanding of information flow and for subsequent audit work required in testing and evaluating internal controls. Usually flowcharts are supplemented by other forms of documentation, such as narratives, policies and procedures, ICQs, or interviews (see Exhibit 3.9 for benefits of flowcharts).

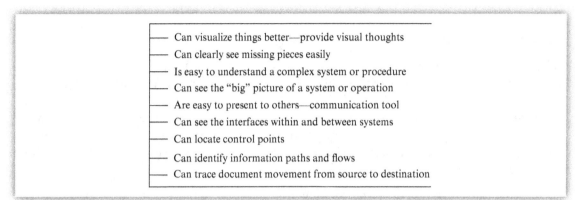

— Can visualize things better—provide visual thoughts
— Can clearly see missing pieces easily
— Is easy to understand a complex system or procedure
— Can see the "big" picture of a system or operation
— Are easy to present to others—communication tool
— Can see the interfaces within and between systems
— Can locate control points
— Can identify information paths and flows
— Can trace document movement from source to destination

EXHIBIT 3.9 Benefits of Flowcharts

Since systems are complex, it is advised to prepare flowcharts in two stages: summary level and detail level. The summary-level flowchart gives a quick synopsis of the entire system, while the detail-level flowchart is used for internal control testing and evaluation. Care should be taken to ensure that these two types of flowcharts do not contradict or duplicate each other in terms of flow of information. For example, a summary flowchart for a revenue cycle can have several detailed flowcharts, such as sales, credit, billing, and accounting receivable functions, and should not contain any unrelated functions.

When a large system is divided into several subsystems, it is important to make sure that interaction between subsystems is kept to a minimum to eliminate overlaps, errors, and confusing flow of documents. Good advice to a flowchart preparer is to keep the interfaces between documents simpler for a clear understanding.

Every flowchart should have at least three key elements: (1) departments involved or activities undertaken; (2) symbols to denote documents, nature of work done (posted, filed), and the sequence of documents related to the activities; and (3) information flow lines that show how documents and records are processed.

Flowcharts are of two types: horizontal and vertical. A flowchart is horizontal when it shows the document movement from source to final destination and from filing to destruction among departments. The information flow is from left to right. A flowchart is vertical when it shows the movement of documents from source to final destination and from filing to destruction within a department or operation. The information flow is from top to bottom. The horizontal flowchart is used to document the procedures followed by several interacting departments; the vertical flowchart does not show such interaction. The horizontal flowchart is more commonly used than the vertical one.

QUESTIONNAIRE VERSUS FLOWCHART

- The questionnaire is a data collection instrument—a means of gathering information about documents processed, forms used, procedures followed, record contents, program logic, and data editing details. However, questionnaires are not useful for document analysis and control evaluation purposes.

- Flowcharts overcome this weakness.

For example, flowcharts developed to describe a computer system can show programmed decisions, master file updates, and computer-generated transactions, in addition to manually generated transactions.

> **USES OF FLOWCHARTS**
>
> Flowcharts make it a lot simpler to see what should be happening. For example, in a computer operation, when something goes wrong, such as figures are not balancing or a job failed in the middle of processing, the flowchart is the first thing that should be checked to see where the job was or what correction needs to be made. A flowchart is a problem-solving tool since it can be used to compare what is and what should be.

For effective control evaluation, auditors need to make sure that the flowchart, whether prepared by the auditors or developed by the auditee, is in fact representative of the actual system in operation. If not, the auditors' conclusions will be questionable. Verification is the process of ensuring that the system described in the flowchart and the actual system is the same. Verification of the transaction or the document flow can be achieved by tracing several different types of transactions or documents taken at random and walking through the entire system. This verification procedure provides a reasonably accurate description of the system and is not intended to provide any reliable information as to whether the systems are operating effectively. Verification procedures provide a partial answer in obtaining observation-type evidence.

For example, the verification procedure can be used to test a small sample of transaction posting from each book of original entry to the general ledger or to trace issuance of credit memos for goods returned by customers, price adjustments, or invoice errors.

(i) Other Uses of Flowcharts

Flowcharts are used in business functions other than auditing. Flowcharts are increasingly the focus now due to total quality management programs. Flowcharting is the most effective way to describe how a process works now, how to fix it when it does not work, and how it is going to be improved in the future. To improve a process, repetitive tasks or activities need to be looked at for streamlining, to improve consistency and quality, and to reduce confusion.

Another use of flowcharting is to improve and facilitate training. People learn more quickly with a flowchart because they can see and understand the process as a whole—a picture is worth 1,000 words.

> **KEY CONCEPTS TO REMEMBER: Flowcharts**
>
> - Flowcharts would most likely be used in the evaluation of controls in a complex system, not in a simple but well-documented system.
>
> - An auditor develops a flowchart primarily to analyze a system and identify internal controls, to determine whether there is inefficiency and lack of controls.
>
> - Flowcharts would be most appropriate during the preliminary stage of an area that has not previously been audited. Flowcharts help auditors in evaluating internal control systems.
>
> - As a means of internal control evaluation, flowcharts allow users to follow information flow more easily than do questionnaires and descriptive narratives.

(ii) Interpreting Charts and Graphs

The basic purpose of a chart or graph is to give a visual comparison between two or more things. For example, changes in budget from one year to the next may be represented in a graph. One significant reason for visualizing a comparison is to reinforce its comprehension.

Charts and graphs are used to dramatize a statement, a fact, a point of view, or an idea. Visual aids assist in the quick comprehension of both simple and complex data, statistics, or problems.

A chart should explain itself in silence; it should be completely understood without the assistance of a caption. The caption must act only as reinforcement to its comprehension.

Various charts, such as tabular charts, column charts, bar charts, pie charts, line charts, layer charts, and radar charts are discussed briefly (see Exhibit 3.10).

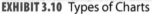

——— Tabular (used to represent items of interest)
——— Column (used for comparison of things)
——— Gantt (bar) (used for milestone scheduling)
——— Pie (used to represent 100% of total)
——— Line (used for comparison of things)
——— Layer (used for accumulation of individual facts)
——— Radar (used to show gaps in performance)

EXHIBIT 3.10 Types of Charts

The **tabular chart** is used to represent items of interest. It requires a fair amount of study in order to grasp the full meaning of the figures. This is because it takes longer to digest the meaning of an itemization of compiled figures than if the same figures are presented graphically. The **column chart** is most commonly used for demonstrating a comparison between two or more things. The column chart is vertical.

The **Gantt chart** is a bar chart and is essentially a column chart on its side; it is used for the same purpose as a column chart. The bar chart is horizontal. It is a tool that allows a manager to evaluate whether existing resources can handle work demand or whether activities should be postponed. The Gantt chart is used for milestone scheduling where each milestone has start and completion dates. A milestone represents a major activity or task to be accomplished (e.g., design phase in a computer system development project).

A Gantt chart is a graphical illustration of a scheduling technique. The structure of the chart shows output plotted against units of time. It does not include cost information. It highlights activities over the life of a project and contrasts actual times with projected times using a horizontal (bar) chart. It gives a quick picture of a project's progress in terms of actual time lines and projected time lines.

The **pie chart** is used to represent a 100% total of two or more items. The **line chart** is exceptionally impressive when comparing several things but could present a visual problem if the comparisons are too many or too close in relation to one another. Advantages are that it is simple to draw. Disadvantages are that if the lines are close to each other, it is difficult to distinguish some of the plotted points.

The **layer chart** is linear in appearance but has a different representation. It depicts the accumulation of individual facts stacked one over the other to create the overall total. This chart is more complex than the others, since it illustrates much more. In addition to showing the comparison of layers that add up to the total, this type of chart also shows how each group of layers relates to subsequent groups. The layer chart requires more work to prepare than the other charts. There is more arithmetic involved, and drawing the chart requires a good deal of concentration.

The radar chart shows gaps between current organization performance and ideal performance. The resulting chart resembles a radar screen.

3.4 Audit and Legal Evidence

The need for audit evidence, including types of evidence, standards of audit evidence, and appropriateness of audit evidence, is discussed. In addition, information sources for audit evidence are presented. Eight types of legal evidence, including the difference between audit evidence and legal evidence, are highlighted.

(a) Audit Evidence

(i) Types of Audit Evidence

Audit evidence is information that provides a factual basis for audit opinions. It is the information documented by the auditors and obtained through observing conditions, interviewing people, examining records, and testing documents. Audit evidence may be categorized as physical, documentary, testimonial, and analytical (see Exhibit 3.11).[4]

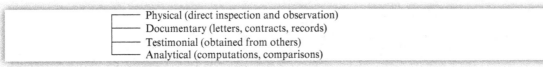

```
├──── Physical (direct inspection and observation)
├──── Documentary (letters, contracts, records)
├──── Testimonial (obtained from others)
└──── Analytical (computations, comparisons)
```

EXHIBIT 3.11 Types of Audit Evidence

Physical evidence is obtained by direct inspection or observation of people, property, or events. Such evidence may be documented in the form of memoranda summarizing the matters inspected or observed, photographs, charts, maps, or actual samples. An auditor's observation of the functioning of an internal control system produces physical evidence.

Examples of physical evidence include: taking a photograph of the auditees' workplace, such as improperly stored materials or unsafe conditions; observing conditions; test counting a batch of inventory; and testing the existence of an asset.

Documentary evidence consists of created information, such as letters, contracts, accounting records, invoices, and management information on performance.

Examples of documentary evidence include a page of the general ledger containing irregularities placed there by perpetrator of a fraud and determining whether erroneous billings occurred when the auditor for a construction contractor finds material costs increasing as a percentage of billings and suspects that materials billed to the company are being delivered to another contractor. A contract is the most appropriate evidence for the auditor to obtain and review when evaluating the propriety of a payment to a consultant.

---

[4] Comptroller General of the United States, *Government Auditing Standards* (Washington, D.C.: US General Accounting Office, 1994).

Testimonial evidence is obtained from others through statements received in response to inquiries, through interviews, or through responses to questionnaires. Testimonial evidence needs to be evaluated from the standpoint of whether the individual may be biased or have only partial knowledge about the area. Testimonial evidence obtained under conditions where persons may speak freely is more credible than testimonial evidence obtained under compromising conditions (e.g., where persons may be intimidated).

Examples of testimonial evidence include: a written, signed statement from an interviewee in response to a question asked by an auditor during an interview; a written statement by or a letter from an auditee in response to a specific inquiry made by an auditor; and a letter from the company's attorney in response to inquiries about possible litigation.

Analytical evidence includes computations, comparisons, reasoning, and separation of information into components.

Examples of analytical evidence include: to evaluate the reasonableness of the quantity of scrap material resulting from a certain production process compared to industry standards, to evaluate the reasonableness of account balances, and concluding that there was an adequate separation of duties in the counting and recording of cash receipts.

(ii) Standards of Audit Evidence

All audit evidence should meet the three standards of sufficiency, competence, and relevance. Evidence is sufficient if it is based on facts. Competent evidence is reliable evidence. The term "relevance" refers to the relationship of the information to its use. When audit evidence does not meet these three standards, additional (corroborative) evidence is required before expressing an audit opinion (see Exhibit 3.12).

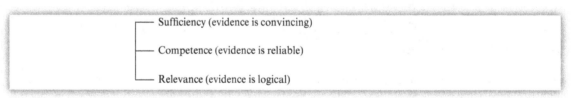

Sufficiency (evidence is convincing)

Competence (evidence is reliable)

Relevance (evidence is logical)

EXHIBIT 3.12 Standards of Evidence

(iii) Appropriateness of Audit Evidence

The phrase "appropriateness of audit evidence" refers to persuasiveness (sufficiency), relevance, and competence (reliability). The next discussion should help auditors determine what constitutes sufficient, relevant, and competent evidence to support their findings and conclusions.

Evidence is **sufficient** if there is enough of it to support the auditors' findings. In determining the sufficiency of evidence, it may be helpful to ask: Is there enough evidence to persuade a reasonable person of the validity of the findings? An essential factor in evaluating the "sufficiency" of evidence is that it must be convincing enough for a prudent person to reach the same decision.

Therefore, *sufficiency deals with the persuasiveness of the evidence* (see Exhibit 3.13 for hierarchy of persuasive evidence). When appropriate, statistical methods may be used to establish sufficiency. When sampling methods are used, the concept of sufficiency of evidence means that the samples selected provide reasonable assurance that they are representative of the sampled population. Interviewing the auditee is not enough to provide sufficient evidence.

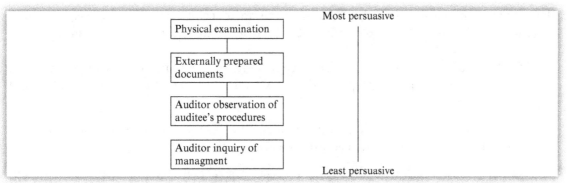

EXHIBIT 3.13 Hierarchy of Persuasive Evidence

Some examples of sufficient evidence are listed next.

- Verifying the quantity of fixed assets on hand by physical observation would provide the most persuasive evidence of quantity on hand.

- Using test data, an auditor has processed both normal and atypical transactions through a computerized payroll system to test calculations of regular and overtime pay amounts. Sufficient competent evidence of controls exists if test data results are compared to predetermined results or expectations.

- The audit procedure that provides the most persuasive evidence about the loan's collectibility is to examine the documentation of a recent, independent appraisal of the real estate that was used a security.

- The most persuasive evidence that the incoming supply counts are made by the receiving department is a periodic observation by the internal auditor over the course of the audit.

- A positive confirmation received directly from the customer is the most persuasive evidence concerning the existence and valuation of a receivable.

- If the audit objective is to gain evidence that payment actually has been made for a specific invoice from a vendor, the most persuasive evidence would be obtained by a canceled check, made out to the vendor and referenced to the invoice, included in a cutoff bank statement that the auditor received directly from the bank.

- If an auditor wants assurance of the existence of inventory stored in a warehouse, the most persuasive evidence is to physically observe the inventory in the warehouse.

- Externally prepared documents (e.g., invoice) would provide the most persuasive evidence regarding an asset value that was acquired.

- A physical examination would provide the most persuasive evidence for testing the existence of an asset.

Evidence used to support a finding is **relevant** if it has a logical, sensible relationship to that finding. Relevant evidence is consistent with the audit objectives and supports audit findings and recommendations. Evidence is **competent** to the extent that it is consistent with fact (i.e., evidence is competent if it is valid). Competent evidence is satisfied by an original signed document, but copies do not provide competent evidence. *Evidence that is both available and reliable is competent. Competent information is reliable and the best available through the use of appropriate audit functions.*

The next presumptions are useful in judging the competence of evidence. However, these presumptions are not to be considered sufficient in themselves to determine competence.

- Evidence obtained from a credible independent source is more competent than that secured from the audited organization. An external source of evidence should impact audit conclusions most.

- Evidence developed under an effective system of management controls is more competent than that obtained where such control is weak or nonexistent.

- Evidence obtained through the auditors' direct physical examination, observation, computation, and inspection is more competent than evidence obtained indirectly. An example of external and internal evidence is when an auditor reviews the count sheets, inventory printouts, and memos from the last inventory during determination of causes of inventory shortages shown by the physical inventories.

Examples of competent evidence are listed next.

- An audit objective of an accounts receivable function is to determine if prescribed standard procedures are followed when credit is granted. An audit procedure providing the most competent evidence would be selecting a statistical sample of credit applications and testing them for conformance with prescribed procedures.

- The most "reliable" (competent) evidence of determining a company's legal title to inventories is paid vendor invoices.

- A contract dispute has arisen between a company and a major supplier. To resolve the dispute, the most competent evidence would be the original contract.

- A positive confirmation of an accounts receivable that proves that it actually exists is competent evidence.

- In deciding whether recorded sales are valid, most "competent" evidence would be obtained by looking at the shipping document, the independent bill of lading, and the invoice for the merchandise.

Auditors should, when they deem it useful, obtain from officials of the audited entity written representations concerning the competence of the evidence they obtain. Written representations ordinarily confirm oral representations given to the auditor, indicate and document the continuing appropriateness of such representations, and reduce the possibility of misunderstandings concerning the matters that are the subject of the representations.

An example of relevant evidence is aging of accounts receivables, which provides relevant evidence regarding the validity of receivables and thus the allowance account.

(iv) Information Sources for Audit Evidence

The auditors' approach to determining the sufficiency, relevance, and competence of evidence depends on the source of the information that constitutes the evidence (see Exhibit 3.14). Information sources include original data gathered by auditors and existing data gathered by either the auditee or a third party. Data from any of these sources may be obtained from computer-based systems.

```
         ——— Data gathered by the auditors
         ——— Data gathered by the auditee
         ——— Data gathered by third parties
         ——— Data gathered from computer-based systems
```

EXHIBIT 3.14 Information Sources for Evidence

(A) Data Gathered by the Auditors Data gathered by the auditors include the auditors' own observations and measurements. Among the methods for gathering these types of data are questionnaires, structured interviews, and direct observations. The design of these methods and the skill of the auditors applying them are the keys to ensuring that these data constitute sufficient, competent, and relevant evidence. When these methods are applied to determine cause, auditors are concerned with eliminating rival explanations of cause. Doing so involves considering three types of validity: (1) internal validity, (2) construct validity, and (3) external validity.

1. **Internal validity** means that A (the program as defined for the particular audit) caused B (the effect measured in the audit).

2. **Construct validity** refers to whether the auditors are measuring or observing what they intend to.

3. **External validity** refers to the ability to generalize the auditors' findings to a broader universe.

(B) Data Gathered by the Auditee Auditors can use data gathered by the auditee as part of their evidence. If those data are significant to the overall body of evidence supporting their findings, auditors should obtain additional evidence regarding the reliability of those data. Statements by auditee management or personnel about the reliability of operations data should be corroborated with other evidence. Auditors can obtain the necessary evidence by testing the effectiveness of the entity's controls over the reliability of the data, by direct tests of the data, or by a combination of the two.

When auditors' tests of data disclose errors in that data, the auditors should consider the significance of those errors in relation to the audit objectives. If the auditors conclude that these errors are so significant that the data are not valid or reliable, they should consider whether to:

- Seek evidence from other sources.

- Redefine the audit's objectives to eliminate the need to use the invalid or unreliable data.

- Use the data, but clearly indicate in their report the data's limitations and refrain from making unwarranted conclusions or recommendations.

Similar considerations apply when the auditors are unable to obtain sufficient, competent, and relevant evidence about the validity and reliability of the auditee's data.

(C) Data Gathered by Third Parties The auditors' evidence may also include data gathered by third parties. In some cases, these data may already have been audited, or the auditors may be able to audit this evidence themselves. Often, however, it is not practical to obtain evidence of the data's validity and reliability.

How the use of unaudited third-party data affects the auditors' report depends on the data's significance to the overall body of evidence supporting the auditors' findings. If it is significant, the auditors should clearly indicate in their report the data's limitations and refrain from making unwarranted conclusions or recommendations based on those data.

(D) Data Gathered from Computer-Based Systems Auditors should obtain sufficient evidence that computer-processed data are valid and reliable when those data are significant to the overall body of evidence supporting the auditors' findings and any conclusions or recommendations. (When the reliability of a computer-based system is the primary objective of the audit, the auditor should conduct a review of the system's general and application controls.) This is necessary regardless of whether the data are provided to auditors or auditors independently extract them. (When the auditor uses computer-processed data or includes them in the report for background or information purposes, and when those data are not significant to the auditor's results, citing the source of the data and stating that they were not verified will satisfy the reporting standards for accuracy and completeness.)

Auditors should determine if other auditors have worked to establish the validity and reliability of the data or the effectiveness of the controls over the system that produced it. If they have, auditors may be able to use that work. If not, auditors can obtain evidence about the validity and reliability of computer-processed data from tests of general and application controls, direct tests of the data, or a combination of both.

(b) Legal Evidence

Eight types of legal evidence exist, which are described below[5] (see Exhibit 3.15). Both legal evidence and audit evidence have common objectives of providing proof and fostering an honest belief about the truth or falsity of any proposition at issue. The focus of audit evidence differs somewhat from that of legal evidence. Legal evidence relies heavily on oral testimony. Audit evidence relies more on documentary evidence. Legal evidence permits certain presumptions. Audit evidence is not bound by any presumptions. This requires auditors to question all evidence until they, themselves, are satisfied with its truth or falsity.

1. Best evidence (the most satisfactory proof of the fact and provides primary evidence)
2. Secondary evidence (inferior to primary evidence and cannot be relied upon)
3. Direct evidence (no presumptions or inferences are required)
4. Circumstantial evidence (does not directly prove the existence of the primary fact)
5. Conclusive evidence (only one conclusion can be drawn and needs no corroboration)
6. Corroborative evidence (additional evidence of a different character)
7. Opinion evidence (based on seeing or hearing and expert opinion is permitted)
8. Hearsay evidence (secondhand evidence; not admissible)

EXHIBIT 3.15 Eight Forms of Legal Evidence

---

[5] Lawrence B. Sawyer, *Sawyer's Internal Auditing* (Altamonte Springs, FL: Institute of Internal Auditors), 1988.

(i) Best Evidence

Best evidence is often referred to as primary evidence and is the evidence that is the most natural and reliable. It is confined to documentary evidence and applies to proof of the content in writing. Oral evidence may not be used to dispute a written instrument such as a contract or a deed; however, oral evidence can be used to explain the meaning of the instrument where such an instrument is capable of more than one interpretation.

Examples of best evidence are listed next.

- The audit procedure providing the best evidence about the collectibility of notes receivable would be an examination of cash receipts records to determine promptness of interest and principal payments.

- Reconciling shipping records to recorded sales is a substantive fieldwork procedure providing best evidence about the completeness of recorded revenues.

- The best evidence in assessing the acceptability of various benefit programs to employees is to evaluate program participation ratios and their trends during an audit of the personnel function, where participation in some of these benefit programs is optional.

- In testing the write-off of a deteriorated piece of equipment, the best evidence of the condition of the equipment would be a physical inspection of the actual piece of equipment.

(ii) Secondary Evidence

Secondary evidence is inferior to primary evidence and cannot be given the same reliance. Examples include a copy of a writing or oral evidence of its contents. A copy of writing is permissible when the original is lost, destroyed, or controlled by a public entity.

(iii) Direct Evidence

Direct evidence proves a fact without having to use presumptions or inference to establish that proof. The testimony of a witness to a fact is direct evidence. The most likely source of evidence indicating employee theft of inventory would be a warehouse employee's verbal charge of theft.

(iv) Circumstantial Evidence

Circumstantial evidence proves an intermediate fact(s) from which one can infer the existence of some primary fact that is significant to the issue under consideration. It provides a logical inference that it exists.

(v) Conclusive Evidence

Conclusive evidence is incontrovertible evidence, irrespective of its nature. It is so strong that it overbears all other evidence. It cannot be contradicted and needs no corroboration.

(vi) Corroborative Evidence

Corroborative evidence is additional evidence of a different character concerning the same point. It is evidence supplementary to that already given and tends to strengthen or confirm it.

Examples of corroborative evidence are listed next.

- Salespersons often order inventory for stock without receiving the approval of the vice president of sales, and a detail testing showed that there are no written approvals on purchase orders for replacement parts. Detail testing is a good example of corroborative evidence.

- Interviews should be corroborated by gathering objective data.

(vii) Opinion Evidence

The opinion rule holds that witnesses must ordinarily testify to fact only—to what they actually saw or heard. Opinions may be biased, self-serving, or uninformed. However, experts are permitted to offer an opinion based on the facts.

(viii) Hearsay Evidence

The hearsay rule renders objectionable any statements made by someone, other than a witness, to prove the truth of the matter stated. It refers to any oral or written evidence brought into court and offered as proof of things said out of court.

Business documents (e.g., sales slips, purchase orders) made during regular business routines are admissible. Photographs represent hearsay evidence but are considered admissible if properly authenticated by witnesses who are familiar with the subject.

3.5 Sample Practice Questions

As mentioned in the Preface of this book, a small batch of sample practice questions is included here to show the flavor of questions and to create a quiz-like environment. The answers and explanations for these questions are shown in a separate section at the end of this book just before the Glossary. If there is a need to practice more questions to obtain a greater confidence, refer to the section "CIA Exam Study Preparation Resources" presented in the front matter of this book.

1. An audit team developed a preliminary questionnaire with the following response choices:

   ■ Probably not a problem.

   ■ Possibly a problem.

   ■ Probably a problem.

   The questionnaire illustrates the use of:

   a. Trend analysis.

   b. Ratio analysis.

   c. Unobtrusive measures or observations.

   d. Rating scales.

2. Which of the following statements describes an internal control questionnaire? It:

   a. Provides detailed evidence regarding the substance of the control system.

   b. Takes less of the auditee's time to complete than other control evaluation devices.

   c. Requires that the auditor be in attendance to properly administer it.

   d. Provides indirect audit evidence that might need corroboration.

3. Which of the following is the **primary** advantage of using an internal control questionnaire?

   a. It provides a clear picture of the interrelationships that exist between the various controls.

   b. It reduces the risk of overlooking important aspects of the system.

   c. It forces an auditor to acquire a full understanding of the system.

   d. Negative responses indicate the only areas needing further audit work.

4. Checklists used to assess audit risk have been criticized for all of the following reasons **except:**

   a. Providing a false sense of security that all relevant factors are addressed.

   b. Inappropriately implying equal weight to each item on the checklist.

   c. Decreasing the uniformity of data acquisition.

   d. Being incapable of translating the experience or sound reasoning intended to be captured by each item on the checklist.

5. When an internal auditor is interviewing to gain information, the auditor will not be able to remember everything that was said in the interview. The **most** effective way to record interview information for later use is to:

   a. Write notes quickly, trying to write down everything in detail, as it is said; then highlight important points after the meeting.

   b. Tape-record the interview to capture everything that everyone says; then type everything said into a computer for documentation.

   c. Hire a professional secretary to take notes, allowing complete concentration on the interview; then delete unimportant points after the meeting.

   d. Organize notes around topics on the interview plan and note responses in the appropriate area, reviewing the notes after the meeting to make additions.

6. When conducting interviews during the early stages of an internal audit, it is more effective to:

   a. Ask for specific answers that can be quantified.

   b. Ask people about their jobs.

   c. Ask surprise questions about daily procedures.

   d. Take advantage of the fact that fear is an important part of the audit.

7. An auditor prepared a working paper that consisted of a list of employee names and identification numbers as well as this statement: "By matching random numbers with employee identification numbers, 40 employee personnel files were selected to verify that they contain all documents required by company policy 501. No exceptions were noted."

The auditor did not place any tick marks on this working paper. Which one of the following changes would improve the auditor's working paper the **most**?

a. Use of tick marks to show that each file was examined.

b. Removal of the employee names to protect their confidentiality.

c. Justification for the sample size.

d. Listing of the actual documents examined for each employee.

8. The standard deviation of a sample will usually decrease with:

a. A decrease in sample size.

b. The use of stratification.

c. An increase in desired precision.

d. An increase in confidence level.

9. Statistical sampling would be appropriate to estimate the value of an auto dealer's 3,000 line-item inventory because statistical sampling is:

a. Reliable and objective.

b. Thorough and complete.

c. Thorough and accurate.

d. Complete and precise.

10. An important difference between a statistical sample and a judgmental sample is that with a statistical sample:

a. No judgment is required, everything is by formula.

b. A smaller sample size can be used.

c. More accurate results are obtained.

d. Population estimates with measurable reliability can be made.

11. Sample size:

a. Increases with the use of higher confidence levels.

b. Decreases with the use of higher confidence levels.

c. Remains unchanged with changes in confidence levels.

d. Increases with the use of lower confidence levels.

12. An auditor becomes concerned that fraud in the form of payments to bogus companies may exist. Buyers, who are responsible for all purchases for specific product lines, are able to approve expenditures up to $50,000 without any other approval. Which of the following audit procedures would be **most** effective in addressing the auditor's concerns?

a. Use generalized audit software to list all purchases over $50,000 to determine whether they were properly approved.

b. Develop a snapshot technique to trace all transactions by suspected buyers.

c. Use generalized audit software to take a random sample of all expenditures under $50,000 to determine whether they were properly approved.

d. Use generalized audit software to list all major vendors by product line; select a sample of paid invoices to new vendors and examine evidence which shows that services or goods were received.

13. An auditor wishes to determine the extent to which invalid data could be contained in a human resources computer system. Examples would be an invalid job classification, age in excess of retirement age, or an invalid ethnic classification. The **best** approach to determine the extent of the potential problem would be to:

a. Submit test data to test the effectiveness of edit controls over the input of data.

b. Review and test access controls to ensure that access is limited to authorized individuals.

c. Use generalized audit software to develop a detailed report of all data outside specified parameters.

d. Use generalized audit software to select a sample of employees. Use the sample to determine the validity of data items and project the result to the population as a whole.

14. A bank internal auditor wishes to determine whether all loans are backed by sufficient collateral, properly aged as to current payments, and properly categorized as current or noncurrent. The **best** audit procedure to accomplish this objective would be to:

a. Use generalized audit software to read the total loan file, age the file by last payment due, and take a statistical sample stratified by the current and aged population. Examine each loan selected for proper collateralization and aging.

b. Take a block sample of all loans in excess of a specified dollar limit and determine if they are current and properly categorized. For each loan approved, verify aging and categorization.

c. Take a discovery sample of all loan applications to determine whether each application contains a statement of collateral.

d. Take a sample of payments made on the loan portfolio and trace them to loans to see that the payments are properly applied. For each loan identified, examine the loan application to determine that the loan has proper collateralization.

15. Governmental auditors have been increasingly called on to perform audits to determine whether individuals are getting extra social welfare payments. One common type of welfare fraud is individuals receiving more than one social welfare payment. This is often accomplished by filing multiple claims under multiple names but using the same address. Which of the following computer audit tools and techniques would be **most** helpful in identifying the existence of this type of fraud?

a. Tagging and tracing.

b. Generalized audit software.

c. Integrated test facility.

d. Spreadsheet analysis.

16. Management has requested an audit of promotional expenses. The sales department has been giving away expensive items in conjunction with new product sales to stimulate demand. The promotion seems successful, but management believes the cost may be too high. Which of the following audit procedures would be the **least** useful to determine the effectiveness of the promotion?

a. A comparison of product sales during the promotion period with sales during a similar nonpromotion period.

b. A comparison of the unit cost of the products sold before and during the promotion period.

c. An analysis of marginal revenue and marginal cost for the promotion period, compared to the period before the promotion.

d. A review of the sales department's reasons for believing that the promotion has been successful.

17. An internal auditor plans to use an analytical review to verify the correctness of various operating expenses in a division. The use of an analytical review as a verification technique would **not** be a preferred approach if:

a. The auditor notes strong indicators of a specific fraud involving this account.

b. The company has relatively stable operations that have not changed much over the past year.

c. The auditor would like to identify large, unusual, or nonrecurring transactions during the year.

d. The operating expenses vary in relation to other operating expenses but not in relation to revenue.

18. During an audit, the internal auditor should consider the following factor(s) in determining the extent to which analytical procedures should be used:

a. Adequacy of the system of internal control.

b. Significance of the area being examined.

c. Precision with which the results of analytical audit procedures can be predicted.

d. All of the above.

19. An auditor performs an analytical review by comparing the gross margins of various divisional operations with those of other divisions and with the individual division's performance in previous years. The auditor notes a significant increase in the gross margin at one division. The auditor does some preliminary investigation and also notes that there were no changes in products, production methods, or divisional management during the year. Based on this information, the **most** likely cause of the increase in gross margin would be:

a. An increase in the number of competitors selling similar products.

b. A decrease in the number of suppliers of the material used in manufacturing the product.

c. An overstatement of year-end inventory.

d. An understatement of year-end accounts receivable.

20. During an operational audit, an auditor compares the inventory turnover rate of a subsidiary with established industry standards in order to:

a. Evaluate the accuracy of the subsidiary's internal financial reports.

b. Test the subsidiary's controls designed to safeguard assets.

c. Determine if the subsidiary is complying with corporate procedures regarding inventory levels.

d. Assess the performance of the subsidiary and indicate where additional audit work may be needed.

21. Which of the following is true of a horizontal flowchart as compared to a vertical flowchart?

a. It provides more room for written descriptions that parallel the symbols.

b. It brings into sharper focus the assignment of duties and independent checks on performance.

c. It is usually longer.

d. It does not provide as broad a picture at a glance.

22. Of the following, which is the **most** efficient source for an auditor to use to evaluate a company's overall control system?

a. Control flowcharts.

b. Copies of standard operating procedures.

c. A narrative describing departmental history, activities, and forms usage.

d. Copies of industry operating standards.

23. Which of the following tools would **best** give a graphical representation of a sequence of activities and decisions?

a. Flowchart.

b. Control chart.

c. Histogram.

d. Run chart.

24. In documenting the procedures used by several interacting departments, the internal auditor will **most** likely use:

a. A horizontal flowchart.

b. A vertical flowchart.

c. A Gantt chart.

d. An internal control questionnaire.

25. Which method of evaluating internal controls during the preliminary review provides the auditor with the **best** visual grasp of a system and a means for analyzing complex operations?

a. A flowcharting approach.

b. A questionnaire approach.

c. A matrix approach.

d. A detailed narrative approach.

26. The auditor wishes to test the assertion that all claims paid by a medical insurance company contain proper authorization and documentation, including but not limited to the validity of the claim from an approved physician and an indication that the claim complies with the claimant's policy. The **most** appropriate audit procedure would be to:

a. Select a random statistical sample of all policyholders and examine all claims for the sampled items during the year to determine if they were handled properly.

b. Select a sample of claims filed and trace to documentary evidence of authorization and other supporting documentation.

c. Select a sample of claims denied and determine that all claims denied were appropriate. The claims denied file is much smaller, and the auditor can obtain greater coverage with the sample size.

d. Select a sample of paid claims from the claims (cash) disbursement file and trace to documentary evidence of authorization and other supporting documentation.

27. In evaluating the validity of different types of audit evidence, which one of the following conclusions is **incorrect**?

a. Recomputation, although highly valid, is limited in usefulness due to its limited scope.

b. The validity of documentary evidence is independent of the effectiveness of the control system in which it was created.

c. Internally created documentary evidence is considered less valid than externally created documentary evidence.

d. The validity of confirmations varies directly with the independence of the party receiving the confirmation.

28. Which of the following is generally **not** true when evaluating the persuasiveness of evidence?
The evidence is considered more persuasive if it is:

a. Verified by internally maintained documents rather than by written inquiry of third party.

b. Obtained under conditions of strong controls rather than weak controls.

c. Known by an auditor's personal knowledge rather than from a third-party confirmation.

d. Obtained from an external source rather than from an internal source.

29. In testing the write-off of a deteriorated piece of equipment, the **best** evidence of the condition of the equipment would be:

a. The equipment manager's statement regarding condition.

b. Accounting records showing maintenance and repair costs.

c. A physical inspection of the actual piece of equipment.

d. The production department's equipment downtime report.

30. Which of the following audit procedures provides the **best** evidence about the collectibility of notes receivable?

a. Confirmation of note receivable balances with the debtors.

b. Examination of notes for appropriate debtors' signatures.

c. Reconciliation of the detail of notes receivable and the provision for uncollectible amounts to the general ledger control.

d. Examination of cash receipts records to determine promptness of interest and principal payments.

31. What standard of evidence is satisfied by an original signed document?

a. Sufficiency.

b. Competence.

c. Relevance.

d. Usefulness.

32. When sampling methods are used, the concept of sufficiency of evidence means that the samples selected provide:

a. Reasonable assurance that they are representative of the sampled population.

b. The best evidence that is reasonably obtainable.

c. Reasonable assurance that the evidence has a logical relationship to the audit objective.

d. Absolute assurance that a sample is representative of the population.

33. An internal auditor takes a photograph of the auditee's workplace. The photograph is a form of what kind of evidence?

a. Physical.

b. Testimonial.

c. Documentary.

d. Analytical.

Sample Practice Questions, Answers, and Explanations

Domain 1: Mandatory Guidance (35–45%)

1. The IIA's definition of internal auditing emphasizes the effectiveness of which of the following?

   a. Value, cost, and benefit propositions.

   Incorrect. See correct answer (c).

   b. Inherent risk, residual risk, and total risk.

   Incorrect. See correct answer (c).

   c. Risk management, control, and governance processes.

   Correct. The definition of internal auditing states the fundamental purpose, nature, and scope of internal auditing. Internal auditing is an independent, objective assurance and consulting activity designed to add value and improve an organization's operations. It helps an organization accomplish its objectives by bringing a systematic, disciplined approach to evaluate and improve the effectiveness of risk management, control, and governance processes.

   d. Purpose, nature, and scope of work.

   Incorrect. See correct answer (c).

2. Which of the following adds value to the others?

   a. Governance processes.

   Incorrect. See correct answer (c).

   b. Risk management processes.

   Incorrect. See correct answer (c).

   c. Internal audit activities.

   Correct. Internal audit activities add value to the organization (and its stakeholders) when they provide objective and relevant assurance and contribute to the effectiveness and efficiency of governance, risk management, and control processes.

   d. Control processes.

   Incorrect. See correct answer (c).

3. All of the following are examples of assurance services **except:**

   a. Financial engagement.

   Incorrect. Financial engagement is part of assurance services.

   b. Compliance engagement.

   Incorrect. Compliance engagement is part of assurance services.

   c. Due diligence engagement.

   Incorrect. Due diligence engagement is part of assurance services.

   d. Training engagement.

   Correct. Training engagement is a part of consulting. The IIA's Glossary defines assurance services as "objective examination[s] of evidence for the purpose of providing an independent assessment on governance, risk management, and control processes for the organization. Examples may include financial, performance, compliance, system security, and due diligence engagements."

4. All of the following are examples of consulting services **except:**

   a. Legal counsel engagement.

   Incorrect. Legal counsel engagement is an example of consulting services.

   b. **System security engagement.**

   Correct. System security engagement is a part of assurance services. The IIA's Glossary defines consulting services as "[a]dvisory and related client service activities, the nature and scope of which are agreed with the client and are intended to add value and improve an organization's governance, risk management, and control processes without the internal auditor assuming management responsibility. Examples include counsel, advice, facilitation, and training."

   c. Advice engagement.

   Incorrect. Advice engagement is an example of consulting services.

   d. Facilitation engagement.

   Incorrect. Facilitation engagement is an example of consulting services.

5. The IIA's Practice Advisories do **not** contain which of the following?

   a. Approaches.

   Incorrect. Approaches are a part of practice advisories.

   b. Considerations.

   Incorrect. Considerations are a part of practice advisories.

   c. **Processes or procedures.**

   Correct. Processes or procedures are part of Practice Guides, not Practice Advisories. The other three choices are part of practice advisories. Practice Advisories assist internal auditors in applying the definition of internal auditing, the Code of Ethics, and the *Standards* and promoting good practices. Practice Advisories address internal auditing's approach, methodologies, and consideration but not detailed processes or procedures. They include practices relating to international, country, or industry-specific issues; specific types of engagements; and legal or regulatory issues.

   d. Methodologies.

   Incorrect. Methodologies are a part of practice advisories.

6. The IIA's Practice Guides do **not** contain which of the following?

   a. **Good practices.**

   Correct. Good practices are part of Practice Advisories, not Practice Guides. Practice Guides provide detailed guidance for conducting internal audit activities. Practice Guides include detailed processes and procedures, such as tools and techniques, programs, and step-by-step approaches as well as examples of deliverables.

   b. Tools and techniques.

   Incorrect. Tools and techniques are part of Practice Guides.

   c. Programs.

   Incorrect. Programs are part of Practice Guides.

   d. Deliverables.

   Incorrect. Deliverables are part of Practice Guides.

7. According to the IIA's Organizational Independence *Standard*, which of the following is **not** a part of functional reporting to the board?

   a. Audit charter.

   Incorrect. See correct answer (c).

   b. Audit risk assessment.

   Incorrect. See correct answer (c).

   c. **Audit budgets.**

   Correct. The chief audit executive, reporting functionally to the board and administratively to the organization's chief executive officer, facilitates organizational independence. Functional reporting to the board typically involves the board approving the internal audit activity's overall charter and approving the internal audit risk assessment and related audit plan. Administrative reporting is the reporting relationship within the organization's management structure that facilitates the day-to-day operations of the internal audit activity. Administrative reporting typically includes audit budgets among other things.

   d. Audit plan.

   Incorrect. See correct answer (c).

8. Which of the following differs between assurance services and consulting services when exercising due professional care?

  a. Costs and benefits.

    Incorrect. Costs and benefits are the same when exercising due professional care in assurance services and consulting services.

  b. Complexity of work.

    Incorrect. Complexity of work is the same when exercising due professional care is assurance services and consulting services.

  c. Extent of work.

    Incorrect. Extent of work is the same when exercising due professional care in assurance services and consulting services.

  d. Materiality.

    Correct. Materiality is considered in assurance services and procedures but is not relevant to consulting services.

9. Which of the following is driving the need for assurance maps?

  a. Risk managers.

    Incorrect. Risk managers do not deal with assurance maps.

  b. Board members.

    Correct. The chief audit executive, senior management, and the board need assurance maps to ensure proper coordination among diverse risk activities. Assurance maps are usually driven by the board due to its oversight responsibility. Assurance maps are organization-wide and coordinated exercises involving mapping assurance coverage provided by multiple parties against the key risks facing the organization so that duplicate efforts, missed risks, and potential gaps can be identified and monitored.

  c. Internal auditors.

    Incorrect. Internal auditors do not deal with assurance maps.

  d. Compliance practitioners.

    Incorrect. Compliance practitioners do not deal with assurance maps.

10. Risk registers describe direct links between which of the following?

  a. Risk acceptance and risk avoidance.

    Incorrect. Risk acceptance and risk avoidance are not related to risk registers.

  b. Risk categories and risk aspects.

    Correct. Risk registers provide direct links among risk categories, risk aspects, audit universe, and internal controls.

  c. Risk assignment and risk sharing.

    Incorrect. Risk assignment and risk sharing are not related to risk registers.

  d. Risk limitation and risk spreading.

    Incorrect. Risk limitation and risk spreading are not related to risk registers.

11. The chief audit executive establishes a method for prioritizing all of the following **except:**

  a. Business units with low risk levels.

    Incorrect. See correct answer (d).

  b. Branch or field office with low risk levels.

    Incorrect. See correct answer (d).

  c. Outstanding risk areas.

    Incorrect. See correct answer (d).

  d. Low inherent risk areas.

    Correct. Audits of lower risk level business units, branch types, or field office types need to be periodically included in the internal audit activity's plan to give them coverage and confirm that their risks have not changed. Also, the internal audit activity establishes a method for prioritizing outstanding risks not yet subject to an internal audit. High inherent risk areas, not low inherent risk areas, are prioritized.

12. All of the following provide effective relationships in the organization's governance framework **except**:

   a. Organizational processes.

   Correct. Governance does not exist as a set of distinct and separate organizational processes and structures. Rather, there are effective relationships among governance, risk management, and internal controls.

   b. Governance.

   Incorrect. Governance provides effective relationships in the organization's governance framework.

   c. Risk management.

   Incorrect. Risk management provides effective relationships in the organization's governance framework.

   d. Internal controls.

   Incorrect. Internal controls provide effective relationships in the organization's governance framework.

13. Which of the following internal audit assessments belong to specific governance processes?

   a. Whistleblower process.

   Correct. Internal audit assessments regarding governance processes are likely to be based on information obtained from numerous audit assignments over time. The internal auditor should consider: (1) the results of audits of specific governance processes (e.g., the whistleblower process, the strategy management process) and (2) governance issues arising from audits that are not specifically focused on governance (e.g., audits of the risk management process, internal control over financial reporting, and fraud risks).

   b. Risk management audit process.

   Incorrect. See correct answer (a).

   c. Internal control over financial reporting.

   Incorrect. See correct answer (a).

   d. Fraud risks.

   Incorrect. See correct answer (a).

14. Ensuring internal audit teams have the right competencies with right level of work experience and designing effective internal audit procedures can reduce the risk of which of the following?

   a. Business risk.

   Incorrect. Business risk is not applicable here.

   b. Audit failures.

   Correct. Audit failures result when there is a (1) failure to evaluate both the design adequacy and the control effectiveness as part of internal audit procedures and (2) use of audit teams that do not have the appropriate level of competence based on experience or knowledge of high-risk areas.

   c. Audit false assurance.

   Incorrect. Audit false assurance is not applicable here.

   d. Audit reputation risk.

   Incorrect. Audit reputation risk is not applicable here.

15. Consulting engagement objectives must be consistent with all of the following **except:**

   a. Organization's goals.

   Correct. Goals are short term in nature while objectives are long term in nature. Hence, consulting engagement objectives must be consistent with the organization's values, strategies, and objectives.

   b. Organization's values.

   Incorrect. See correct answer (a).

   c. Organization's strategies.

   Incorrect. See correct answer (a)

   d. Organization's objectives.

   Incorrect. See correct answer (a).

16. Which of the following is the **major** purpose of performing analytical procedures in internal audits?

  a. To perform additional audit procedures.

  Incorrect. Performing additional audit procedures is part of obtaining audit evidence.

  b. To plan the audit engagement.

  Incorrect. Planning the audit engagement is part of obtaining audit evidence.

  c. To obtain audit evidence.

  Correct. Analytical procedures often provide the internal auditor with an efficient and effective means of obtaining audit evidence. The assessment results from comparing information with expectations identified or developed by the internal auditor.

  d. To study relationships among elements of information.

  Incorrect. Studying relationships among elements of information is part of obtaining audit evidence.

17. According to the IIA *Standards*, which of the following is **not** included in the scope of the internal audit function?

  a. Appraising the effectiveness and efficiency of operations and programs.

  Incorrect. Appraising the effectiveness and efficiency of operations and programs is included in the scope of internal auditing as stated in the IIA *Standards*.

  b. Reviewing the strategic management process, assessing the quality of management decision making both quantitatively and qualitatively and reporting the results to the audit committee.

  Correct. The scope of the internal audit function does not include an assessment of the company's strategic management process.

  c. Reviewing the means of safeguarding assets.

  Incorrect. Reviewing the means of safeguarding assets is included in the scope of internal auditing as stated in the IIA *Standards*.

  d. Complying with the laws, regulations, policies, procedures, and contracts.

  Incorrect. Complying with the laws, regulations, policies, procedures, and contracts is included in the scope of internal auditing as stated in the IIA *Standards*.

18. An internal auditor is auditing the financial operations of an organization. Which of the following is **not** specified by the IIA *Standards* for inclusion in the scope of the audit?

  a. Reviewing the reliability and integrity of financial and operational information.

  Incorrect. Reviewing the reliability and integrity of financial and operational information is the basic element of the audit.

  b. Reviewing the compliance with laws, regulations, policies, procedures, and contracts.

  Incorrect. The *Standards* include compliance, and there are compliance aspects in financial operations.

  c. Appraising the effectiveness and efficiency of operations and programs.

  Incorrect. The auditor would review the economy, efficiency, and effectiveness of the financial functions.

  d. Reviewing the financial decision-making process.

  Correct. This element of the audit is not included in *IIA Standard 2130— Control*.

19. The audit committee of an organization has charged the chief audit executive (CAE) with bringing the department into full compliance with the IIA *Standards*. The CAE's first task is to develop a charter. Identify the item that should be included in the statement of objectives:

  a. Report all audit findings to the audit committee every quarter.

  Incorrect. Only significant audit findings should be discussed with the audit committee.

  b. Notify governmental regulatory agencies of unethical business practices by organization management.

  Incorrect. Internal auditors are not required to report deficiencies in regulatory compliance to the appropriate agencies. However, Institute members and Certified Internal Auditors may not knowingly be involved in illegal acts.

  c. Determine the adequacy and effectiveness of the organization's systems of internal controls.

  Correct. This is a primary function of any internal auditing department.

  d. Submit departmental budget variance reports to management every month.

  Incorrect. This choice is not a primary objective of the internal auditing department. It is a budgetary control that management may require on a periodic basis.

20. If an auditee's operating standards are vague and thus subject to interpretation, the auditor should:

    a. Seek agreement with the auditee as to the standards to be used to measure operating performance.

    Correct. This is what is required by _IIA Standard 2210—Engagement Objectives_.

    b. Determine best practices in this area and use them as the standard.

    Incorrect. The auditor should seek to understand the operating standards as they are applied to the organization.

    c. Interpret the standards in their strictest sense because standards are otherwise only minimum measures of acceptance.

    Incorrect. Agreement is necessary.

    d. Omit any comments on standards and the auditee's performance in relationship to those standards, because such an analysis would be meaningless.

    Incorrect. The auditor should first seek to gain an understanding with the auditee on the appropriate standards.

21. In which of the following situations does the auditor potentially lack objectivity?

    a. An auditor reviews the procedures for a new electronic data interchange connection to a major customer before it is implemented.

    Incorrect. IIA _Standards_ says that the internal auditor's objectivity is not adversely affected when the auditor reviews procedures before they are implemented.

    b. A former purchasing assistant performs a review of internal controls over purchasing four months after being transferred to the internal auditing department.

    Correct. _IIA Standard 1130—Impairment to Independence or Objectivity_ says that persons transferred to the internal auditing department should not be assigned to audit those activities they previously performed until a reasonable period of time has elapsed.

    c. An auditor recommends standards of control and performance measures for a contract with a service organization for the processing of payroll and employee benefits.

    Incorrect. IIA _Standards_ say that the internal auditor's objectivity is not adversely affected when the auditor recommends standards of control for systems before they are implemented.

    d. A payroll accounting employee assists an auditor in verifying the physical inventory of small motors.

    Incorrect. Use of staff from other areas to assist the internal auditor does not impair objectivity, especially when the staff is from outside of the area being audited.

22. Which of the following actions would be a violation of auditor independence?

    a. Continuing on an audit assignment at a division for which the auditor will soon be responsible as the result of a promotion.

    Correct. *IIA Standard 1130—Impairment to Independence or Objectivity* **specifies that an auditor who has been promoted to an operating department should not continue on an audit of the new department.**

    b. Reducing the scope of an audit due to budget restrictions.

    Incorrect. *IIA Standard 1130—Impairment to Independence or Objectivity* states that budget restrictions do not constitute a violation of an auditor's independence.

    c. Participating on a task force which recommends standards for control of a new distribution system.

    Incorrect. *IIA Standard 1130—Impairment to Independence or Objectivity* states that an auditor may participate on a task force that recommends new systems. However, designing, installing, or operating such systems might impair objectivity.

    d. Reviewing a purchasing agent's contract drafts prior to their execution.

    Incorrect. *IIA Standard 1130—Impairment to Independence or Objectivity* states that an auditor may review contracts prior to their execution.

23. The IIA's Code of Ethics includes which of the following two essential components?

    a. Definition of internal auditing and administrative directives.

    Incorrect. See correct answer (b).

    b. Principles and Rules of Conduct.

    Correct. The IIA's Code of Ethics extends beyond the definition of internal auditing to include two essential components:

    1. Principles that are relevant to the profession and practice of internal auditing.

    2. Rules of Conduct that describe behavior norms expected of internal auditors. These rules are an aid to interpreting the Principles into practical applications and are intended to guide the ethical conduct of internal auditors.

    Note that the IIA's Bylaws and Administrative Directives are applicable to IIA members and Certified Internal Auditor designation holders. Integrity, objectivity, confidentiality, and competency are part of the Principles and the Rules of Conduct.

    c. Integrity and objectivity.

    Incorrect. See correct answer (b).

    d. Confidentiality and competency.

    Incorrect. See correct answer (b).

24. A Certified Internal Auditor (CIA) is working in a non–internal audit position as the director of purchasing. The CIA signs a contract to procure a large order from the supplier with the best price, quality, and performance. Shortly after signing the contract, the supplier presents the CIA with a gift of significant monetary value. Which of the following statements regarding the acceptance of the gift is correct?

a. Acceptance of the gift would be prohibited only if it were noncustomary.

Incorrect. Acceptance of the gift could easily be presumed to have impaired independence and thus would not be acceptable.

b. Acceptance of the gift would violate the IIA Code of Ethics and would be prohibited for a CIA.

Correct. As long as an individual is a CIA, he or she should be guided by the profession's Code of Ethics in addition to the organization's code of conduct. Objectivity (Rules of Conduct) of the Code of Ethics would preclude such a gift because it could be presumed to have influenced the individual's decision.

c. Since the CIA is no longer acting as an internal auditor, acceptance of the gift would be governed only by the organization's code of conduct.

Incorrect. There is not sufficient information given to judge possible violations of the organization's code of conduct. However, the action could easily be perceived as a kickback.

d. Since the contract was signed before the gift was offered, acceptance of the gift would not violate either the IIA Code of Ethics or the organization's code of conduct.

Incorrect. There is not sufficient information given to judge possible violations of the organization's code of conduct. However, the action could easily be perceived as a kickback.

25. An auditor, nearly finished with an audit, discovers that the director of marketing has a gambling habit. The gambling issue is not directly related to the existing audit, and there is pressure to complete the current audit. The auditor notes the problem and passes the information on to the chief audit executive but does no further follow-up. The auditor's actions would:

a. Be in violation of the IIA Code of Ethics for withholding meaningful information.

Incorrect. The auditor is not withholding information because he or she has passed the information along to the chief audit executive. The information may be useful in a subsequent audit in the marketing area.

b. Be in violation of the *Standards* because the auditor did not properly follow-up on a red flag that might indicate the existence of fraud.

Incorrect. The auditor has documented a red flag that may be important in a subsequent audit. This does not violate the *Standards*.

c. Not be in violation of either the IIA Code of Ethics or the *Standards*.

Correct. There is no violation of either the Code of Ethics or the *Standards*.

d. Both a and b.

Incorrect. See correct answer (c).

26. As used by the internal auditing profession, the IIA *Standards* refer to all of the following **except**:

a. Criteria by which the operations of an internal audit department are evaluated and measured.

Incorrect. This is the definition of the IIA *Standards*.

b. Criteria which dictate the minimum level of ethical actions to be taken by internal auditors.

Correct. The IIA's Code of Ethics defines the minimum ethical standards for the internal auditor.

c. Statements intended to represent the practice of internal auditing, as it should be.

Incorrect. The *Standards* define the practice of internal auditing "as it should be."

d. Criteria that is applicable to all types of internal audit departments.

Incorrect. The IIA *Standards* are equally applicable across all industries and all types of internal audit organizations globally.

27. Which of the following situations would be a violation of the IIA Code of Ethics?

a. An auditor was subpoenaed in a court case in which a merger partner claimed to have been defrauded by the auditor's company. The auditor divulged confidential audit information to the court.

Incorrect. Article II prohibits members and Certified Internal Auditors from being party to illegal activities. Failure to comply with a subpoena would be illegal.

b. An auditor for a manufacturer of office products recently completed an audit of the corporate marketing function. Based on this experience, the auditor spent several hours one Saturday working as a paid consultant to a hospital in the local area, which intended to conduct an audit of its marketing function.

Incorrect. A part-time job would not be a problem since it was not with a competitor or supplier.

c. An auditor gave a speech at a local IIA chapter meeting outlining the contents of a program the auditor had developed for auditing electronic data interchange connections. Several auditors from major competitors were in the audience.

Incorrect. Giving a speech is not a violation of the Code of Ethics. In fact, the IIA's motto is "progress through sharing."

d. During an audit, an auditor learned that the company was about to introduce a *new* product that would revolutionize the industry. Because of the probable success of the new product, the product manager suggested that the auditor buy additional stock in the company, which the auditor did.

Correct. Confidentiality (Rules of Conduct) of the IIA's Code of Ethics states that members and Certified Internal Auditors shall not use confidential information for any personal gain.

28. In applying the standards of conduct set forth in the Code of Ethics, internal auditors are expected to:

a. Exercise their individual judgment.

Correct. The IIA's Code of Ethics contains basic principles, such as integrity, which require individual judgment to apply.

b. Compare them to standards in other professions.

Incorrect. While the comparison might be interesting, it would not help determine how to apply the Code.

c. Be guided by the desires of the auditee.

Incorrect. Application might not be in the best interest of the auditee.

d. Use discretion in deciding whether to use them or not.

Incorrect. Judgment may be applied to their use but not to whether to use them of their involvement, as well as future objectivity and independence issues.

29. Reinforcing the Code of Conduct and ethical behavior standards for all internal auditors can protect which of the following?

a. Business risk.

Incorrect. See correct answer (d).

b. Audit failures.

Incorrect. See correct answer (d).

c. Audit false assurance.

Incorrect. See correct answer (d).

d. Audit reputation risk.

Correct. A leading practice to protect the reputation of internal audit's "brand" name is to reinforce the Code of Conduct and ethical behavior standards for all internal auditors.

Domain 2: Internal Control and Risk (25–35%)

1. An exception report for management is an example of which of the following?

    a. Preventive control.

    Incorrect. See correct answer (c).

    b. Detective control.

    Incorrect. See correct answer (c).

    c. Corrective control.

    Correct. Detecting an exception in a business transaction or process is detective in nature, but reporting it is an example of a corrective control. Both preventive and directive controls do not detect or correct an error; they simply stop the error, if possible.

    d. Directive control.

    Incorrect. See correct answer (c).

2. Organizational procedures allow employees to anticipate problems. This type of control is known as:

    a. Feedback control.

    Incorrect. This is a retrospective control based on the outcome of a completed activity.

    b. Strategic control.

    Incorrect. This is a broader-based control that should go hand in hand with strategic planning.

    c. Feed-forward control.

    Correct. Procedures provide guidance on how tasks should be accomplished.

    d. Performance appraisal.

    Incorrect. This is a retrospective control.

3. As part of a total quality control program, a firm not only inspects finished goods but also monitors product returns and customer complaints. Which type of control best describes these efforts?

    a. Feedback control.

    Correct. Feedback control ensures that past mistakes are not repeated.

    b. Feed-forward control.

    Incorrect. The controls mentioned occur after processing and therefore cannot provide feed-forward control.

    c. Production control.

    Incorrect. Complaints are not part of production control.

    d. Inventory control.

    Incorrect. The question is not limited to inventory.

4. To be successful, large companies must develop means to keep the organization focused in the proper direction. Organization control systems help keep companies focused. These control systems consist of which of the following components?

    a. Budgeting, financial ratio analysis, and cash management.

    Incorrect. These are means of financial control.

    b. Objectives, standards, and an evaluation-reward system.

    Correct. These items are the basic components of complex organizational control systems in large companies.

    c. Role analysis, team building, and survey feedback.

    Incorrect. These are several types of organizational development interventions.

    d. Coaching, protection, and challenging assignments.

    Incorrect. Mentoring fulfills several types of career enhancement functions, including these.

5. **Control** has been described as a closed system consisting of six elements. Identify one of the six elements.

    a. Setting performance standards.

    Correct. Setting performance standards is one of the six elements.

    b. Adequately securing data files.

    Incorrect. This choice is not an element of a closed control system.

    c. Approval of audit charter.

    Incorrect. This choice is not an element of a closed control system.

    d. Establishment of independent audit function.

    Incorrect. This choice is not an element of a closed control system.

6. The three basic components of all organizational control systems are:

   a. **Objectives, standards, and an evaluation-reward system.**

      Correct. These are the three basic components of a control system.

   b. Plans, budgets, and organizational policies and procedures.

      Incorrect. These three terms are all used to describe subsystems of a control system.

   c. Statistical reports, audits, and financial controls.

      Incorrect. These three terms are used to describe either a subsystem of a control process or a tool used in a control system.

   d. Inputs, objectives, and an appraisal system.

      Incorrect. While "objectives" is a correct answer, the other two terms are incorrect. "Inputs" is a good distracter because it is part of the "input-process-output" relationship used to describe a system.

7. Which of the following management control systems measures performance in terms of operating profits minus the cost of capital invested in tangible assets?

   a. Open-book management system.

      Incorrect. The open-book management system focuses on sharing company's financial information to all employees.

   b. **Economic value added system.**

      Correct. The economic value added system is a new system to measure corporate performance.

   c. Activity-based costing system.

      Incorrect. The activity-based costing system identifies various activities needed to produce a product or service and determines the cost of those activities.

   d. Market value added system.

      Incorrect. The market value added system determines the market value of a firm based on its market capitalization rate.

8. A comprehensive management control system that considers both financial and nonfinancial measures relating to a company's critical success factors is called a(n):

   a. **Balanced scorecard system.**

      Correct. The balanced scorecard system is a comprehensive management control system that balances the traditional accounting (financial) measures with the operational (nonfinancial) measures.

   b. Economic value added system.

      Incorrect. See correct answer (a).

   c. Activity-based costing system.

      Incorrect. See correct answer (a).

   d. Market value added system.

      Incorrect. See correct answer (a).

9. According to the IIA Planning *Standard*, the term "risk appetite" means which of the following?

   a. Risk avoidance.

      Incorrect. Risk avoidance is eliminating the risk cause and/or consequence.

   b. Risk limitation.

      Incorrect. Risk limitation implements controls to minimize the adverse impact of a threat.

   c. **Risk acceptance.**

      Correct. Risk acceptance is the level of risk that an organization is willing to accept, and it is referred to as risk appetite.

   d. Risk spreading.

      Incorrect. Risk spreading is sharing the risk with other divisions or business units of the same organization.

10. According to the IIA Planning *Standard*, residual risk is also known as which of the following?

a. Audit risk.

Incorrect. Audit risk results when an auditor fails to detect a material error or event, and an auditor may fail to detect significant error or weakness during an examination.

b. Pure risk.

Incorrect. Pure risks are those in which there is a chance of loss or no loss only.

c. Current risk.

Correct. Residual risk is current risk, which is the risk remaining after management takes action to reduce the impact and likelihood of an adverse event, including control activities in responding to a risk. Current risk is often defined as the risk managed within existing controls or control systems. Current risk cannot be ignored; instead, it should be managed well so it can become a managed risk.

d. Inherent risk.

Incorrect. Inherent risk is a built-in risk; an example is the susceptibility of information or data to a material misstatement.

11. Residual risk is calculated as which of the following?

a. Known risks minus unknown risks.

Incorrect. See correct answer (d).

b. Actual risks minus probable risks.

Incorrect. See correct answer (d).

c. Probable risks minus possible risks.

Incorrect. See correct answer (d).

d. Potential risks minus covered risks.

Correct. Potential risks include all possible and probable risks. Countermeasures cover some but not all risks. Therefore, the residual risk is potential risks minus covered risks.

12. Which of the following is closely linked to risk acceptance?

a. Risk detection.

Incorrect. See correct answer (c).

b. Risk prevention.

Incorrect. See correct answer (c).

c. Risk tolerance.

Correct. Risk tolerance is the level of risk that an entity or a manager is willing to assume or accept in order to achieve a potential desired result. Some managers accept more risk than others do due to their personal affinity to risk.

d. Risk correction.

Incorrect. See correct answer (c).

13. Which of the following risk concepts can be assumed to have **no** mitigating controls?

a. Business risk.

Incorrect. Business risk is total risk facing an organization.

b. Residual risk.

Incorrect. Residual risk is current risk.

c. Inherent risk.

Correct. Two fundamental risk concepts are inherent risk and residual risk (also known as current risk). Inherent risk is a built-in risk. To financial/external auditors, inherent risk can be summarized as the susceptibility of information or data to a material misstatement, assuming that there are no related mitigating controls.

d. Current risk.

Incorrect. Inherent risk is the susceptibility of a management assertion to a material misstatement.

14. The internal audit charter normally requires the internal audit activity to focus on areas consisting of which of the following?

a. **High inherent risk and high residual risk.**

Correct. The internal audit charter normally requires the internal audit activity to focus on areas of high risk, including both inherent and residual risk. The internal audit activity needs to identify areas of high inherent risk, high residual risks, and the key control systems upon which the organization is most reliant.

b. High audit risk and high current risk.

Incorrect. See correct answer (a).

c. Low inherent risk and low audit risk.

Incorrect. See correct answer (a).

d. Low inherent risk and high outstanding risk.

Incorrect. See correct answer (a).

15. Internal auditors would be more likely to detect fraud if they developed/strengthened their ability to:

a. **Recognize and question changes which occur in organizations.**

Correct. The recognition and questioning of change is critical to the detection of fraud.

b. Interrogate fraud perpetrators to discover why the fraud was committed.

Incorrect. Interrogation of fraud perpetrators occurs after detection.

c. Develop internal controls to prevent the occurrence of fraud.

Incorrect. The controls mentioned are preventive, not detective.

d. Document computerized operating system programs.

Incorrect. Documentation of operating systems is not within the scope of internal auditing and would do little to enhance fraud detection skills.

16. According to the IIA *Standards*, which of the following **best** describes the two general categories or types of fraud that concern most internal auditors?

a. Improper payments (i.e., bribes and kickbacks) and tax fraud.

Incorrect. These are examples of kinds of fraud within the two general categories or types given in the *Standards*.

b. **Fraud designed to benefit the organization and fraud perpetrated to the detriment of the organization.**

Correct. These are the two overall categories or types of fraud given in the IIA *Standards*.

c. Acceptance of bribes or kickbacks and improper related-party transactions.

Incorrect. These are examples of kinds of fraud within the two general categories or types given in the *Standards*.

d. Acceptance of kickbacks or embezzlement and misappropriation of assets.

Incorrect. These are examples of kinds of fraud within the two general categories or types given in the *Standards*.

17. A company hired a highly qualified accounts payable manager who had been terminated from another company for alleged wrongdoing. Six months later, the manager diverted $12,000 by sending duplicate payments of invoices to a relative. A control that might have prevented this situation would be to:

a. **Adequately check prior employment backgrounds for all new employees.**

Correct. This practice might give some leads to previous shortcomings.

b. Not hire individuals who appear overqualified for a job.

Incorrect. Individuals in their declining years may be forced to accept jobs below their full capabilities.

c. Verify educational background for all new employees.

Incorrect. This does not include checking prior employment.

d. Check to see if close relatives work for vendors.

Incorrect. This is not an adequate control in this scenario.

18. Red flags are conditions that indicate a higher likelihood of fraud. Which of the following would **not** be considered a red flag?

    a. **Management has delegated the authority to make purchases under a certain dollar limit to subordinates.**

    Correct. This is an acceptable control procedure aimed at limiting risk while promoting efficiency. It is not, by itself, considered a red flag.

    b. An individual has held the same cash-handling job for an extended period without any rotation of duties.

    Incorrect. Lack of rotation of duties or cross-training for sensitive jobs is one of the red-flag list factors.

    c. An individual handling marketable securities is responsible for making the purchases, recording the purchases, and reporting any discrepancies and gains/losses to senior management.

    Incorrect. This would be an example of an inappropriate segregation of duties, which is an identified red flag.

    d. The assignment of responsibility and accountability in the accounts receivable department is not clear.

    Incorrect. This is an identified red flag.

19. Internal auditors and management have become increasingly concerned about computer fraud. Which of the following control procedures would be **least** important in preventing computer fraud?

    a. Program change control that requires a distinction between production programs and test programs.

    Incorrect. This is one of the elements of good program change control.

    b. Testing of new applications by users during the systems development process.

    Incorrect. Testing of new applications by users is one of the most important controls to help prevent computer fraud.

    c. Segregation of duties between the applications programmer and the program librarian function.

    Incorrect. An adequate control structure over program changes is one of the most important control procedures in a computerized environment.

    d. **Segregation of duties between the programmer and systems analyst.**

    Correct. This would be the least important control procedure. The analyst is responsible for communicating the nature of the design to the programmer. There is no control reason not to combine these functions.

Domain 3: Conducting Internal Audit Engagements—Audit Tools and Techniques (28–38%)

1. An audit team developed a preliminary questionnaire with the following response choices:

   - Probably not a problem.
   - Possibly a problem.
   - Probably a problem.

   The questionnaire illustrates the use of:

   a. Trend analysis.

   Incorrect. Trend analysis is a specialized form of analytical review procedure, used primarily to analyze the changes in account balances over time.

   b. Ratio analysis.

   Incorrect. Ratio analysis is a subset of trend analysis used in analytical review. It is unrelated to the subject.

   c. Unobtrusive measures or observations.

   Incorrect. Observing means seeing and noticing, not passing over. It implies a careful, knowledgeable look at people and things. It means a visual examination with a purpose, a mental comparison with standards, an evaluative sighting. Use of rating scales requires the participant to actively participate; it is not unobtrusive.

   d. **Rating scales.**

   Correct. The auditors are using a numerical rating scale for the organization audited.

2. Which of the following statements describes an internal control questionnaire? It:

   a. Provides detailed evidence regarding the substance of the control system.

   Incorrect. "Yes" and "no" answers may be very general and not specific as to degree.

   b. Takes less of the auditee's time to complete than other control evaluation devices.

   Incorrect. Such questionnaires are tiring for auditees to complete due to their length.

   c. Requires that the auditor be in attendance to properly administer it.

   Incorrect. The structured questionnaire asks for specific "yes" or "no" answers plus brief explanations.

   d. **Provides indirect audit evidence that might need corroboration.**

   Correct. The evidence provided is indirect and therefore could require corroboration in some way.

3. Which of the following is the **primary** advantage of using an internal control questionnaire?

a. It provides a clear picture of the interrelationships that exist between the various controls.

Incorrect. This is an advantage of flowcharts.

b. It reduces the risk of overlooking important aspects of the system.

Correct. An internal control questionnaire can be prepared in advance and functions very much like a checklist.

c. It forces an auditor to acquire a full understanding of the system.

Incorrect. This is an advantage of flowcharts.

d. Negative responses indicate the only areas needing further audit work.

Incorrect. Positive responses must also be tested to determine compliance.

4. Checklists used to assess audit risk have been criticized for all of the following reasons **except:**

a. Providing a false sense of security that all relevant factors are addressed.

Incorrect. This choice is a criticism of checklists.

b. Inappropriately implying equal weight to each item on the checklist.

Incorrect. This choice is a criticism of checklists.

c. Decreasing the uniformity of data acquisition.

Correct. Checklists increase the uniformity of data acquisition.

d. Being incapable of translating the experience or sound reasoning intended to be captured by each item on the checklist.

Incorrect. This choice is a criticism of checklists.

5. When an internal auditor is interviewing to gain information, the auditor will not be able to remember everything that was said in the interview. The **most** effective way to record interview information for later use is to:

a. Write notes quickly, trying to write down everything in detail, as it is said; then highlight important points after the meeting.

Incorrect. Extensive note taking may interfere with communication with respondents, since the auditor cannot maintain eye contact or notice nonverbal as well when occupied taking notes.

b. Tape-record the interview to capture everything that everyone says; then type everything said into a computer for documentation.

Incorrect. Tape recording might be used for controversial material but generally will not elicit positive feelings from respondents. For most organizational purposes, auditors will not need exact quotes, which are the major benefit of a recording.

c. Hire a professional secretary to take notes, allowing complete concentration on the interview; then delete unimportant points after the meeting.

Incorrect. Aside from cost, this option would not work because of confidentiality and negative reaction from respondents. This interview is the auditor's job, not someone else's.

d. Organize notes around topics on the interview plan and note responses in the appropriate area, reviewing the notes after the meeting to make additions.

Correct. Organizing note taking ahead of time helps auditors have time during the interview to listen and evaluate the responses and the reactions of respondents.

6. When conducting interviews during the early stages of an internal audit, it is more effective to:

   a. Ask for specific answers that can be quantified.

   Incorrect. Later fieldwork will cover information that can be quantified. Building rapport is more important in the early interviews.

   b. Ask people about their jobs.

   Correct. Individuals feel more important when they are asked people questions rather than control questions. This will improve the important interpersonal part of building the audit relationship.

   c. Ask surprise questions about daily procedures.

   Incorrect. Unless fraud is suspected or the audit deals with cash or negotiable securities, it is more effective to defuse the anxiety of anticipating the audit by providing information ahead of time that explains the audit process and how to prepare for it.

   d. Take advantage of the fact that fear is an important part of the audit.

   Incorrect. Auditee fear may be a natural part of anticipating the audit, but the auditor should keep it from being an important continuing part of the audit by using good interpersonal skills to build a positive participative relationship with auditees.

7. An auditor prepared a working paper that consisted of a list of employee names and identification numbers as well as this statement: "By matching random numbers with employee identification numbers, 40 employee personnel files were selected to verify that they contain all documents required by company policy 501. No exceptions were noted."

   The auditor did not place any tick marks on this working paper. Which one of the following changes would improve the auditor's working paper the **most**?

   a. Use of tick marks to show that each file was examined.

   Incorrect. It is not necessary to use tick marks in this case because the same procedures were applied to all sample selections and no exceptions were detected.

   b. Removal of the employee names to protect their confidentiality.

   Incorrect. The audit working papers are themselves kept confidential so it is not necessary to remove employee names.

   c. Justification for the sample size.

   Correct. The working paper should specify the sampling risk and the confidence level or precision achieved by the sample or the method of determining size.

   d. Listing of the actual documents examined for each employee.

   Incorrect. In this case, reference to the company policy is equivalent to listing the documents that were examined.

8. The standard deviation of a sample will usually decrease with:

   a. A decrease in sample size.

   Incorrect. A larger sample might more closely approximate the population standard deviation, but that could be either higher or lower depending on the point of reference. A smaller sample might go either way without the increased reliability.

   b. The use of stratification.

   Correct. Because high-value items can be sampled 100%, a large segment of variability can be eliminated.

   c. An increase in desired precision.

   Incorrect. To the extent that sample size is affected, the results might be the same as in choice (a).

   d. An increase in confidence level.

   Incorrect. To the extent that sample size is affected, the results might be the same as in choice (a).

9. Statistical sampling would be appropriate to estimate the value of an auto dealer's 3,000 line-item inventory because statistical sampling is:

a. **Reliable and objective.**

Correct. This fits the definition.

b. Thorough and complete.

Incorrect. Statistical sampling is neither thorough nor complete.

c. Thorough and accurate.

Incorrect. Statistical sampling is neither thorough nor accurate.

d. Complete and precise.

Incorrect. Statistical sampling is precise but not complete.

10. An important difference between a statistical sample and a judgmental sample is that with a statistical sample:

a. No judgment is required, everything is by formula .

Incorrect. Judgment is needed for sample size.

b. A smaller sample size can be used.

Incorrect. A large sample may be needed.

c. More accurate results are obtained.

Incorrect. There is no way to determine whether more accurate results are obtained.

d. **Population estimates with measurable reliability can be made.**

Correct. A statistical sample is the only way to measure reliability.

11. Sample size:

a. **Increases with the use of higher confidence levels.**

Correct. In its simplest form, the sample-size formula shows that sample size is equal to [(Confidence level factor squared × Estimated standard deviation squared)/(Precision squared)]; thus any increase in confidence level would be accompanied by an increase in sample size.

b. Decreases with the use of higher confidence levels.

Incorrect. See correct answer (a).

c. Remains unchanged with changes in confidence levels.

Incorrect. See correct answer (a).

d. Increases with the use of lower confidence levels.

Incorrect. See correct answer (a).

12. An auditor becomes concerned that fraud in the form of payments to bogus companies may exist. Buyers, who are responsible for all purchases for specific product lines, are able to approve expenditures up to $50,000 without any other approval. Which of the following audit procedures would be **most** effective in addressing the auditor's concerns?

a. Use generalized audit software to list all purchases over $50,000 to determine whether they were properly approved.

Incorrect. This would provide evidence only on purchases above $50,000, which must be approved by someone other than the buyer.

b. Develop a snapshot technique to trace all transactions by suspected buyers.

Incorrect. This would provide information only on whether the transactions that were authorized by the buyer were properly processed. It does not provide evidence on whether the transaction should have been processed.

c. Use generalized audit software to take a random sample of all expenditures under $50,000 to determine whether they were properly approved.

Incorrect. This would provide information on whether transactions under $50,000 contained the buyer's authorization. That is not the question here; the question is whether there is support for the expenditure. Further, this procedure is limited because it is not directed to the specific indicators that a fraud might exist.

d. **Use generalized audit software to list all major vendors by product line; select a sample of paid invoices to new vendors and examine evidence which shows that services or goods were received.**

Correct. This is the most comprehensive procedure because it identifies major vendors, concentrates on new vendors, and searches for underlying support that goods or services were provided by the vendor.

13. An auditor wishes to determine the extent to which invalid data could be contained in a human resources computer system. Examples would be an invalid job classification, age in excess of retirement age, or an invalid ethnic classification. The **best** approach to determine the extent of the potential problem would be to:

a. Submit test data to test the effectiveness of edit controls over the input of data.

Incorrect. Test data would provide evidence on whether the edit controls are currently working. The concern, however, is that data may have entered the system earlier and may be corrupted.

b. Review and test access controls to ensure that access is limited to authorized individuals.

Incorrect. Access controls are important, but they do not address the auditor's major concern, which is to determine the extent of the potential problem as a precursor for planning the extent to which additional audit work is necessary.

c. **Use generalized audit software to develop a detailed report of all data outside specified parameters.**

Correct. This is both the most effective and the most efficient procedure as it provides a comprehensive analysis of the extent that obviously incorrect data are included in the database.

d. Use generalized audit software to select a sample of employees. Use the sample to determine the validity of data items and project the result to the population as a whole.

Incorrect. This is a valid procedure, but given the auditor's more limited objective, choice (c) provides more comprehensive and efficient evidence.

14. A bank internal auditor wishes to determine whether all loans are backed by sufficient collateral, properly aged as to current payments, and properly categorized as current or noncurrent. The **best** audit procedure to accomplish this objective would be to:

a. **Use generalized audit software to read the total loan file, age the file by last payment due, and take a statistical sample stratified by the current and aged population. Examine each loan selected for proper collateralization and aging.**

Correct. This is the best procedure because it takes a sample from the total loan file and tests to determine that the loan is properly categorized as well as properly collateralized.

b. Take a block sample of all loans in excess of a specified dollar limit and determine if they are current and properly categorized. For each loan approved, verify aging and categorization.

Incorrect. This sample deals only with large-dollar items and does not test for proper collateralization.

c. Take a discovery sample of all loan applications to determine whether each application contains a statement of collateral.

Incorrect. This is an inefficient audit procedure because it samples from loan applications, not loans approved.

d. Take a sample of payments made on the loan portfolio and trace them to loans to see that the payments are properly applied. For each loan identified, examine the loan application to determine that the loan has proper collateralization.

Incorrect. This would be an ineffective procedure because it is based only on loans in which payments are currently being made—it does not include loans that should have been categorized differently because payments are not being made.

15. Governmental auditors have been increasingly called on to perform audits to determine whether individuals are getting extra social welfare payments. One common type of welfare fraud is individuals receiving more than one social welfare payment. This is often accomplished by filing multiple claims under multiple names but using the same address. Which of the following computer audit tools and techniques would be **most** helpful in identifying the existence of this type of fraud?

a. Tagging and tracing.

Incorrect. Tagging and tracing is most effective to determine that items properly submitted are processed correctly.

b. **Generalized audit software.**

Correct. Generalized audit software could be used to develop a list of multiple recipients at one address. The list could then be investigated further to determine the possibility of fraud.

c. Integrated test facility.

Incorrect. The integrated test facility is most effective to determine that items properly submitted are processed correctly.

d. Spreadsheet analysis.

Incorrect. This would not be the most effective technique.

16. Management has requested an audit of promotional expenses. The sales department has been giving away expensive items in conjunction with new product sales to stimulate demand. The promotion seems successful, but management believes the cost may be too high. Which of the following audit procedures would be the **least** useful to determine the effectiveness of the promotion?

a. A comparison of product sales during the promotion period with sales during a similar nonpromotion period.

Incorrect. This comparison would help highlight the effectiveness of the promotion in increasing sales.

b. **A comparison of the unit cost of the products sold before and during the promotion period.**

Correct. There is no indication that the cost of the products sold has changed. The challenge is to address the effectiveness of the promotion.

c. An analysis of marginal revenue and marginal cost for the promotion period, compared to the period before the promotion.

Incorrect. This is the key analysis, as it would show the extent of additional revenue versus cost.

d. A review of the sales department's reasons for believing that the promotion has been successful.

Incorrect. This would be helpful because the sales department may have useful information on new customers and repeat purchases.

17. An internal auditor plans to use an analytical review to verify the correctness of various operating expenses in a division. The use of an analytical review as a verification technique would **not** be a preferred approach if:

a. **The auditor notes strong indicators of a specific fraud involving this account.**

Correct. If the auditor already suspects fraud, a more directed audit approach would be appropriate.

b. The company has relatively stable operations that have not changed much over the past year.

Incorrect. Relatively stable operating data are a good scenario for using analytical review.

c. The auditor would like to identify large, unusual, or nonrecurring transactions during the year.

Incorrect. Analytical review would be useful in identifying whether large, nonrecurring, or unusual transactions occurred.

d. The operating expenses vary in relation to other operating expenses but not in relation to revenue.

Incorrect. Analytical review only needs to have accounts related to other accounts or other independent data. It does not require that they be related to revenue.

18. During an audit, the internal auditor should consider the following factor(s) in determining the extent to which analytical procedures should be used:

    a. Adequacy of the system of internal control.

    Incorrect. Adequacy of the system of internal control would be used to determine the extent of analytical audit procedures to be completed.

    b. Significance of the area being examined.

    Incorrect. The significance of the area being examined would be a factor in determining the extent of the analytical audit procedures to be used.

    c. Precision with which the results of analytical audit procedures can be predicted.

    Incorrect. The precision of the prediction of the internal audit results would be a factor in determining the extent of analytical audit procedures to be used.

    d. All of the above.

    Correct. All of the listed factors would be considered in determining the extent of analytical audit procedures to be used.

19. An auditor performs an analytical review by comparing the gross margins of various divisional operations with those of other divisions and with the individual division's performance in previous years. The auditor notes a significant increase in the gross margin at one division. The auditor does some preliminary investigation and also notes that there were no changes in products, production methods, or divisional management during the year. Based on this information, the **most** likely cause of the increase in gross margin would be:

    a. An increase in the number of competitors selling similar products.

    Incorrect. An increase in the number of competitors would result in price competition and a likely decrease in gross margin.

    b. A decrease in the number of suppliers of the material used in manufacturing the product.

    Incorrect. A decrease in the number of suppliers would cause less price competition on the incoming side and, all else being equal, would result in a decreased gross margin.

    c. An overstatement of year-end inventory.

    Correct. An overstatement of year-end inventory would result in an increase in the gross margin.

    d. An understatement of year-end accounts receivable.

    Incorrect. A decrease in accounts receivable would be very unlikely to signal an increase in the gross margin.

20. During an operational audit, an auditor compares the inventory turnover rate of a subsidiary with established industry standards in order to:

    a. Evaluate the accuracy of the subsidiary's internal financial reports.

    Incorrect. Comparison with industry standards will not test the accuracy of internal reporting.

    b. Test the subsidiary's controls designed to safeguard assets.

    Incorrect. Comparison with industry standards will not test the controls designed to safeguard the inventory.

    c. Determine if the subsidiary is complying with corporate procedures regarding inventory levels.

    Incorrect. A comparison with industry standards will not test compliance.

    d. Assess the performance of the subsidiary and indicate where additional audit work may be needed.

    Correct. Such an analytical procedure will provide an indication of the efficiency and effectiveness of the subsidiary's management of the inventory.

21. Which of the following is true of a horizontal flowchart as compared to a vertical flowchart?

    a. It provides more room for written descriptions that parallel the symbols.

    Incorrect. A vertical flowchart usually is designed to provide for written descriptions.

    b. It brings into sharper focus the assignment of duties and independent checks on performance.

    Correct. By emphasizing the flow of processing between departments and/or people, it more clearly shows any inappropriate separation of duties and lack of independent checks on performance.

    c. It is usually longer.

    Incorrect. A horizontal flowchart is usually shorter because space for written descriptions is not provided.

    d. It does not provide as broad a picture at a glance.

    Incorrect. More of the flow of processing can be depicted on one page than in a vertical flowchart with written descriptions.

22. Of the following, which is the **most** efficient source for an auditor to use to evaluate a company's overall control system?

   a. **Control flowcharts.**

      Correct. Control flowcharting provides an efficient and comprehensive method of describing relatively complex activities, especially those involving several departments.

   b. Copies of standard operating procedures.

      Incorrect. Copies of procedures and related forms do not provide an efficient method of reviewing the processing activities.

   c. A narrative describing departmental history, activities, and forms usage.

      Incorrect. A narrative review covering the department's history and forms usage is not as efficient or comprehensive as flowcharting for communicating relevant information about controls.

   d. Copies of industry operating standards.

      Incorrect. Industry standards do not provide a picture of existing practice for subsequent audit activity.

23. Which of the following tools would **best** give a graphical representation of a sequence of activities and decisions?

   a. **Flowchart.**

      Correct. According to its definition, a flowchart is a graphical representation of a sequence of activities and decisions.

   b. Control chart.

      Incorrect. A control chart is used to monitor actual versus desired quality measurements during repetition operation.

   c. Histogram.

      Incorrect. A histogram is a bar chart showing conformance to a standard bell curve.

   d. Run chart.

      Incorrect. A run chart tracks the frequency or amount of a given variable over time.

24. In documenting the procedures used by several interacting departments, the internal auditor will **most** likely use:

   a. **A horizontal flowchart.**

      Correct. A horizontal (systems) flowchart highlights the interaction between departments.

   b. A vertical flowchart.

      Incorrect. A vertical flowchart does not highlight the interaction of departments.

   c. A Gantt chart.

      Incorrect. A Gantt chart is not a procedure-oriented documenting tool.

   d. An internal control questionnaire.

      Incorrect. An internal control questionnaire does not highlight the interaction of departments.

25. Which method of evaluating internal controls during the preliminary review provides the auditor with the **best** visual grasp of a system and a means for analyzing complex operations?

   a. **A flowcharting approach.**

      Correct. A flowchart provides a visual grasp of the system and a means of analysis that cannot be achieved by other methods.

   b. A questionnaire approach.

      Incorrect. A questionnaire approach provides only an agenda for evaluation.

   c. A matrix approach.

      Incorrect. A matrix approach does not provide the visual grasp of the system that a flowchart does.

   d. A detailed narrative approach.

      Incorrect. A detailed narrative does not provide the means of evaluating complex operations that a flowchart does.

26. The auditor wishes to test the assertion that all claims paid by a medical insurance company contain proper authorization and documentation, including but not limited to the validity of the claim from an approved physician and an indication that the claim complies with the claimant's policy. The **most** appropriate audit procedure would be to:

a. Select a random statistical sample of all policyholders and examine all claims for the sampled items during the year to determine if they were handled properly.

   Incorrect. Sampling from a population of policyholders would be very inefficient for the audit assertion, as many policyholders may not have any activity during the year.

b. Select a sample of claims filed and trace to documentary evidence of authorization and other supporting documentation.

   Incorrect. A sample of claims filed does provide evidence on the overall processing of claims and thus provides some evidence related to the assertion. However, given the assertion, choice (a) is more efficient because it deals with paid claims.

c. Select a sample of claims denied and determine that all claims denied were appropriate. The claims denied file is much smaller, and the auditor can obtain greater coverage with the sample size.

   Incorrect. The claims denied filed provides evidence on the claims denied, but the auditor cannot conclude that all claims that were not denied should have been paid.

d. **Select a sample of paid claims from the claims (cash) disbursement file and trace to documentary evidence of authorization and other supporting documentation.**

   Correct. The auditor is interested in whether the actual claims paid are properly supported. The most appropriate population from which to sample is the claims-paid file.

27. In evaluating the validity of different types of audit evidence, which one of the following conclusions is **incorrect**?

a. Recomputation, although highly valid, is limited in usefulness due to its limited scope.

   Incorrect. This choice is a true statement.

b. **The validity of documentary evidence is independent of the effectiveness of the control system in which it was created.**

   Correct. The validity of documentary evidence depends on the internal control system.

c. Internally created documentary evidence is considered less valid than externally created documentary evidence.

   Incorrect. This choice is a true statement.

d. The validity of confirmations varies directly with the independence of the party receiving the confirmation.

   Incorrect. This choice is a true statement.

28. Which of the following is generally **not** true when evaluating the persuasiveness of evidence?

a. **Verified by internally maintained documents rather than by written inquiry of third party.**

   Correct. Written inquiry/confirmation obtained from outside third parties is more persuasive than internal company documents.

b. Obtained under conditions of strong controls rather than weak controls.

   Incorrect. Evidence obtained under conditions of strong control is always more persuasive than if controls had been weak.

c. Known by an auditor's personal knowledge rather than from a third-party confirmation.

   Incorrect. Personal knowledge is generally more persuasive than knowledge obtained from other parties.

d. Obtained from an external source rather than from an internal source.

   Incorrect. Generally, evidence from outside the organization is more persuasive than evidence obtained from organizational sources. These justifications are based on the general theory of audit evidence.

29. In testing the write-off of a deteriorated piece of equipment, the **best** evidence of the condition of the equipment would be:

a. The equipment manager's statement regarding condition.

Incorrect. Testimonial evidence, standing alone, is not conclusive.

b. Accounting records showing maintenance and repair costs.

Incorrect. The record of repair and maintenance costs is an internal record providing little evidence of current condition.

c. **A physical inspection of the actual piece of equipment.**

Correct. A physical inspection provides the best evidence of current condition.

d. The production department's equipment downtime report.

Incorrect. As an internal document, the production department's downtime report provides little persuasive evidence of current condition.

30. Which of the following audit procedures provides the **best** evidence about the collectibility of notes receivable?

a. Confirmation of note receivable balances with the debtors.

Incorrect. Confirmation establishes existence, not collectibility.

b. Examination of notes for appropriate debtors' signatures.

Incorrect. Inspection helps verify the validity (not collectibility) of the notes.

c. Reconciliation of the detail of notes receivable and the provision for uncollectible amounts to the general ledger control.

Incorrect. This merely tests bookkeeping procedures.

d. **Examination of cash receipts records to determine promptness of interest and principal payments.**

Correct. This procedure provides the best evidence of the collectibility of notes receivable.

31. What standard of evidence is satisfied by an original signed document?

a. Sufficiency.

Incorrect. Sufficiency has to do with factual, adequate, and convincing evidence. The information contained on the document may be none of those things.

b. **Competence.**

Correct. Competent evidence is reliable. It is the best available. An original document is the prime example of such evidence, per the IIA *Standards*.

c. Relevance.

Incorrect. Relevancy has to do with the relationship of the evidence to some objective of the audit. Since no audit objective is disclosed in the stem of the question, the observer has no way to tell whether the information on the document is or is not relevant to the investigation.

d. Usefulness.

Incorrect. Usefulness is achieved if the item of evidence helps the organization (the auditor, in this case) to accomplish predetermined goals. Since no such goals are specified, there is no way to determine whether the information on the document will help the auditor accomplish some goal established for the audit.

32. When sampling methods are used, the concept of sufficiency of evidence means that the samples selected provide:

a. **Reasonable assurance that they are representative of the sampled population.**

Correct. A sample need only provide reasonable assurance. Due to of cost/benefit considerations, absolute assurance is not necessary.

b. The best evidence that is reasonably obtainable.

Incorrect. The best reasonably obtainable is a test of competence.

c. Reasonable assurance that the evidence has a logical relationship to the audit objective.

Incorrect. The logical relationship is a test of relevance.

d. Absolute assurance that a sample is representative of the population.

Incorrect. Due to cost/benefit considerations, absolute assurance is not necessary.

33. An internal auditor takes a photograph of the auditee's workplace. The photograph is a form of what kind of evidence?

a. Physical.

Correct. All graphic evidence is classified as physical evidence. This includes other forms of graphic evidence, such as graphs, charts, and maps.

b. Testimonial.

Incorrect. Testimonial evidence is restricted to the written response to inquiry or interview.

c. Documentary.

Incorrect. Documentary evidence is nongraphical. It takes the form of records, memoranda, correspondence, and related written material.

d. Analytical.

Incorrect. Analytical evidence is the result of the division of a complex entity into its constituent parts, with the subsequent review of each subset of the original whole.

# Glossary

This glossary contains key terms useful to CIA Exam candidates. Reading the glossary terms prior to studying the theoretical subject matter covered in the review books and prior to answering the online test bank's practice questions can help the candidate understand the domain contents better. In addition, this glossary is a good source for answering multiple-choice questions on the CIA Exam. Certain glossary terms are repeated in the Part 1, Part 2 , and Part 3 glossary sections for students' convenience due to their common topics and the fact that each Part Exam must be passed separately.

Abuse
Abuse occurs when the conduct of an activity or function falls short of expectations for prudent behavior. Abuse is distinguished from noncompliance in that abusive conditions may not directly violate laws or regulations. Abusive activities may be within the letter of the laws and regulations but violate either their spirit or the more general standards of impartial and ethical behavior.

Activity reports
Activity reports of the internal auditing department highlight significant audit findings and recommendations and inform senior management and the board of any significant deviations from approved audit work schedules, staffing plans, and financial budgets, and the reasons for them.

Add value
The internal audit activity adds value to the organization (and its stakeholders) when it provides objective and relevant assurance, and contributes to the effectiveness and efficiency of governance, risk management, and control processes.

Adequate control
Adequate control is a level of control that is present if management has planned and organized in a manner that provides reasonable assurance that the organization's risks have been managed effectively and that the organization's goals and objectives will be achieved efficiently and economically.

Alternative risk-transfer tools
There are five alternative risk-transfer tools:

> **Captive insurance methods.** A noninsurance firm is created for the purpose of accepting the risk of the parent firm who owns an insurer. Here, a parent firm establishes a subsidiary (called captive insurance company) to finance its retained losses. Captives combine risk transfer and risk retention.

Financial insurance contracts. These contracts are based on spreading risk over time, as opposed to across a pool of similar exposures. These contracts usually involve a sharing of the investment returns between the insurer and the insured.

Multiline/multiyear insurance contracts. These contracts combine a broad array of risks (multiline) into a contract with a policy period that extends over multiple years (multiyear). For example, a pure risk may be combined with a financial risk.

Multiple-trigger policies. These policies reflect the source of the risk and are not as important as the impact of the risk on the earnings of the firm. A pure risk is combined with a financial risk. The policy is "triggered," and payment is made, only upon the occurrence of an adverse event.

Risk securitization. This method involves the creation of securities, such as bonds, or derivatives contracts, options, swaps, or futures, that have a payout or price movement linked to an insurance risk. Examples include catastrophe options, earthquake bonds, catastrophe bonds, and catastrophe equity puts.

Multiple-trigger policies and risk securitization tools are more commonly used.

Analytical procedures

Analytical auditing procedures are performed by studying and comparing relationships among both financial and nonfinancial information. The application of analytical auditing procedures is based on the premise that, in the absence of known conditions to the contrary, relationships among information may reasonably be expected to exist and continue. Examples of contrary conditions include unusual or nonrecurring transactions or events; accounting, organizational, operational, environmental, and technological changes; inefficiencies; ineffectiveness; errors; irregularities; or illegal acts.

Anecdotal records

Such records constitute a description or narrative of a specific situation or condition.

Appreciation

"Appreciation" means the ability to recognize the existence of problems or potential problems and to determine the further research to be undertaken or the assistance to be obtained.

Assurance maps

Assurance maps are organization-wide and coordinated exercises involving mapping assurance coverage provided by multiple parties against the key risks facing the organization so that duplicate efforts, missed risks, and potential gaps can be identified and monitored. The chief audit executive, senior management, and the board need assurance maps to ensure proper coordination among diverse risk activities.

Assurance services

These services are an objective examination of evidence for the purpose of providing an independent assessment on governance, risk management, and control processes for the organization. Examples may include financial, performance, compliance, system security, and due diligence engagements.

Attribute

An attribute is a characteristic that describes a person, thing, or event. It is an inherent quality that an item either has or does not have.

Attribute listing

An attribute listing emphasizes the detailed observation of each particular characteristic or quality of an item or situation. Attempts are then made to profitably change the characteristic or to relate it to a different item.

Attribute sampling

Attribute sampling is the measurement or evaluation of selected sampling units to determine whether they have the attribute of interest, and the computation of some statistical measure (statistic) from these measurements to estimate the proportion of the population that has the attribute.

Auditable activities

Auditable activities consist of those subjects, units, or systems that are capable of being defined and evaluated. Auditable activities may include (1) policies, procedures, and practices; (2) cost centers, profit centers, and investment centers; (3) general ledger account balances; (4) information systems (manual and computerized); (5) major contracts and programs, (6) organizational units such as product or service lines; (7) functions such as information technology, purchasing, marketing, production, finance, accounting, and human resources; (8) transaction systems for activities such as sales, collection, purchasing, disbursement, inventory and cost accounting, production, treasury, payroll, and capital assets; (9) financial statements; and (10) laws and regulations.

Auditee

The term "auditee" includes any individual, unit, or activity of the organization that is audited.

Audit objectives

Audit objectives are broad statements developed by internal auditors and define intended audit accomplishments.

Audit procedures

Audit procedures are the tasks the internal auditor undertakes for collecting, analyzing, interpreting, and documenting information during an audit. Audit procedures are the means to attain audit objectives.

Audit program

An audit program is a document that lists the audit procedures to be followed during an audit and states the objectives of the audit.

Audit report

An audit report is a signed, written document that presents the purpose, scope, and results of the audit. Results of the audit may include findings, conclusions (opinions), and recommendations.

Audit risk

Audit risk is the risk that the auditor may unknowingly fail to appropriately modify his or her opinion on financial statements that are materially misstated. It is also defined as the risk that an auditor may fail to detect a significant error or weakness during an examination.

Audit risk is equal to inherent risk multiplied by control risk and multiplied by detection risk. Inherent risk is the susceptibility of a management assertion to a material misstatement, assuming that there are no related internal control structure policies or procedures. Control risk is the risk that a material misstatement in a management assertion will not be prevented or detected on a timely basis by the entity's internal control structure policies or procedures. Detection risk is the risk that the auditor will not detect a material misstatement present in a management assertion.

Audit scope

Audit scope refers to the activities covered by an internal audit. Audit scope includes (a) audit objectives, (b) nature and extent of auditing procedures performed, (c) time period audited, and (d) related activities not audited in order to delineate the boundaries of the audit.

Audit working papers

Audit working papers record the information obtained, the analyses made, and conclusions reached during an audit. Audit working papers support the bases for the findings and recommendations to be reported.

Audit work schedules

Audit work schedules include (a) what activities are to be audited; (b) when they will be audited; and (c) the estimated time required, taking into account the scope of the audit work planned and the nature and extent of audit work performed by others.

Authorization

Authorization implies that the authorizing authority has verified and validated that the activity or transaction conforms to established policies and procedures.

Authorizing

Authorizing includes initiating or granting permission to perform activities or transactions.

Bias

The word "bias" refers to the existence of a factor that causes an estimate made on the basis of a sample to differ systematically from the population parameter being estimated. Bias may originate from poor sample design, deficiencies in carrying out the sampling process, or an inherent characteristic of the measuring or estimating technique used.

Board

A board is an organization's governing body, such as a board of directors, supervisory board, head of an agency or legislative body, board of governors or trustees of a nonprofit organization, or any other designated body of the organization, including the audit committee, to which the chief audit executive functionally reports.

Cause

Cause is the reason for the difference between the expected and actual conditions (why the difference exists).

Charter (internal audit)

The internal audit charter is a formal document that defines the internal audit activity's purpose, authority, and responsibility. The charter establishes the internal audit activity's position within the organization; authorizes access to records, personnel, and physical properties relevant to the performance of engagements; and defines the scope of internal audit activities.

Chief audit executive (CAE)

CAE refers to a person in a senior position responsible for effectively managing the internal audit activity in accordance with the internal audit charter and the definition of internal auditing, the Code of Ethics, and the *Standards*. The CAE or others reporting to the CAE will have appropriate professional certifications and qualifications. The specific job title of the CAE may vary across organizations.

Civil acts

Civil acts are illegal acts for which penalties that do not include incarceration are available for a statutory violation. Penalties may include monetary payments and corrective actions.

Cluster sample

A cluster sample is a simple random sample in which each sampling unit is a collection of elements.

Code of Ethics

The Code of Ethics of The Institute of Internal Auditors are principles relevant to the profession and practice of internal auditing, and Rules of Conduct that describe behavior expected of internal auditors. The Code of Ethics applies to both parties and entities that provide internal audit services. The purpose of the Code of Ethics is to promote an ethical culture in the global profession of internal auditing.

Coefficient of variation

The coefficient of variation is the ratio produced by dividing the standard deviation by the mean value. It provides an indication of the consistency of the data.

Compliance

"Compliance" refers to the ability to reasonably ensure conformity and adherence to an organization's policies, plans, procedures, laws, regulations, contracts, and other requirements.

Compliance requirement

"Compliance requirement" refers to conditions established by management for the organization. The term also refers to conditions that may be imposed on the organization by law or regulation or agreed to by contractual agreement. These conditions affect the manner in which an organization's operations are conducted and objectives are achieved. Compliance requirements include those established, imposed, or agreed to for the purpose of safeguarding organization assets including prevention and/or detection of unauthorized acquisition, use, or disposition of resources.

Conclusions (opinions)

Conclusions (opinions) are the internal auditor's evaluations of the effects of the findings on the activities reviewed. Conclusions usually put the findings in perspective based on their overall implications.

Condition

A condition is the factual evidence that the internal auditor found in the course of the examination (what does exist).

Confidence coefficient

The confidence coefficient is a measure (usually expressed as a percentage) of the degree of assurance that the estimate obtained from a sample differs from the population parameter being estimated by less than the measure of precision (sampling error).

Confidence interval

A confidence interval is an estimate of a population parameter that consists of a range of values bounded by statistics called upper and lower confidence limits.

Confidence level

The confidence level is a number, stated as a percentage, that expresses the degree of certainty associated with an interval estimate of a population parameter. It is the probability that an estimate based on a random sample falls within a specified range.

Confidence limits

Confidence limits are two statistics that form the upper and lower bounds of a confidence interval.

Conflict of interest

A conflict of interest is any relationship that is, or appears to be, not in the best interest of the organization. Such a relationship would prejudice an individual's ability to perform his or her duties and responsibilities objectively.

Consulting services

Consulting services are advisory and related client service activities, the nature and scope of which are agreed with the client, that are intended to add value and improve an organization's governance, risk management, and control processes without the internal auditor assuming management responsibility. Examples include counsel, advice, facilitation, and training.

Control

Control is any action taken by management, the board, and other parties to manage risks and to increase the likelihood that established objectives and goals will be achieved. Management plans, organizes, and directs the performance of sufficient actions to provide reasonable assurance that objectives and goals will be achieved. Thus, control is the result of proper planning, organizing, and directing by management. The control environment includes six elements: (1) integrity and ethical values, (2) management's philosophy and operating style, (3) organizational structure, (4) assignment of authority and responsibility, (5) human resource policies and practices, and (6) competence of personnel.

Control environment

The control environment is the attitude and actions of the board and management regarding the importance of control within the organization. It provides the discipline and structure for the achievement of the primary objectives of the system of internal control. The control environment includes these elements: (1) integrity and ethical values; (2) management's philosophy and operating style; (3) organizational structure; (4) assignment of authority and responsibility; (5) human resource policies and practices; and (6) competence of personnel.

Control processes

Control processes are the policies, procedures, and activities that are part of a control framework, designed to ensure that risks are contained within the risk tolerances established by the risk management process.

Cost/benefit relationship

The term "cost/benefit relationship" means that the potential loss associated with any exposure or risk is weighed against the cost to control it.

Criminal acts

Criminal acts are illegal acts for which incarceration, as well as other penalties, is available if the organization obtains a guilty verdict.

Criteria

Criteria are the standards, measures, or expectations used in making an evaluation and/or verification (what should exist).

Degrees of freedom

A random sample of size n is said to have $n - 1$ degrees of freedom for estimating the population variance, in the sense that there are $n - 1$ independent deviations from the sample mean on which to base such an estimate.

Detective controls

Detective controls are actions taken to detect and correct undesirable events that have occurred.

Deviation

Deviation is the difference between the particular number and the average of the set of number under consideration.

Directing

Directing involves, in addition to accomplishing objectives and planned activities, authorizing and monitoring performance, periodically comparing actual with planned performance, and documenting these activities to provide additional assurance that systems operate as planned.

Directive controls

Directive controls are actions taken to cause or encourage a desirable event to occur.

Director of internal auditing

The term "director of internal auditing" is used for the top position in an internal auditing department. The term is also called general auditor, chief internal auditor, chief audit executive, and inspector general.

Dispersion

Dispersion refers to the extent to which the elements of a sample or the elements of a population are not all alike in the measured characteristic, are spread out, or vary from one another. Items that measure dispersion include range, deviation, mean absolute deviation, variance, standard deviation, and coefficient of variation.

Dynamic risk

Dynamic risk, in contrast to static risk, is produced because of changes in society. Dynamic risks also can be either pure or speculative. Examples of sources of dynamic risk include urban unrest, increasingly complex technology, and changing attitude of legislatures and courts about a variety of issues.

Economical performance

Economical performance accomplishes objectives and goals at a cost commensurate with the risk.

Effect

Effect is the risk or exposure the auditee organization and/or others encounter because the condition is not the same as the criteria (the impact of the difference).

Effective control

Effective control is present when management directs systems in such a manner as to provide reasonable assurance that the organization's objectives and goals will be achieved.

Efficient performance

Efficient performance accomplishes objectives and goals in an accurate and timely fashion with minimal use of resources.

Engagement

The term "engagement" refers to a specific internal audit assignment, task, or review activity, such as an internal audit, control self-assessment review, fraud examination, or consultancy. An engagement may include multiple tasks or activities designed to accomplish a specific set of related objectives.

Engagement objectives

Engagement objectives are broad statements developed by internal auditors that define intended engagement accomplishments.

Engagement work program

An engagement work program is a document that lists the procedures to be followed during an engagement, designed to achieve the engagement plan.

Error

The term "error," as it relates to internal audit reports, is an unintentional misstatement or omission of significant information in a final audit report. Errors are unintentional noncompliance with applicable laws and regulations and/or misstatements or omissions of amounts or disclosures in financial statements.

External auditors

The term "external auditors" refers to those audit professionals who perform independent annual audits of an organization's financial statements.

External reviews

External reviews of the internal auditing department are performed to appraise the quality of the department's operations. External reviews should be performed by qualified persons who are independent of the organization and who do not have either a real or apparent conflict of interest.

External service provider

An external service provider is a person or firm outside of the organization that has special knowledge, skill, and experience in a particular discipline.

Financial engineering

The goal of financial engineering is to reduce financial risks which, in part, are achieved through financial instruments such as derivative securities (e.g., hedging with forward contracts). Financial engineering can also be applied to insurance and reinsurance areas using alternate risk transfer methods (e.g., captive insurance), as part of a company's risk mitigation strategy. In a way, financial engineering is related to risk engineering in terms of sharing common goals such as risks, hedging, insurance, and captive insurance.

Financial risk

Financial risks are risks arising from volatility in foreign currencies, interest rates, and commodities. They include credit risk, liquidity risk (bankruptcy risk), interest rate risk, and market risk.

Findings

Findings are pertinent statements of fact. Audit findings emerge by a process of comparing what should be with what is.

Finite population correction (FPC) factor

The FPC factor is a multiplier that makes adjustments for the sampling efficiency gained when sampling is without replacement and when the sample size is large (greater than 5% or 10%) with respect to the population size. This multiplier reduces the sampling error for a given sample size or reduces the required sample size for a specified measure of precision (in this case, desired sampling error).

Flowchart

A flowchart is a representation, primarily through the use of symbols, of the sequence of activities in a system (process, operation, function, or activity).

Follow-up

Follow-up by internal auditors is defined as a process by which they determine the adequacy, effectiveness, and timeliness of actions taken by management on reported audit findings. Such findings also include relevant findings made by external auditors and others.

Formal internal reviews

Formal internal reviews are periodic self-assessments of the internal auditing department to appraise the quality of the audit work performed. These reviews generally are performed by a team or an individual selected by the director of internal auditing.

Fraud

Fraud encompasses an array of irregularities and illegal acts characterized by intentional deception. Fraud is the obtaining of something of value, illegally, through willful misrepresentation. Thus, fraud is a type of illegal act characterized by deceit, concealment, or violation of trust. Fraudulent acts are not dependent on the threat of violence or physical force. Frauds are perpetrated by parties and organizations to: obtain money, property, or services; avoid payment or loss of services; or secure personal or business advantage.

Goals

Goals are specific objectives of specific systems. They also may be referred to as operating or program objectives or goals, operating standards, performance levels, targets, or expected results.

Governance

The term "governance" refers to the combination of processes and structures implemented by the board to inform, direct, manage, and monitor the activities of the organization toward the achievement of its objectives.

Hazard

Hazard is a condition that creates or increases the probability of a loss. Three types of hazards exist: (1) physical hazard, (2) moral hazard, and (3) morale hazard. Physical hazard is a condition of the subject of insurance that creates or increases the chance of loss, such as structural defects, occupancy, or similar conditions. Moral hazard is a dishonest predisposition on the part of an insured that increases the chance of loss. Morale hazard is a careless attitude on the part of an insured that increases the chance of loss or causes losses to be greater than would otherwise be the case.

Hazard risk

Hazard risks are risks that are insurable, such as natural disasters, various insurable liabilities, impairment of physical assets and property, and terrorism.

Hedge or hedging

Hedge or hedging is taking a position opposite to the exposure or risk. This can be done with financial derivatives, such as futures contracts, forward contracts, options, and swaps. A perfect hedge is not possible because financial derivatives used to hedge do not move together, leaving some risk. The idea behind hedging is to minimize risk. Value is created for shareholders if corporate hedging does not duplicate the shareholders' "homemade" hedging.

Illegal acts

The term "illegal acts" refers to violations of laws and governmental regulations. Illegal acts are a type of noncompliance; specifically, they are violations of laws or regulations. They are failures to follow requirements of laws or implementing regulations, including intentional and unintentional noncompliance and criminal acts.

Impairment

Impairment to organizational independence and individual objectivity may include personal conflict of interest, scope limitations, restrictions on access to records, personnel, and properties, and resource limitations (funding).

Independence

Independence refers to the freedom from conditions that threaten the ability of the internal audit activity to carry out internal audit responsibilities in an unbiased manner.

Independence allows internal auditors to carry out their work freely and objectively. This concept requires that internal auditors be independent of the activities they audit. Independence is achieved through organizational status and objectivity.

Information

Information is data the internal auditor obtains during an audit to provide a sound basis for audit findings and recommendations. Information should be sufficient, competent, relevant, and useful.

Information technology (IT) controls

These are controls that support business management and governance as well as provide general and technical controls over IT infrastructures, such as applications, information, infrastructure, and people.

Information technology (IT) governance

IT governance consists of the leadership, organizational structures, and processes that ensure that the enterprise's IT supports the organization's strategies and objectives.

Insurance

Insurance is an economic device whereby an individual or a corporation substitutes a small certain cost (the premium) for a large uncertain financial loss (the claim, or contingency insured against) that would exist if it were not for the insurance policy (contract). Insurance is most appropriate for situations in where there is a low frequency and a high severity of occurrence. Insurance is a risk transfer mechanism.

Insurable interest

An insurable interest is an interest that might be damaged if the peril insured against occurs; the possibility of a financial loss to an individual or a corporation that can be protected against through insurance.

Internal audit activity

The term "internal audit activity" refers to a department, division, team of consultants, or other practitioner(s) that provides independent, objective assurance and consulting services designed to add value and improve an organization's operations. The internal audit activity helps an organization accomplish its objectives by bringing a systematic, disciplined approach to evaluate and improve the effectiveness of governance, risk management, and control processes.

Internal auditing

Internal auditing is an independent, objective assurance and consulting activity designed to add value and improve an organization's operations. It helps an organization accomplish its objectives by bringing a systematic disciplined approach to evaluate and improve the effectiveness of risk management, control, and governance processes.

Internal auditing department

Internal auditing department includes any unit or activity within an organization that performs internal auditing functions.

Internal auditor

An internal auditor is an individual within an organization's internal auditing department who is assigned the responsibility of performing internal auditing functions.

Internal control

Internal control is a process within an organization designed to provide reasonable assurance regarding the achievement of five primary objectives: (1) the reliability and integrity of information; (2) compliance with policies, plans, procedures, laws, regulations, and contracts; (3) the safeguarding of assets; (4) the economical and efficient use of resources; and (5) the accomplishment of established objectives and goals for operations or programs. The auditor verifies that these processes are established.

International Professional Practices Framework (IPPF)

The *International Standards for the Professional Practice of Internal Auditing* (*Standards*) is the conceptual framework that organizes the authoritative guidance promulgated by the IIA's internal auditing standards (IASB). These *Standards* include Attribute *Standards* and Performance *Standards* from the IPPF.

Interval estimate

"Interval estimate" is a general term for an estimate of a population parameter that is a range of numerical values. It is the estimation of a parameter in terms of an interval, called an interval estimate, for which one can assert with a given probability (or degree of confidence) that it contains the actual value of the parameter.

Interval variable

The interval variable is a quantitative variable the attributes of which are ordered and for which the numerical differences between adjacent attributes are interpreted as equal.

Irregularities

Irregularities are intentional noncompliance with applicable laws and regulations and/or misstatements or omissions of amounts or disclosure in financial statements with significant information in accounting records, financial statements, other reports, documents or records. Irregularities include fraudulent financial reporting, which renders financial statements misleading, and misappropriation of assets. They involve: (1) falsification or alteration of accounting or other records and supporting documents; (2) intentional misapplication of accounting principles; and (3) misrepresentation or intentional omission of events, transactions, or other significant information.

Judgment sample

Unlike a probability sample, a judgment sample is one in which personal judgment plays a significant part. Although judgment samples are sometimes required by practical considerations and may lead to satisfactory results, they do not lend themselves to analysis by standard statistical methods.

Legal concepts

Several legal concepts exist as they apply to managers, executives, officers, and board of directors in any organization. For example, officers and directors need to follow duty of due care, duty of loyalty, and duty of obedience, not duty of absolute care or duty of utmost care. Only reasonable and ordinary care is expected of the officers and the board of directors because no one can anticipate all problems or protect from all disasters or losses. Especially, officers and board of directors are expected to follow the highest levels of legal concepts due to their fiduciary and governance responsibilities (i.e., duty of loyalty and duty of obedience). Examples of legal concepts follow:

Due process means following rules and principles so that an individual is treated fairly and uniformly at all times with basic rights protected. It also means fair and equitable treatment to all concerned parties so that no person is deprived of life, liberty, or property without due process of the law, which is the right to notice and a hearing. Due process means each person is given an equal and a fair chance of being represented or heard and that everybody goes through the same process for consideration and approval. It means all people are equal in the eyes of the law. Due law covers due process and due care. Due process requires due care and due diligence.

Two types of due process exist: procedural due process and substantive due process. Procedural due process ensures that a formal proceeding is carried out regularly and in accordance with the established rules and principles. Substantive due process deals with a judicial requirement that enacted laws may not contain provisions that result in the unfair, arbitrary, or unreasonable treatment of an individual. It protects personal property from governmental interference or possession.

Due care means reasonable care in promoting the common good, maintaining the minimal and customary practices, and following the best practices. Due law covers due process and due care. For example, it is the responsibility that managers and their organizations have a duty to provide for information security to ensure that the type of control, the cost of control, and the deployment of control are appropriate for the system being managed. Another related concept of due care is good faith, which means showing "honesty in fact" and "honesty in intent." Both due care and due diligence are similar to the "prudent man" or "reasonable person" concept.

Due diligence reviews involve pre-assessment, examination, analysis, and reporting on major activities with due care before they are finalized or approved by management. Its purpose is to minimize potential risks from undertaking new businesses and ventures and involving in mergers, acquisitions, and divestitures. Due diligence requires organizations to develop and implement an effective system of controls, policies, and procedures to prevent and detect violation of policies and laws. It requires that the organization has taken minimum and necessary steps in its power and authority to prevent and detect violation of policies and laws. In other words, due diligence is the care that a reasonable person exercises under the circumstances to avoid harm to other persons or to their property. Due diligence is another way of saying due care. Both due care and due diligence are similar to the "prudent man" or "reasonable person" concept. A due diligence defense is available to a defendant in that it makes the defendant not liable if the defendant's actions are reasonable and they are proven.

Due professional care calls for the application of the care and skill expected of a reasonably prudent and competent person in the same or similar circumstances. For example, due professional care is exercised when internal audits are performed in accordance with the IIA *Standards*. The exercise of due professional care requires that: (1) internal auditors be independent of the activities they audit, (2) internal audits be performed by those persons who collectively possess the necessary knowledge, skills, and disciplines to conduct the audit properly, (3) audit work be planned and supervised, (4) audit reports be objective, clear, concise, constructive, and timely, and (5) internal auditors follow up on reported audit findings to ascertain that appropriate action was taken.

Duty of loyalty is applicable to the officers and the directors of a corporation not to act adversely to the interests of the corporation and not to subordinate their personal interests to those of the corporation and its shareholders.

Duty of care is the legal obligation that each person has to others not to cause any unreasonable harm or risk of harm resulting from careless acts. A breach of the duty of care is negligence. An example is that corporate directors and officers must use due care and due diligence when acting on behalf of a corporation. Duty of reasonable care is same as the duty of care.

Duty of obedience is expected of officers and directors of a corporation to act within the authority conferred upon them by the state corporation statute, the articles of incorporation, the corporate bylaws, and the resolutions adopted by the board of directors.

Management

The term "management" includes those individuals with responsibilities for setting and/or achieving the organization's objectives.

Mean

Mean is the sum of all the values in a set of observations divided by the number of observations. Mean is also known as "average" or "arithmetic mean," as it indicates the typical value for a set of observations. For example, if five students make the grades 15, 75, 80, 95, and 100, the mean is 73.

Mean absolute deviation (MAD)

MAD is a measure of the difference between the individual items in a population and the mean value. It is the average of the total unsigned differences. The average distance of each value in a distribution from the mean value of the distribution (sum of the differences divided by the number of items in the distribution).

Median

Median is the exact midpoint of a distribution, with an equal number of items below it and above it. For example, if five students make the grades 15, 75, 80, 95, and 100, the median is 80.

Mode

Mode is a measure of central tendency; a statistic used primarily with nominal variables. It is the number that occurs most frequently in a series. For example, if more students (of a given group) make 75 than any other one grade, 75 is the mode.

Monitoring

Monitoring encompasses supervising, observing, and testing activities and appropriately reporting to responsible individuals. Monitoring provides an ongoing verification of progress toward achievement of objectives and goals.

Must

The IIA *Standards* use the word "must" to specify an unconditional requirement.

Natural hedges

Natural hedges are created from the relationship between revenues and costs of a business unit or a subsidiary. The more revenues over the cost, the better protection is. The key is the extent to which cash flows adjust naturally to currency changes due to exchange-rate fluctuations. One way to explore the likelihood of a natural hedge is to determine whether a subsidiary's revenue and cost functions are sensitive to domestic or global business conditions.

Many types of risks may be relatively correlated with each other. Consequently, combining these risks produces a form of natural hedging. The traditional silo approach actually could reduce the overall efficiency of the firm's risk management activities by destroying the natural hedging that exists at the enterprise-wide level.

Nominal variable

A nominal variable is a quantitative variable the attributes of which have no inherent order.

Noncompliance

Noncompliance is a failure to follow requirements, or a violation of prohibitions, contained in laws, regulations, contracts, governmental grants, or organization's policies and procedures.

Objective risk

Objective risk differs from subjective risk primarily in the sense that it is more precisely observable and therefore measurable. In general, objective risk is the probable variation of actual from expected experience.

Objectives

Objectives are the broadest statements of what the organization chooses to accomplish.

Objectivity

The term "objectivity" refers to an unbiased mental attitude that allows internal auditors to perform engagements in such a manner that they believe in their work product and that no quality compromises are made. Objectivity requires that internal auditors do not subordinate their judgment on audit matters to others.

Operational risk

Operational risk is a risk related to the organization's internal systems, products, services, processes, technology, and people.

Operations

The term "operations" refers to the recurring activities of an organization directed toward producing a product or rendering a service. Such activities may include, but are not limited to, marketing, sales, production, purchasing, human resources, finance and accounting, and governmental assistance.

Ordinal variable

An ordinal variable is a quantitative variable the attributes of which are ordered but for which the numerical difference between adjacent attributes is not necessarily interpreted as equal.

Outlier

An outlier is an extremely large or small observation; it applies to ordinal, interval, and ratio variables.

Outside service provider

The term "outside service provider" refers to a person or firm, independent of the organization, that has special knowledge, skill, and experience in a particular discipline. Outside service providers include, among others, actuaries, accountants, appraisers, environmental specialists, fraud investigators, lawyers, engineers, geologists, security specialists, statisticians, information technology specialists, the organization's external auditors, and other auditing organizations. An outside service provider may be engaged by the board, senior management, or the director of internal auditing.

Parameter

A parameter is a number that describes a population. It is a measure, such as mean, median, standard deviation, or proportion, that is calculated or defined by using every item in the population.

Peril

Peril is the cause of possible loss, the event insured against. "Open peril" is a term used to describe a broad form of property insurance in which coverage applies to loss arising from any fortuitous cause other than those perils or causes specifically excluded.

Point estimate

A point estimate is an estimate of a population parameter that is a single numerical value.

Population

A population is a set of persons, things, or events about which there are questions. It is all the numbers of a group to be studied as defined by the auditor; the total collection of individuals or items from which a sample is selected. Population is also called a universe.

Portfolio risk

Portfolio risk considers risk and return of a firm when it is investing in acquisition or expansion projects. Management needs to find the relationship between the net present values (NPVs) for new projects and the NPVs for existing projects. In a portfolio framework, the trade-off between risk and expected NPV for different combinations of investments can be analyzed.

Practice Advisories

Practice Advisories assist internal auditors in applying the definition of internal auditing, the Code of Ethics, and the *Standards* and promoting good practices. Practice Advisories address internal auditing's approach, methodologies, and consideration but not detail processes or procedures. They include: practices relating to international, country, or industry-specific issues; specific types of engagements; and legal or regulatory issues.

Practice Guides

Practice Guides provide detailed guidance for conducting internal audit activities. They include detailed processes and procedures, such as tools and techniques, programs, and step-by-step approaches, as well as examples of deliverables.

Precision

Each estimate generated from a probability sample has a measurable precision, or sampling error, that may be expressed as a plus or minus figure. A sampling error indicates how closely we can reproduce from a sample the results that we would obtain if we were to take a complete count of the population using the same measurement methods. By adding the sampling error to and subtracting from the estimate, we can develop upper and lower bounds for each estimate. This range is called a confidence interval. Sampling errors and confidence intervals are stated at a certain confidence level. For example, a confidence interval at the 95% confidence level means that in 95 of 100 instances, the sampling procedure we used would produce a confidence interval containing the population value we are estimating. Note that precision is the same as sampling error.

Preventive Controls
Preventive controls are actions taken to deter undesirable events from occurring.

Process mapping
Process mapping uses three tools to help map a process, activity, or function to understand it and to improve it: relationships maps, cross-functional process maps, and flowcharts.

Proficiency
"Proficiency" means the ability to apply knowledge to situations likely to be encountered and to deal with them without extensive recourse to technical research and assistance.

Programs
Programs are special-purpose activities of an organization. Such activities include, but are not limited to, the raising of capital, sale of a facility, fund-raising campaigns, new product or service introduction campaigns, capital expenditures, and special-purpose government grants.

Pure risk
Risk is a possibility of loss. Many types of risks exist, including pure risk, speculative risk, static risk, dynamic risk, subjective risk, and objective risk. Pure risk is a condition in which there is the possibility of loss or no loss (e.g., default of a debtor or disability). Pure risks are of several types. Including personal risks, property risks, liability risks, and performance risks. Risk management is a scientific approach to the problem of dealing with the pure risks facing an individual or an organization. Insurance is viewed as simply one of several approaches for dealing with such risks. The techniques of insurance and self-insurance are commonly limited to the treatment of pure risks, such as fire, product liability, and worker's compensation. Traditionally, risk management tools—avoidance, loss control, and transfer—have been applied primarily to the pure or hazard risks facing a firm.

Purpose statements
Purpose statements in audit reports describe the audit objectives and may, where necessary, inform the reader why the audit was conducted and what it was expected to achieve.

Quality assurance
Quality assurance is a program by which the director of internal auditing evaluates the operations of the internal auditing department. The purpose of the quality assurance program is to provide reasonable assurance that internal auditing work conforms to the IIA *Standards*, the internal auditing department's charter, and other applicable standards. The quality assurance program should include these elements: (1) supervision, (2) internal reviews, and (3) external reviews.

Random number sampling
Random number sampling is a sampling method in which combinations of random digits, within the range of the number of items in a population, are selected by using one of the random number generation methods until a given sample size is obtained. For example, if a sample of 60 items is required from a population numbered 1 through 2,000, then 60 random numbers between 1 and 2,000 are selected.

Random selection
Random selection is a selection method that uses an acceptable method of generating random numbers in a standard manner. The method minimizes the influence of nonchance factors in selecting the sample items.

Range

The term "range" refers to the distance (or difference) between the highest and lowest values. This is a quick measure of the dispersion (spread) of the distribution. It is a statistic used primarily with interval-ratio variables.

Ratio analysis

Ratio analysis is the study of financial condition and performance through ratios derived from items in the financial statements or from other financial or nonfinancial information.

Ratio estimate

A ration estimate is an estimate of a population parameter that is obtained by multiplying the known population total for another variable by a ratio of appropriate sample values of the two variables.

Ratio variable

A ratio variable is a quantitative variable the attributes of which are ordered, spaced equally, and have a true zero point.

Reasonableness test

A reasonableness test is a comparison of an estimated amount, calculated by the use of relevant financial and nonfinancial information, with a recorded amount.

Recommendations

Recommendations are actions the internal auditor believes necessary to correct existing conditions or improve operations.

Regression analysis

Regression analysis is a mathematical procedure used to determine and measure the predictive relationship between one variable (dependent variable) and one or more other variables (independent variable).

Residual risk

Residual risk is the risk remaining after management takes action to reduce the impact and likelihood of an adverse event, including control activities in responding to a risk. Residual risk is current risk, which, in turn, is called managed risk with existing control systems. Residual risk is calculated as potential risks minus covered risks, resulting in uncovered risk.

Several equations are available to express residual risks:

Residual risks = Total risks − Mitigated risks

Residual risks = Potential risks − Covered risks

Residual risks = Total risks − Control measures applied

Residual risks = Potential risks − Countermeasures applied

Residual risks = Uncovered or Unaddressed risks

Risk

The term "risk" means the possibility of an event occurring that will have an impact on the achievement of objectives. Risk is measured in terms of impact and likelihood. It is the probability that an event or action may adversely affect the organization or activity under audit. Risks can be classified or categorized into three types: static versus dynamic, subjective versus objective, and pure versus speculative. Risk is uncertainty about loss. Risks should be avoided where possible; if not, they should be managed well. There are at least six types of risks, including pure, strategic, operational, financial, hazard, and speculative.

Risk acceptance
The term "risk acceptance" means accepting a potential risk and continuing with operating a process or system. It is like accepting risks as part of doing business (a kind of self-insurance). Risk acceptance is also called risk tolerance and risk appetite in order to achieve a desired result.

Risk appetite
The risk appetite of an organization is the level of risk that it is willing to accept.

Risk assessment
Risk assessment includes identification, analysis, measurement, and prioritization of risks. Risk assessment (or risk analysis) is the process of identifying the risks and determining the probability of occurrence, the resulting impact, and additional safeguards that would mitigate this impact.

Risk assignment
Risk assignment consists of transferring or assigning risk to a third party by using other options to compensate for the loss, such as an insurance company or outsourcing firm.

Risk avoidance
Risk avoidance eliminates the risk causes and/or consequences (e.g., add controls that prevent the risk from occurring, remove certain functions of the system, or shut down the system when risks are identified). It is like reducing, avoiding, or eliminating risks by implementing cost-effective safeguards and controls. Risk situations that have high severity and high frequency of loss should be either avoided or reduced. Risk reduction is appropriate when it is possible to reduce either risk severity or frequency. Otherwise, the risk should be avoided or transferred. Examples of risk avoidance controls include (1) separating threats from assets or assets from threats to minimize risks and (2) separating resource allocation from resource use to prevent resource misuse.

Risk control
Risk control identifies the presence or lack of effective controls in the form of prevention, detection, and correction of risks. Risk control focuses on minimizing the risk of loss to which an organization is exposed. The situation of high frequency and low severity should be managed with additional controls (loss control). Risk control includes risk avoidance and risk reduction.

Risk engineering
The goal of risk engineering is to reduce risks in traditional and non-traditional insurance activities which, in part, are achieved through risk financing to fund financial losses. Risk financing includes internal funds for risks (e.g., self insurance and residual risk) and external transfer of risks (e.g., insurance, hedging, and captive insurance). In a way, risk engineering is related to financial engineering in terms of sharing common goals such as risks, hedging, insurance, and captive insurance.

Risk factors
Risk factors are the criteria used to identify the relative significance of and likelihood that conditions and/or events may occur that could adversely affect the organization.

Risk financing
Risk financing concentrates on arranging the availability of internal funds to meet occurring financial losses. It also involves external transfer of risk. Risk financing includes risk retention and risk transfer, which is a tool used by captive insurers. Risk retention applies to risks that have a low expected frequency and a low potential severity. Risk transfer applies to risks that have a low expected frequency and a high potential severity (e.g., buying insurance). Insurance should be purchased for losses in excess of a firm's risk retention level.

When losses have both high expected frequency and high potential severity, it is likely that risk retention, risk transfer, and loss control all will need to be used in varying degrees. Common methods of loss control include reducing the probability of losses (i.e., frequency and severity reduction) and decreasing the cost of losses that do occur (i.e., cost reduction). Note that "high" and "low" loss frequency and severity rates are defined differently for different firms.

Risk financing includes internal funding for risks (self-insurance and residual risk) and external transfer of risks, such as insurance and hedging. It can be unfunded or funded retention. The unfunded retention is treated as part of the overall cost of doing business. A firm may decide to practice funded retention by making various pre-loss arrangements to ensure that money is readily available to pay for losses that occur. Examples of funded retention include use of credit, reserve funds, self-insurance, and captive insurers.

Risk limitation

"Risk limitation" means limiting or containing risks by implementing controls that minimize the adverse impact of a threat's exercising a vulnerability (e.g., use of supporting, preventive, and detective controls) or by authorizing operation for a limited time during which additional risk mitigation efforts by other means is installed.

Risk management

Risk management is the total process of identifying, assessing, controlling, and mitigating risks as it deals with uncertainty. It includes risk assessment (risk analysis); cost/benefit analysis; the selection, implementation, testing, and evaluation of safeguards (risk mitigation); risk financing (risk funding); and risk monitoring (reporting, feedback, and evaluation). It is expressed as:

Risk management = Risk assessment + Risk mitigation + Risk financing + Risk monitoring

The ultimate goal of risk management is to minimize the adverse effects of losses and uncertainty connected with pure risks. Risk management is broken down into two major categories: risk control and risk financing.

Risk mapping

Risk mapping involves profiling risk events to their sources (i.e., threats and vulnerabilities), determining their impact levels (i.e., low, medium, or high), and evaluating the presence of or lack of effective controls to mitigate risks.

Risk mitigation

Risk mitigation involves implementation of preventive, detective, and corrective controls along with management, operational, and technical controls to reduce the effects of risks. Risk mitigation includes designing and implementing controls and control-related procedures to minimize risks.

Risk monitoring

Risk monitoring addresses internal and external reporting and provides feedback into the risk assessment process, continuing the loop.

Risk registers

Risk registers document the risks below the strategic level and include inherent risks (high or higher) and unchanged residual risks, lack of or ineffectiveness of key internal controls, and lack of mitigating factors (e.g., contingency plans and monitoring activities). Risk registers provide direct links among risk categories, risk aspects, audit universe, and internal controls.

Risk retention

Risk retention is most appropriate for situations in which there is a low probability of occurrence (frequency) with a low potential severity. These are situations that seldom occur, and, when they do happen, the financial impact is small or negligible. Severity dictates whether a risk should be retained. If the potential severity is more than the organization can afford, retention is not recommended. Frequency determines whether the risk is economically insurable. The higher the probabilities of loss, the higher the expected value of loss and the higher the cost of transfer.

Risk spreading or sharing

Risk spreading or sharing involves spreading or sharing risks with other divisions or business units of the same organization. It is viewed as a special case of risk transfer, in which the risk is transferred from an individual to a group, from one division to another, or from one business unit to another. Risk sharing is a form of risk retention, depending on the success of the risk-sharing arrangement.

Risk transfer

Risk transfer involves payment by one party (the transferor) to another party (the transferee, or risk bearer). The five forms of risk transfer are: (1) hold-harmless agreements, (2) incorporation, (3) diversification, (4) hedging, and (5) insurance. Risk transfer is most likely ideal for a risk with a low expected frequency and a high potential severity.

Sample

The term "sample" refers to a portion of a population that is examined or tested in order to obtain information or draw conclusions about the entire population.

Sampling distribution

A sampling distribution is the distribution of a statistic.

Sampling error or precision

Each estimate generated from a probability sample has a measurable precision, or sampling error, that may be expressed as a plus or minus figure. A sampling error indicates how closely we can reproduce from a sample the results that we would obtain if we were to take a complete count of the population using the same measurement methods. By adding the sampling error to and subtracting it from the estimate, we can develop upper and lower bounds for each estimate. This range is called a confidence interval. Sampling errors and confidence intervals are stated at a certain confidence level. For example, a confidence interval at the 95% confidence level means that in 95 of 100 instances, the sampling procedure we used would produce a confidence interval containing the population value we are estimating.

Sampling frame

A sampling frame is a means of access to a population, usually a list of the sampling units contained in the population. The list may be printed on paper, on a magnetic tape/disk file, or in a physical file of such things as payroll records or accounts receivable.

Scope limitation

Scope limitation is a restriction placed on the internal auditing department that precludes the department from accomplishing its objectives and plans. Among other things, a scope limitation may restrict the: (1) scope defined in the charter; (2) department's access to records, personnel, and physical properties relevant to the performance of audits; (3) approved audit work schedule; (4) performance of necessary auditing procedures; and (5) approved staffing plan and financial budget.

Self-insurance

Self-insurance is a risk-retention program that incorporates elements of the insurance mechanism where the self-insured organization pays the claims rather than an insurance company.

Senior management

"Senior management" refers to those individuals to whom the director of internal auditing is responsible.

Should

The IIA *Standards* use the word "should" where conformance is expected unless, when applying professional judgment, circumstances justify deviation.

Simple random sample

A simple random sample is a probability sample in which each member of the population has an equal chance of being drawn to the sample.

Significance

The term "significance" refers to the relative importance of a matter within the context in which it is being considered, including quantitative and qualitative factors, such as magnitude, nature, effect, relevance, and impact. Professional judgment assists internal auditors when evaluating the significance of matters within the context of the relevant objectives.

Significant

The term "significant" refers to the level of importance or magnitude assigned to an item, event, information, or problem by the internal auditor.

Significant audit findings

Significant audit findings are those conditions that, in the judgment of the director of internal auditing, could adversely affect the organization. Such audit findings may include conditions dealing with irregularities, illegal acts, errors, inefficiency, waste, ineffectiveness, conflicts of interest, and control weaknesses.

Speculative risk

Speculative risk exists when there is uncertainty about an event that could produce either a profit or a loss. It involves the chance of loss or gain (e.g., hedging, options, and derivatives).

Spread

"Spread" is a general term for the extent of variation among cases.

Standard

A standard is a criterion by which the operations of an internal auditing department are evaluated and measured. A standard is intended to represent the practice of internal auditing as it should be.

Standard deviation

Standard deviation is a numerical measure of the spread of a group of values about their mean. It is a statistic used with interval-ratio variables. It is also called root mean square deviation and is the square root of the variance. We take the square root to account for the fact that we squared the differences in computing the variance. It is the measure of variability of a statistical sample that serves as an estimate of the population variability. This is the most common and useful of the dispersion measures.

Standard error of the mean

The standard error of the mean is the standard deviation of the sampling distribution of a sample statistic. It is a measure of the variability within a sample.

Standards

Professional pronouncements promulgated by the IIA's Internal Auditing Standards Board (IASB) that delineates the requirements for performing a broad range of internal audit activities and for evaluating internal audit performance. They include Attribute *Standards* and Performance *Standards*.

Static risk

Static risk, which can be either pure or speculative, stems from an unchanging society that is in stable equilibrium. Examples of pure static risk include the uncertainties due to such random events as lightning, windstorms, and death. Business undertakings in a stable economy illustrate the concept of speculative static risk.

Statistic
A statistic is a number computed from data on one or more variables.

Statistical estimate
A statistical estimate is a numerical value assigned to a population parameter on the basis of evidence from a sample.

Strata
The term "strata" refers to two or more mutually exclusive subdivisions of a population defined in such a way that each sampling unit can belong to only one subdivision or stratum.

Strategic risk
Strategic risk is a high-level and corporate-wide risk, which includes strategy risk, political risk, economic risk, regulatory risk, reputation risk, global risk, leadership risk, customer risk, and market brand management risk. It is also related to failure of strategy and changing customer needs and business conditions.

Stratified random sample
If the population to be sampled is first subclassified into several subpopulations called strata, the sample may be drawn by taking random samples from each stratum. The samples need not be proportional to the strata sizes.

Subjective risk
"Subjective risk" refers to the mental state of an individual who experiences doubt or worry as to the outcome of a given event. In addition to being subjective, a particular risk may be either pure or speculative and either static or dynamic.

Supervision
Supervision is a process that begins with planning and continues throughout the examination, evaluation, report, and follow-up phases of the audit assignment. Supervision includes: (1) ensuring that the auditors assigned possess the requisite knowledge and skills; (2) providing appropriate instructions during the planning of the audit and approving the audit program; (3) seeing that the approved audit program is carried out unless changes are both justified and authorized; (4) determining that audit working papers adequately support the audit findings, conclusions, and reports; (5) ensuring that audit reports are accurate, objective, clear, concise, constructive, and timely; (6) ensuring that audit objectives are met; and (7) providing opportunities for developing internal auditors' knowledge and skills.

Survey
A survey is a process for gathering information, without detailed verification, on the activity being examined. The main purposes of a survey are to: (1) understand the activity under review; (2) identify significant areas warranting special emphasis; (3) obtain information for use in performing the audit; and (4) determine whether further auditing is necessary.

Symmetric measure of association
A symmetric measure of association is measure of association that does not make a distinction between independent and dependent variables.

System
A system (process, operation, function, or activity) is an arrangement, a set, or a collection of concepts, parts, activities, and/or people that are connected or interrelated to achieve objectives

and goals. (This definition applies to both manual and automated systems.) A system may also be a collection of subsystems operating together for a common objective or goal.

Systematic selection with a random start

Systematic selection with a random start is a sampling method in which a given sample size is divided into the population size in order to obtain a sampling interval. A random starting point between 1 and the sampling interval is obtained. This item is selected first; then every item whose number or location is equal to the previously selected item plus the sampling interval is selected, until the population is used up.

Technology-based audit techniques

The term "technology-based audit techniques" refers to any automated audit tool, such as generalized audit software, test data generators, computerized audit programs, specialized audit utilities, and computer-assisted audit techniques.

Tolerable error

Tolerable error is the specified precision or the maximum sampling error that will still permit the results to be useful. It is also called bound on error.

Trend analysis

Trend analysis is the analysis of the changes in a given item of information over a period of time.

Understanding

"Understanding" means the ability to apply broad knowledge to situations likely to be encountered, to recognize significant deviations, and to be able to carry out the research necessary to arrive at reasonable solutions.

Unobtrusive measures

Unobtrusive measures are measures that are not readily noticeable to others.

Variable sampling

The term "variable sampling" refers to sampling in which the selected sampling units are measured or evaluated (in terms of dollars, pounds, days, etc.), and some statistical measure (statistic) is computed from these measurements to estimate the population parameter or measure.

Variance

Variance is sometimes called the average squared deviation. It is computed by taking the difference between individual value and the mean, squaring it, then adding all the squared differences and dividing by the number of items.

Work measurement

Work measurement is an industrial engineering program that applies some of the general principles of creative problem solving to the simplification of operations or procedures.

Index

Purpose, Authority, and
 Responsibility (Standard
 1000), 3
 Recognition of the Definition
 of Internal Auditing, the
 Code of Ethics, and the
 Standards in the Internal
 Audit Charter (Standard
 1010), 3, 4

Q
Quality Assurance and
 Improvement Program
 (Standard 1300), 13, 14
 Disclosure of Nonconformance
 (Standard 1322), 22
 External Assessments
 (Standard 1312), 16–20
 Internal Assessments (Standard
 1311), 15, 16
 Reporting on the Quality
 Assurance and
 Improvement Program
 (Standard 1320), 21
 Requirements of the
 Quality Assurance and
 Improvement Program
 (Standard 1310), 14, 15
 Use of "Conforms with the
 International Standards for
 the Professional Practice
 of Internal Auditing"
 (Standard 1321), 21, 22
Questionnaires
 agree-or-disagree scale, 158
 bias, 158
 closed-ended questions,
 150–154
 confidentiality, 142
 constraints, 149
 corroboration, 155, 156
 data analysis, 147
 data collection, 147
 data design, 147
 data validation, 155
 descriptive questions, 148
 expert review of, 155
 feedback methods, 160
 fill-in-the blank questions, 154

free-choice questions, 153
Gutman format, 158
impact (cause-and-effect)
 questions, 148
instructions, 157
intensity scale format, 158–160
interviews compared, 149, 150
key concepts, 161
Likert scale, 158–160
multiple-choice questions, 153
nonresponses, analysis of, 156,
 157
normative questions, 148
open-ended questions, 150, 151
pretesting, 155
purpose of, 147
quality of, 154
ranking questions, 157, 158
rating scales, use of, 157, 158,
 160
reliability, 155, 156
structured, 149
use of in data gathering, 148,
 149
verification, 155, 156

R
Range check, 95
Range test, 95
Ratio estimation, 185, 186
Ratio test, 97
Reasonable assurance, 14, 23, 24,
 31, 47, 50, 107–110, 113–
 115, 133, 194
Reasonableness tests, 94, 186, 187
Record count, 95
Recovery logging, 99
Red flags of fraud, 129, 131–134.
 See also Fraud
Reference values/codes kept
 outside the program, 93
Relationship maps, 189
Relationship test, 97
Report files, 87
Reporting on the Quality
 Assurance and
 Improvement Program
 (Standard 1320), 21
Reports
 annual reports, 15, 16, 21, 26

audit trail, 98, 100, 104, 105
control report, 98
error report, 98
exception report, 98
Reporting on the Quality
 Assurance and
 Improvement Program
 (Standard 1320), 21
Reporting to Senior
 Management and the
 Board (Standard 2060),
 32, 33
Requirements of the Quality
 Assurance and
 Improvement Program
 (Standard 1310), 14, 15
Residual risk, 24–26, 30, 67, 120,
 122, 123
Resolution of Senior
 Management's Acceptance
 of Risks (Standard 2600),
 67
Resource allocation, 50
Resource management, 24, 26, 27,
 40, 44, 167
Resource Management (Standard
 2030), 26, 27
Results, communicating. *See*
 Communicating Results
 (Standard 2400)
Risk (domain 2)
 fraud. *See* Fraud risk (domain 2)
 sample practice questions, 139,
 140
 vocabulary and concepts,
 120–125
Risk, described, 120
Risk acceptance
 described, 121
 Resolution of Senior
 Management's Acceptance
 of Risks (Standard 2600),
 67
Risk appetite, 22–24, 33, 35, 36,
 49, 121
Risk assessments, 22–24, 27–29,
 46–49, 110, 111, 114,
 120–122
Risk assignment, 121
Risk avoidance, 121